Praise for "Flipside: A Tourist's Gui

"Richard has written a terrific book
highly recommend it. Love the suc(
better angle on their post-death responsibility."
Robert Thurman ("Why the Dalai Lama Matters")

"Inspiring, well written and entertaining. The kind of book where once you have read it, you will no longer be able to see the world in the same way again."
Gary E. Schwartz Ph.D. ("The Sacred Promise")

"Everyone should have a Richard Martini in their life. I've known him a long time and I'm convinced he's from another planet. So what he's saying about the afterlife is entirely possible."   **Charles Grodin** ("Just When I Thought I'd Heard Everything!")

"We viewed (the documentary) "Flipside" last night and we were blown away about how good it is.... The visual lead-ins were just outstanding; I loved the way you interspersed visual images and graphic illustrations of the topic being discussed. The care taken in putting it all together really shows."
Michael Newton "Journey of Souls"

"Martini's book is deeply thought provoking, poignant and profound. He brings the gift of a great story teller to the table and oh, what a story he tells! Like him, I'm a skeptic. But he does a better job than any book that I've ever read on bringing "structure" and clarity to what happens next. To the extent there's science around what happens to us when we die, Martini captures it. Read this book." Amazon review by **"J.C. Rogers"**

"Richard does a skillful job weaving the physical world with the other dimensions of consciousness. He draws on Drs. Brian Weiss and Michael Newton as well as several other pioneers in the field. This is also a love story. After reading this work, you may feel the bonds we all share as we choose to enter this world, especially if you've suffered a traumatic loss of a loved one. This is a must read if you are a believer of reincarnation or just open minded...." **"Jim"**

"Flipside is probably the best book I've read on reincarnation since Carol Bowman's "Children's Past Lives." Starting as a skeptic, you come to believe, as Martini does, that consciousness not only endures, but expands and grows. His quest, his need to know, to understand, comes across as completely genuine. I think he has pushed his soul's agenda forward with this book. I loved it." **"Trish"**

"One of the most fascinating books I've read on after life experiences. The author delves into the between-life adventure, past life regressions, where supposedly the soul group decides what particular lesson is important to learn in the upcoming incarnation. I found it astounding." **"J. Silver"**

"This book has changed my views and truly rocked my world. "Flipside" brought it together for me in one big "aha" moment. I loved the balance of real world experience combined with sessions and quotes from experts. Martini indicates this is a journey based on one man's quest to find answers; I thoroughly enjoyed that quest and learned so much along the way!" **"Shan"**

"A powerful journey into heaven that holds the reader's interest from beginning to end. Martini's revelations of the "other side of the veil" allow us to travel with him into heaven as he and other individuals experience lives between lives. Dr. Michael Newton shares his research that gives this credence. For those with open minds, "Flipside" offers confirmation for what people the world over have suspected. Our soul exists after this life on Earth; death is nothing to fear. **"J. Holcomb"**

"I heard Richard Martini interviewed on Coast to Coast AM and was compelled to get his book. I found it fascinating and illuminating. His accounts of Newton's 30 year studies of over 7,000 subjects, all with similar characteristics was extremely interesting. If you have ever felt a little "Deja vu" or had dreams of a previous life, you won't be able to put this one down. Illuminating." **"CargoPylot"**

"If you've ever wondered what it would be like to go to "the other side" without actually dying, this book is for you. Fascinating, highly informative on what it's like to die, then find you are just continuing life in another realm, experiencing and embracing love and acceptance of a magnitude that is unknown in their lives but familiar; like "coming home." A helpful guide to the afterlife. Its title is well named!" **"L. Mull"**

"By being regressed himself, Martini gives a depth of knowledge that's astounding. Our current life might not always make sense, but it does when combined with our many lives. The book ends with the chapter, "What's It All Add Up To?" I recommend reading this chapter first. This book is a wonderful addition to our knowledge of who and what we really are. **"Robin"**

"Wow!! "Flipside" the most inspired and inspiring book I've read in a long time; an impressive introduction into reincarnation, "Past life regression" and "Life between lives." He may have started out as a skeptic but that doesn't stop Martini from taking the reader on an exciting journey, with a stunning glimpse of the afterlife. Personal and moving, mind-boggling for sure, but truly uplifting. I just couldn't put it down." **"Gert"**

It's a Wonderful Afterlife

Volume 1

Further Adventures into the Flipside

By

Richard Martini

Homina Publishing
PO Box 248
Santa Monica, CA 90406
HominaPublishing.com

CONTENTS

FOREWORD BY CHARLES GRODIN

"See you in the next life, Jack." Charles Grodin to Robert De Niro's character Jack Walsh in "Midnight Run." (Photo: Walter Matthau, Charles Grodin pointing out where "craft service has gone" on the set of "Movers & Shakers")

If you would have told me that someday I would have among my small group of close male friends a guy with a last name of Martini, I would have said "Well... that seems unlikely, I've never even heard of anyone, anywhere with the name of Martini." But the fact is one of my best friends for the last thirty five years is a guy named Richard Martini.

There's always a lot of laughs with him around. It started many years ago when the maître d' of a restaurant I used to go to in Los Angeles called me and said "Mr. Grodin, you're a very good tipper, but you've got to tip the captain." I asked "Who's the captain?" He said "Me."

I wasn't aware of who you tip. Generally I just leave a tip and expect the restaurant to distribute it. Richard Martini does the maître d's bit with me on the phone every time I call him. "Mr. Grodin, where's my tip?"

At some point in the mid-nineties he worked for me on my CNBC cable show. He was in Los Angeles, and we presented him as our Hollywood correspondent. He would say something like "I went to a big Hollywood premier last night and saw Julia Roberts." I would then ask "What did she have to say?" He would then say "Well... she was very beautiful, but I was in the back of the theater, so I didn't get a chance to actually talk to her." He was constantly reporting about big show business events he went to and how wonderful everyone looked, but never got a chance to talk to anybody or pass along any Hollywood gossip.

My favorite experience with Richard Martini is when he came with me when I was doing a movie in Morocco.[1] Richard and I went out one day to look at some rugs. They were very expensive. Richard later told the story of how he had gone back to the rug dealer and literally begged for a discount for his own rug.

So I asked Richard to go back to the rug dealer and do the same for a rug I wanted. He got on his knees and grabbed hold of the rug dealer's leg and begged "Pleeeeeeeze!" The rug dealer laughed and gave him a good price. Then the first rug dealer and Richard went to a second, tougher looking rug dealer who had another rug I had seen. Richard and the first rug dealer fell to their knees and begged for a discount. "Pleeeeeeeze!" The second rug dealer was not amused.

For the last several years Richard has been promoting his book he wrote called "Flipside," and now he's written two new volumes called "It's a Wonderful Afterlife." He's done a lot of research that he says proves there is an afterlife.

Recently he called me from Syracuse, New York and asked if he could quote me for an opening line in front of the audience for his book talk. I said "Tell them I don't know whether or not I believe *there is* an afterlife, but I do believe *you're* from another planet. So it's entirely possible."

That's some Martini, that Martini.

Charles Grodin

Charles Grodin is an actor, playwright, director, talk show host and author. Known best for his roles in Beethoven (1992), Midnight Run (1988) and The Heartbreak Kid (1972), he has two children and is married to author Elissa Grodin.

---

[1] "Ishtar" with Warren Beatty and Dustin Hoffman, directed by Elaine May.

Introduction:

It's A Wonderful Afterlife

"No man is a failure who has friends." Inscription written on a book given to George Bailey by his guardian angel Clarence in "It's A Wonderful Life." (Photo: Luana Anders in Rockefeller Plaza circa 1985)

Welcome to Bedford Falls.

Most people don't realize that the genesis of the film "It's a Wonderful Life" is from director Frank Capra's own near death experience. In the classic sense of the term, Capra wasn't in a hospital and didn't die, but he had a transformative spiritual experience that changed his life, which spawned the beloved movie.

Capra's film "It Happened One Night" swept the Oscars in 1934. And like most successful artists who hit a pinnacle early in their career, he had a hell of a time thinking up his next film. He was courted by everyone, and all asked "What's your next hit going to be?" It caused a series of panic attacks, as described in his autobiography "Name above the Title." People would call to say "We have a meeting set up for you with so and so," and Frank would say "I'm sorry, I'm just not feeling up to it."

Eventually Frank Capra started to not actually feeling well. He admits it was likely psychosomatic, but in the late 30's, that wasn't a common term. Despite visits from numerous doctors, Capra could not get out of bed. It was shortly thereafter that he had a spiritual experience that changed the course of his life.

He said a man came into his home that he'd never seen before. He was a short bald man that Frank's assistant Max saw as well. The man appeared in "our second-floor den... completely bald, wearing thick glasses." Max said the man insisted on seeing Capra, who finally crawled out of his bed to see him. Capra said he could barely walk into the room next door, where the bald man said "Please sit down, sir." Capra sat down. The little man sat opposite him and said: "Mr. Capra, you are a coward."

"A what?" Capra asked. "A coward, sir. But infinitely sadder. You are an offense to God. You hear that man in there?" Capra's assistant Max had turned on the radio in the next room and Hitler's voice was shrieking out of it. "That evil man is desperately trying to poison the world with hate. How many can he talk to?" Fifteen million – twenty million? And for how long – twenty minutes? You, sir, you can talk to hundreds of millions, for two hours – and in the dark."

He continued. "The talents you have, Mr. Capra, are not your own, not self-acquired. God gave you those talents; they are His gift to you, to use for His purpose. And when you don't use the gifts God blessed you with – you are an offense to God – and to humanity. Good day, sir."

The little "faceless man" left. Capra wrote "What had just happened? Who was this faceless little man who told me I was a coward and an offense to God? I didn't know, never would know, never wanted to know."[2]

The next day Capra crawled out of his bed, called his writing partner and got into his car. They drove out to the desert where they wrote the most famous "near death experience" film of all time, "It's A Wonderful Life." The movie was a flop when it was released. It wasn't until the advent of television that people started watching it religiously. [3]

---

[2] "Name Above The Title" by Frank Capra. De Capo Press 1997 Pg. 176. Bedford Falls is the name of the fictitious town in "It's A Wonderful Life."

But the film didn't only save Frank Capra's life.

Reagan cabinet minister Robert McFarlane had just attempted suicide when he received an anonymous gift in the mail.

> Among the Belgian chocolate truffles and the Bibles, the flowers and cards, the call from President Reagan and the visit from President of Egypt's widow Jihan Sadat, there was one especially welcome get-well greeting that Robert C. McFarlane received after his suicide attempt three weeks ago. A sympathetic stranger from New York mailed the former national security adviser a video cassette of the Frank Capra movie, "It's a Wonderful Life," with the simple message, "Watch this!"

> "So we did," said Jonda McFarlane, sitting on the couch beside her husband in their suburban Maryland home, her hand on his knee. As he recuperated from his attempt to take his life through an overdose of Valium, Mr. McFarlane took to heart the message of the film, in which an angel saves a beleaguered Jimmy Stewart from killing himself and shows him the ways the world would have been worse off if he had never lived.[4]

I wonder if the fellow who sent McFarlane the film was also a short bald "faceless" man.

Often people who've had a near death experience (NDE) have a hard time assimilating their experience. They've experienced something profound – a connectedness to everyone, a feeling of bliss or purpose - but when they come back from their experiences, those intense feelings can dissipate.

As one near death experiencer said to me:

> It's like suddenly finding the love of your life and the next morning finding out that person has moved to Mars. They still exist, they still love you and you still love them - but they are far away and you don't know how to reconnect.

---

[3] They also optioned the self-published book "The Greatest Gift" and script credits go to Michael Wilson, Frank Capra, Albert Hackett, Frances Goodrich, and Jo Swerling. imdb.com).

[4] From NY Times "The White House Crisis: McFarlane suicide attempt" by Maureen Dowd March 2nd, 1987

For me it was like nothing in this world could compare to the beauty of "there." Everything back here seemed dull and almost dead. The energy and the beauty and the feeling of "there" was beyond anything you can express, and coming back here was almost painful.

You know it's still there, it hasn't gone away, you just don't know how to get back there. I think this life would be easier for those who have had near death experiences if they knew they could revisit at will or even occasionally travel back "there."

But to be cut off from it - for some - can be very difficult. The lucky ones are those who can take the "there" with them, and not pine for it. But to use that experience to make *this* world like *that* world.

Hence why I like to refer to near death events as "near *life* experiences." The experience is one where people feel that they suddenly understand the meaning of life. They feel they can suddenly understand the purpose of their existence, they say that they can see the connectedness between all people and things. And when they return to a world where the rest of the people can't or don't see that – it can feel like being stuck in mud.

Some who've had NDE's are able to revisit and process them with the help of a hypnotherapist. In this volume David Bennett (in the chapter called "Voyage of Purpose") had an NDE and then later was able to examine details with more clarity during a life between lives (LBL) session while under deep hypnosis.

David has been interviewed by Dr. Bruce Greyson[5] at the University of Virginia, the "father of near death research" and has recounted his story in his book "Voyage of Purpose."[6] David drowned and then found himself enveloped in a feeling of "unconditional love" and being "welcomed home" by light beings.

---

[5] (Charles) Bruce Greyson is Professor of Psychiatry at the University of Virginia. He is co-author of Irreducible Mind (2007) and co-editor of The Handbook of Near-Death Experiences (2009). Greyson has written many journal articles, and has given media interviews, on the subject of near death experiences. Greyson is Chester F. Carlson Professor of Psychiatry and the division director of The Division of Perceptual Studies (DOPS), formerly the Division of Personality Studies, at the University of Virginia. He is also a Professor of Psychiatric Medicine in the Department of Psychiatric Medicine, Division of Outpatient Psychiatry, at the University of Virginia. (Wikipedia)

[6] Co-written with his wife Cindy Griffith-Bennett

Later, during his LBL with a Michael Newton trained therapist, he was able to see those beings more clearly and recognized them as members of his "soul group" - the people he's been with since the beginning of his existence.

I mention David's journey because he had a near death experience, was examined by a scientist about it, and later had a between-life experience where he could examine it more fully. By revisiting the event, he was able to process it and the LBL helped with his integration back into his life.

So how is it a "wonderful" afterlife?

As a cultural reference, we've made the afterlife seem strange, creepy or fantastical. "I see dead people," "Don't speak ill of the dead," "Walking dead" are all references to something that refers to people who are gone. Logic tells us that if we're communicating with someone, then they cannot *be* dead. If they're communicating with us and we aren't creating the illusion of communication, then death is not, could not, be the correct word to use.

When characters show up in films or television from the flipside, they're usually accompanied by eerie music and zombie makeup. When children try to tell their parents they saw "grandpa," often their parents say "that's just your imagination" or "Grandpa's dead, Billy. There's no such thing as ghosts." I heard the same information as a child, but by the time I got around to actually seeing a ghost or two, I'd already decided that whoever told me there was "no such things as ghosts" hadn't seen one themselves.

Religion, for the most part, has painted the afterlife as a place where sins are punished, karma is righted, or people are given their just due for their transgressions. On the bright side, we also have stories of pearly gates, golden thrones and bliss. Just what the heck is going on up there anyway?

In the two volumes of "It's A Wonderful Afterlife," we'll hear consistent claims that there is little or no evil in the afterlife, there is relatively no judgment doled out for transgressions – and how a soul learns and grows from the experiences it's had over many lifetimes. What this afterlife research demonstrates is that these hallmarks are both consistent and replicable. That contrary to popular opinion, we don't die. That we are no more dead after our journey here, than we are alive while we're here.

Dr. Greyson published a study in 1983 which demonstrated the hallmarks of the NDE could be documented. People reported encountering a "bright light" or "seeing other individuals" or a sense of "time standing still." As it says in his ground breaking report: "Near death experiences have been described consistently since antiquity and more rigorously in recent years."[7]

My point is that if near death experiences can be catalogued scientifically, then so can "between-life" (LBL) reports, if they are consistent and replicable.

In the LBL, people claim to find "spirit guides," "escorts" or "guardians" that keep an eye on them throughout their lifetimes. They claim there are "soul groups" with other individuals they normally incarnate with. Often, they report visiting a "library" to examine their many lifetimes. (Not a physical place – as every account of a library I've heard or examined is different. But the word is the same.) People claim we have elders, or wise beings that help us "review our lifetimes" but that by and large, we are responsible for our journey on Earth.

Those who've read "Flipside" know my personal journey to this research began with the death of my close friend Luana Anders in 1996. Just prior to her death she told me about a recurring dream she had where she was in a "classroom in another galaxy. Everyone was dressed in white, speaking a language I've never heard before but completely understood." The day after she passed, her friend called to tell me she had a dream where she saw Luana in a "classroom in the 4th dimension, and everyone was dressed in white, and she seemed really happy."

The night she died she came to visit me in a dramatic dream. I wondered if it was possible she might still reside somewhere in the universe – how could she visit me if she didn't still exist?

Luana had been a Buddhist, so I studied Tibetan philosophy to see if that was a path to find her. I began researching what people said during near death experiences, what scientists had written about reincarnation (Dr. Ian Stevenson, Dr. Jim Tucker, Carol Bowman and others) and finally I found the work of Dr. Michael Newton...

A quick reminder of his work; Dr. Newton was a psychologist practicing in the 1950's who didn't believe in past lives – and refused to do any regressions in his

---

[7] "The Near-Death Experience Scale" by Bruce Greyson, M.D. Journal of Nervous and Mental Disease. Vol 171, No 6. 1983

practice. He thought it was useless until one of his clients spontaneously went into the past life of being a British soldier. In that case, as outlined in his interview in "Flipside," Newton says that he at first didn't believe what his client was saying and grilled him about details from that life, asking his name, rank, serial number, mother's maiden name, etc. And afterwards Newton checked with the British War office to discover this man's story was true; there was such a man who existed and his story matched the detail's he'd given.

That experience opened his practice to past life regressions, but it wasn't until the late 60's when a woman came into his practice for a session that took him to the between lives realm. She'd come to examine her loneliness – and during that session, when he asked her to "go to the source of your loneliness, especially if there's a group around," she went to the between lives realm where she saw and identified what she claimed was her "soul group" in the "between lives realm."

> Dr. Newton: "Well, one day a woman had come to me with a presenting problem of depression, claiming she felt isolated from society and that she felt a terrible yearning to be with her old friends. I asked her if these old friends, who were no longer around, were childhood friends and she said "No, I don't see them in my current life, just in my dreams."

> I took this woman into deep hypnosis and asked her if these missing friends were perhaps people she had known at any time during her adult life. "No," she said. Were they missing childhood friends? "No," she again said. Then we began to explore a number of past lives and a couple of these dear friends began to crop up. But she kept saying that she hadn't seen most of them and that what she really wanted was to see them all together. This, according to her, was why she felt so isolated. At this point, I had no idea where we were and was getting frustrated.

> I didn't realize that this was a highly receptive woman who was taking herself deeper, in a way I was to later learn was the proper procedure for getting somebody into what I call a superconscious state. I had been inadvertently using words with her that I later found were "key words" in facilitating the spiritual regression process. In this instance, it was the word "group."

> I finally asked her if there was ever a time in her existence that she was not lonely because she was with her "group" of friends and she

immediately exclaimed "YES!" So I simply said, "Go there" and in the next moment, with her eyes closed, she was laughing and pointing to my office wall saying "I see them all right now!" I asked her where we were - were we in a past life? "No", she said. "I'm in the spirit world!"

This opened the door for me. I had already been involved with past life regression, something that I had never before used in my traditional practice, so you could say I was ready to "come to the party" as regard to metaphysical work. However, the results of this session changed everything for me. I became obsessed with what had occurred, replaying the tape over and over and over, making refinements with other clients, and slowly this complex jigsaw puzzle began to come together. [8]

Michael Newton spent roughly the next 25 years only seeing clients who could take him to this realm and collected the data from what they said about it. He published his first book "Journey of Souls" in 1994.

When I picked up Newton's book, what jumped out at me was an account of a session where a man said that in-between lives he was "in a classroom and everyone was dressed in white." (Sound familiar?)

I realized if I was going to find the spirit of my friend Luana, it should begin with an investigation into this world. I was granted Michael Newton's last interview – he's alive and well, but retired – and that began a documentary about his work and between-life sessions. The filming of those between-life sessions became the transcripts for "Flipside: A Tourist's Guide on How to Navigate the Afterlife" and the footage became the documentary "Flipside: A Journey into the Afterlife."

I've continued to film sessions and interview people under deep hypnosis. I've gathered so much material, it made sense to release the new research in two volumes. I wasn't sure what to call the new book. My son suggested "The Flipside of Flipside." I liked "Thinning of the veil," but it sounded like an episode of "Game of Thrones."

I was visiting literary agent Joel Gotler one day with professor/author Gary Schwartz Ph.D. Gary asked Joel, "How would you feel if someone could prove beyond a shadow of doubt, that there is an afterlife, that life continues on?" Joel said "I would feel like Jimmy Stewart in "It's a Wonderful Life" the moment he

[8] "Interview with Michael Newton," Mary Arsenault Wisdom Magazine 2008

gets his life back! Everything would be new, everything would be completely changed forever, and I'd be so appreciative for being here on the planet."

I laughed and said "That's the title of the next book." They both looked at me. "It's a Wonderful Afterlife."

But mark my words; this won't be an easy ride.

"Lasciate ogni speranza chi voi entrate." (Abandon all hope ye who enter here.) Sign posted over the gates of hell in Dante's "Inferno."

"Reality Ends Here" Sign posted over the entrance to the USC film school when I was in attendance.

"The truth is coming and it cannot be stopped." Edward Snowden

Chapter One: The Veil Is Thinning

"I do not feel obliged to believe that the same God who has endowed us with sense, reason, and intellect has intended us to forgo their use." - Galileo Galilei, physicist and astronomer

The other day someone asked me: "Why is this information about the afterlife becoming so prevalent and in the *zeitgeist*?"[9] You can't change the channel on the television without hearing about ghosts, resurrection, or the flipside in general. My answer; "Because the veil appears to be thinning."

What is this veil? I first heard the metaphor of the veil in terms of a "veil of forgetfulness;" the idea that when we come to the planet, there's a veil or block that keeps us from remembering our previous lifetimes or experiences. And every time a person under deep hypnosis begins to remember those lifetimes, or the between-life realm, that veil gets thinner.

Using another metaphor, it's like electronic interference with our cell phones. We've all had the experience; the cell reception is bad and a person's voice stops and starts, or disappears altogether. So for a moment, think of the veil as an FM

[9] "The defining spirit or mood of a particular period of history as shown by the ideas and beliefs of the time."

tuner – when the channel is off kilter, there is no communication, but if you are able to fine tune it, at first you get part of a station, and the station eventually comes in clearer the closer you are to the transmitter.

This is reminiscent of one of the sessions in "Flipside." An old friend and successful entertainment executive agreed to do a between-life session. He was fairly adamant he could not be hypnotized and was "less than convinced" he'd get anywhere.

But during his session he said he spoke to his departed mother. As anyone who has experienced a between-life session can attest, it doesn't matter whether or not the experience is real; it really feels as if your loved one is standing in front of you, expressing thoughts and feelings and concepts that are new.

And about his experience of seeing his departed mother, she reportedly said:

> Trying to reach us over here is just like the way a cell phone works. You pick it up and push buttons, not knowing how the process works, but the phone reaches your loved one. It's the same way in the afterlife, you think about us, say a prayer to us, we receive the communication even if it's across the galaxy. We may not be able to reply directly, or at that moment, but we will eventually. We do hear you.

Recently my wife attended a class where two mediums were helping people develop their own psychic ability. The exercise was simple; bring a photograph of a loved one or friend who had passed away and give it to someone else in class to see if anything might come forth about that person. My wife brought along a photograph of an old friend, a prominent attorney in Los Angeles, who spent his life defending and believing in those who had been charged with crimes he believed they did not commit.

One of the mediums held his picture and spoke accurately about this attorney's life. She quoted him as saying that he's visits his wife when she walks or jogs every day. But when asked point blank why he was coming to the classroom so clearly, he replied, "Because the veil is thinning."

Or the reception is getting better.

As we'll see, thousands of people under deep hypnosis are saying relatively the same things about the afterlife and our journey there. Thousands of people who've had near death experiences are speaking up about them, and saying the same basic things about their journey into the afterlife. Many are from different countries, different religions. But they're all saying essentially the same things.

This book will attempt to tie these reports together; showing that scientific reports are nearly identical to the sessions under hypnosis, that near death reports are nearly identical to the between-life reports.[10] And when examined without the prejudice of materialist science, or the element of mythology or religion, there's only one logical conclusion:

That *we* don't die.

One can argue the veil is thinning because we are becoming aware of it: instead of dismissing these reports as we did for centuries, we are now choosing to examine them. For thousands of years, if someone reported an experience that was beyond perception, people acted adversely to it. Children were spanked, slapped or had other "enhanced interrogation techniques" applied to them to get them to forget they had an "imaginary friend" or spoke to their departed grandparents.

Adults were accused of witchcraft, heresy and were strung up or put to the torch. By admitting they saw a ghost, heard a report of a previous lifetime, or experienced some out of the ordinary event, people put their lives in their hands to report it. Joan of Arc heard voices that told her to lead an army in France. Her reward? The stake. In Salem, people who heard voices, saw ghosts, or had visions were strapped to a chair and dunked in the pond. If they drowned, they were innocent. But if they survived, they were deemed guilty and executed.[11]

Giordano Bruno was a 16th century philosopher born with an amazing memory – perhaps it was a case of *hyperthymesia*,[12] where he exhibited something very few

---

[10] "Deep hypnosis" refers to the method that Michael Newton's group uses, four to six hour sessions with specific questions about the between-life journey.

[11] About eighty people were accused of practicing witchcraft in a witch-hunt that lasted throughout New England from 1648-1663. Thirteen women and two men were executed. The Salem witch trials followed in 1692–3, culminating in the executions of 19 people. It has been estimated that tens of thousands of people were executed for witchcraft in Europe and the American colonies over several hundred years. "List of people executed for witchcraft." Wikipedia.

[12] Hyperthymesia is the condition of possessing an extremely detailed autobiographical memory. Hyperthymesiacs remember an abnormally vast number of their life experiences. (Wikipedia)

people can do; recalling memories of every event in their lifetime. Bruno claimed to have an out of body experience where he flew through outer space and realized that the sun was just like all the other stars. He also claimed he "saw spirits" and that they were the souls of the dead, waiting to re-inhabit bodies on Earth. Bruno's observations were feted by royal courts until he ran afoul of the Inquisition. He was burned at the stake.

Throughout human history, religious figures have reported experiences with other realms, visions of people who've died, described a heaven like arena where people "live forever." Whether they called these realms "Heaven" or "Nirvana," whether they contained "angels" or "virgins," they share characteristics with what people report during NDEs and LBLs. Even the descriptions of the Viking's *Valhalla* or the Greek's *Mt. Olympus* include non-reincarnating deities who drink nectars that keep them alive and powerful forever. Is it possible these descriptions of another realm might be observations, or have some basis in reality?

Just where did these depictions of heaven come from?

Who was the first person who claimed to see small flying cherubs, or mandolin wielding angels singing angelic choruses behind "pearly" gates? If they're constructed fantasies, where did the descriptions originate? Why do they include flying, feelings of bliss or celestial music?

As we'll see in the various between-life experiences or near death experiences examined in this book, the cliché's we've been using for eons to describe the afterlife are not that far off from what people actually report. Materialist science would argue the reason for that, is that people have read or seen these descriptions in the past and during a dramatic life altering event, conjure them up for purposes of comfort. But there's evidence that's not the case, or rather, that it *could not be* the case.

Nowadays when people experience these journeys and report about them, they're no longer chastised, laughed at, or put on display in front of a frightened populace. All they have to do is turn to the internet. One result of the World Wide Web is that people who might have kept their psychic or extra sensory experiences to themselves, now feel free to share online. Forums, blogs, and comments allow people to speak of their own experiences without fear of being dunked or roasted.

The internet is a place (reportedly like the afterlife) where we can connect to other souls, share information and see the connections we all have. Perhaps one reason why "the veil" is thinning; medical studies show that when a person watches footage of themselves stuttering or having a tantrum –they're able to forge new pathways in their brains to solve their physical problems.

Perhaps by discussing the afterlife and the subconscious memories of previous lifetimes, we untie the Gordian Knot of mechanisms that prevent our brains from remembering this knowledge. We may not have to actually experience a near death event to learn the lessons from having one.

When I began my documentary about Michael Newton's work, I was offered to have my own between-life session. In a George Plimpton like moment, I realized I couldn't write about other's experiences going off into another realm if I didn't actually go there myself. (Plimpton was famous for writing books about adventures he'd actually accomplished, like being a professional baseball player for a day.)[13] I've had four such adventures.

As recounted in "Flipside," the first was conducted by Michael Newton trained hypnotherapist Jimmy Quast of Maryland. Prior to returning to consciousness, Jimmy asked if there was any particular message I could bring back to the planet from my excursion that would be helpful to people.

The answer was; "Just let go." (Hey, sounds like a great idea for a Disney song.)

Perhaps part of that letting go, is letting go of the veil that prevents us from seeing into the afterlife, or from experiencing feelings, thoughts and emotions that we've felt before. That letting go isn't just about releasing anger, jealousy, fear or resentment, but also letting go of our ingrained perceptions of what reality might actually be.

At some point in the film "The Matrix," the character of Neo realizes that even bullets are merely a mental construct in his universe, and he's able to put up his hand and watch them fall harmlessly to the ground. In his case, I guess the veil seems to have disappeared altogether.

Don't believe me? Just turn the page.

[13] "Paper Lion: Confessions of a Last String Quarterback" George Plimpton 1968

"The key to happiness: learn to let go." The Buddha

Chapter Two - *"Voyage of Purpose"*

Interview with David Bennett

"However vast the darkness, we must supply our own light." Stanley Kubrick

I met David Bennett at the NY upstate International Association of Near Death Studies (IANDS) group in Liverpool, N.Y. A tall, gentle, ever-smiling fellow, David was the Chief Engineer of the ocean research vessel, *The Aloha* when he had a near death experience off the coast of Ventura, California. Initially, he only told his wife about it, and her reaction was so negative that he kept his story to himself for over a decade.

It was an incident that happened years later that caused him to remember the event in vivid detail. As mentioned, he was interviewed by Dr. Bruce Greyson,[14]

[14] Bruce Greyson is Professor of Psychiatry at the University of Virginia. He is co-author of Irreducible Mind (2007) and co-editor of The Handbook of Near-Death Experiences (2009). Greyson has written many journal articles, and has given media interviews, on the subject of near death experiences.

and recently, did a between-life session with Michael Newton trained hypnotherapist Virginia "Kiki" Waldron.[15]

We spent about an hour in his local café near Seneca Falls, which reportedly is the town Frank Capra modeled Bedford Falls after in "It's A Wonderful Life." We talked about his book "Voyage of Purpose" which he co-wrote with his new wife and author Cindy Griffith-Bennett.

David Bennett

RM: I've just finished reading your book "Voyage of Purpose;" it's an incredible journey. Tell us how you came upon your near death experience.

David: In March of 1983 I was chief engineer of the research vessel "The Aloha." That night there was a storm and the harbor master wouldn't allow our ship into Ventura harbor, in California, but we needed to dock because we had an engineer on board who needed to get to the airport.

So the Captain decided to launch a Zodiac, a rubber boat. The sea state was pretty rough, 25-30 foot seas, and when you're two miles off shore, they're big rollers and you don't really see the surf. And as a matter of course, we launch small research vessels or submarines in seas like that all the time, and then we use the Zodiac to pick them up. It's a very durable craft and we didn't think it would be a big deal. So there was this scientist who needed to make it to the airport, and we thought we'd take him in to the beach instead of the harbor.

As chief engineer I would normally stay with the ship; I never go on the small rubber boats as a first mate usually takes people in. But I knew the harbor pretty well as I'd gone in and out of it a lot, and because this night it was so rough, the Captain asked me to take him in. You could say I really wasn't supposed to be there.

We started heading in, going on top of these 30 foot waves, and we'd roll down the trough and back up; this is how we were going to track our way in. The wind was blowing hard, and we totally lost track of the harbor buoy, but we could see the lights of the shoreline. We just figured we'd do a beach landing somehow, some way. We didn't know it, but the wind had blown us south of the harbor

[15] GateKeeperGuidance.com

where there's a sandbar. We slid off a 30 footer, and I yelled to the mate "Turn us around, let's go back out to sea where we're a lot safer" and at that moment this giant foam ridge was above our heads, and it came crashing down on top of us. It folded the Zodiac like a sandwich, and I was hanging onto this old WWII life vest.

I'm a commercial diver, so I wasn't freaking out. I'm used to being underwater, I've logged thousands of hours doing dives, so I was holding my breath, and my faith was that the life vest would eventually bring me to the surface. But it didn't.

I went through this period where I was thinking "I'm going to die." I'd totally lost my orientation, the sea was tossing me like a rag doll. So I started thinking, "Well, at least my wife will be taken care of, the insurance is paid." And then I reached a point where the oxygen deprivation created euphoria; it's the moment when you believe you can breathe, and you just breathe in the salt water.

It's not pleasant. There's a burning sensation and then "boom" you're gone. There's something in the brain that allows you to escape that severe agony.

I found myself in this pitch darkness. Being a trained diver, I've gone through oxygen deprivation where we learn not to freak out when these things happen – but I was really curious, because I had just come from this violent world of 30 foot raging seas to this calm environment with total darkness.

It really didn't freak me out at all, in fact I was curious. "What is this?" I hadn't experienced anything like this in our training. But it felt like I wasn't alone – it felt like there was more to this darkness. **And it was darkness which had a richness to it, more than just… - it wasn't emptiness; it was a void that was full of everything. It's hard to explain in our terms or vocabulary, but that's the perception I can convey.**[16]

Then I saw this light appear. It was off in the distance and I was drawn to it; I felt like I was moving toward it. It was not a tunnel, just a light and as I got closer and closer it grew, until it was infinite. I could see it was like millions upon millions of fragments of light all moving and dancing and coalescing together.

Is there anything like that in nature you can think of?

---

[16] Emphasis added throughout the text to point out where concepts are repeated during various NDEs and LBLs.

Yes, have you ever seen a school of sardines or anchovies and how they work together? When they get close to the surface, they refract the light – kind of like what the fragments conveyed to me, coming together, moving apart. They were moving in a like-mind. I was in complete awe of this light. And then I was coming closer and closer and three fragments broke away from the light and they came to me.

Three out of how many?

Thousands of fragments, and infinite number. They came toward me and they conveyed this profound feeling of **"Welcome home."** **As I was getting closer to this light, I kept feeling these waves of love; it was like they were embracing me in a warm blanket.**

And I was so comfortable with this love, it was such a warm embrace that when these three... – I talk about them as light beings, because they were fragments of light heading towards me and they were welcoming me home. (He wipes away a tear) It's still tough to talk about it, it was over 30 years ago and it still chokes me up. **Because it was a feeling of home unlike any I've ever, ever, ever felt before.** I had a really dysfunctional childhood growing up, thrown from one family to another... But to feel this love and welcoming was not what I had experienced in life.[17]

Interesting you used the word "home" as the word itself means something different to each individual.

Well this was more of a home of my being; this was like "Welcome back to your being, to your essence, to your totality." And then eventually about a dozen of these fragments of light were there greeting me. And then we moved; there was no conveyance of "Let's go, let's do something," it was just more an understanding; "We've got to go over here."

A Life Review

And we went to this other area that felt spherical. And then we (joined the others and) started to re-experience my life. And it wasn't just me experiencing it; they were experiencing it as well and they were very excited about doing so.

All of your soul group?

---

[17] The idea of "home" comes up often in both NDE and LBL experiences.

All twelve experienced my life - not just from my point of view - but from every interaction I'd ever had, from the *other person's point of view*. It was ripples upon ripples of memory that would cascade outwards from us.

Where you aware of what those memories were, or was it odd to you what you wound up focusing on?

Again I was in complete awe of all this. But it was a little disturbing because as a young boy I was kind of "rough around the edges" growing up as a young man. Mainly because I was thrown from so many different families, I had taken on the philosophy of "You cut your swath through life." And it's a very brutal and protective-of-yourself perspective and you try not to let anyone in.

So I got to see all of my interactions and how I had hurt other people. But I also got to see when I did open up and I did have experiences of just being openhearted and giving freely of my love and my heart. Those memories were ones that created some of the biggest ripples.

Oddly enough, the things I took the most pride in, like becoming chief engineer, and what that meant to me, didn't have such big ripples. **The bigger ones were when I would help someone.**

Do you remember any instances?

One that really sticks out - for a period of time I lived in Arizona outside Sedona, and worked in Clarkdale in a Fairway Foods Market behind the meat counter. It was interesting; it was one of those jobs that really teaches you a lot about life. There was this one lady who used to come in the store, a lady that everyone hated to deal with because of her demeanor. She was such a grumpy, little old lady. And I don't know why, but I felt like I needed to see if I could please her in some way, and make her smile.

Every time she'd come in, I'd give her the service of her life. And I relived his experience where this one time she came in and told me she was going to have a dinner party and needed to make rump roast. So I made sure she got the best we had, and I thanked her; she stood there stoic, no reaction, took her package and stomped off.

But the next time she came in, there was this lightness that was with her that you could actually kind of feel. And suddenly there was that smile. And it lit up the room and she told me how I had gone above and beyond, "it was the best roast," she started to convey this happiness.

I realized then it was a pivotal moment in my life, as I got to really experience it in this life review – that open-hearted act planted a seed in my being; when we do things for each other we're expanding our connections, we're expanding that positive energy. I didn't know that until I'd experienced this, where I had done this act from my own free will open heartedly; I got to experience her joy.

And on the flipside? A negative experience?

On the flipside, a few years later, I was in a cowboy bar, a guy came up to me and propositioned me. I didn't understand that lifestyle at that time and I had a very bad reaction. It was a very conservative cowboy bar and when I was yelling at him and screaming because of this proposition; they all knew what was going on. **Interestingly, in the life review I got to see the fight not only from my and his perspective, but everyone who was observing the fight - the bartender and the other patrons. In the life review, I could feel their rage feeding me, I could feel that energy feeding into me which was heightening my rage even more. So I would say that's a pretty negative experience.**

I take it this was before the film "Brokeback Mountain." (A bit of comedy, trying to lessen his stress over telling this story).

Yeah, way before.

It's interesting, as an observation, I did read about that incident in your book - but when you're talking about examination of energy – sometimes there's a benefit for everyone involved. It doesn't mitigate his pain or the negativity of the experience, but at the same time you got to experience that – it was a gift from him so that you could learn how negative that experience was and how you felt.... you got to learn from him – if you're trying to learn what energy is.

I still suffer from that incident.[18]

---

[18] I spoke to David about another past life memory that I recounted in "Flipside." And it was reported by Kenneth Ring on a fellow who had an NDE and during it recalled an incident when he was cut off in traffic, ran over to the offending driver and pulled him out of the car. He said he relived the experience from the point of view of the person being hit – he could "taste the blood and feel the broken teeth and humiliation" of the person he was pounding. And David said "Yes, I know that incident; that was my friend Tom Sawyer," (his real name) who spoke about his NDE extensively.

Well, let's at least give you credit for doing a good job of examining it.

One of my lifetime goals is learning to accept compliments – I have a hard time with that.

You mentioned in the book there's a point of being out of control in your life, and I'd offer it's the same when getting a compliment – you're not in control of what a person's going to say about your work or life. But on the other hand, it's also just energy – a person acknowledges their own experience; even using words that are about how your work influenced them. Reminds me of the old Hollywood joke, "Okay, enough about me, now tell me what you think of me." Why was it so hard for you to recount your NDE?

I lived and worked in a macho environment, it was a world of...

"Popeye?"

Living on board a ship, doing underwater exploration, it's a very macho world. I was an engineer, so this experience rocked my world. Until then, I saw things as black and white and factual, and suddenly I had this other world experience outside my world view. I tried to share it with my first wife, which went kind of badly – so I just shut up. I didn't feel like I could share it with my co-workers, we put each other's lives in each other's hands daily.

I think it's interesting that I met your friend last night at the IANDS event, as he was the first person you shared your NDE story with.... I told him "You two look like brothers." It took you 11 years to meet him.

Well, yeah, now that you mention it. I had a second experience that led up to our meeting. I had tried to suppress it all those years. I put it so far back in my brain that I had wrapped it up with duct tape and had written on it "do not open" with a marker. I did not know how much I was actually changing from the NDE; there were things in that experience that you just could not put away. I came around to calling it my "acceptance, tolerance and truth" experience.

Return to the light

Each one of those concepts I went in depth trying to comprehend – because what I experienced in the light was total acceptance, tolerance and truth. I tried to start living my life a little bit differently afterwards, I tried to understand it. But the rest of it, the light, the soul family, the loving embraces and talking to the light – that was just beyond anything I'd experienced.

So you had another experience in Sedona? Spirit spoke to you and told you what?

Return to the light.

What does that mean?

When I lived in Arizona some of "the grandmothers"[19] taught me how to get to a sacred space through meditation, and **I was doing this meditation and I heard the light tell me to return to the light.** And I did. I relived everything, the life review, not only experiencing my entire life and the interim since the NDE, I started experiencing my future, my future potential.

It was unusual as everything I had lived in the life review was crystal sharp and clear, the repercussions were crystal clear – but when I got to this experience of my future life the core path was clear but then outside of that core it was a little hazy and the further I went it got hazier.

My perception was that this core path was an example of all our potential, **I was told I have this purpose, that path is pretty clearly laid out for us but we can deviate around the path, or weave across the path.** And sometimes those areas are a little grey, but until we put intention, it doesn't solidify with that crystal clarity.

During your NDE you heard the light tell you that you had to go back because your life had a purpose. During this reliving the NDE, did you get a sense of what that purpose was?

I was told "You must return and have purpose." In the 2nd experience I got to see those 11 years after the NDE in crystal clarity and it showed me how much I had changed, even though I didn't know how much I had changed.

And has there been an answer to that sentence? What do you perceive is the purpose?

---

[19] David explained to me later that his reference to "Grandmothers" were Native American women in Sedona that he had come to know.

For years I was asking myself "What is this purpose?" It seemed clear during my NDE when I was there, but when I came back from it, it wasn't clear. And then after the 2nd experience, I started hearing spirit more clearly. I started having an intuitive knowing, or a clear sense of guidance in my life.

I started following that clear sense, I didn't fight it anymore. I started seeing the purpose unfold, I truly believe we're not meant to know our (essential) "soul purpose," but we have every day purposes that we're a part of. And we don't recognize most of them, and I think a lot of folks, if we were to know them, it would take the mystery away. Being separate is a great opportunity for the totality that exists in the light to play a little bit and to stretch and to go in directions that we normally wouldn't.

They asked Victor Frankl, Holocaust survivor, psychiatrist, the meaning of life – and he asked his students to write down what they thought the meaning of his life was. And one student got it right; the meaning of his life was to show others the meaning of their lives. So that was his purpose. Tell me how it came to be that you did a between-life LBL?

A dear friend of mine was being trained by the Newton Institute, Margaret "Kiki" Waldron, and she was looking for subjects, and knew of me and my NDE and we both worked closely with IANDS, the International Association of Near Death studies. So she was excited, and asked me if I'd like to a between-life session.

I was curious, as I'd read "Journey of Souls" after my NDE, and felt it was one of the closest books to explain my experience, with its description of soul groups. It reminded me of my soul journey, it so paralleled what people were experiencing.

During my NDE, I wasn't able to really get anyone's names, aside from my main person, Peter. The others weren't as clear. So I felt the regression would be a great way to examine that. What I wasn't prepared for was going into a past life.

During the five hour regression, Virginia took me into a past life, where I saw myself as this old Indian who was very embittered.

In your book, while you were in Sedona reliving your NDE you visualized an elder Indian man. Was he the same fella?

That's very possible – their dress was very similar.

Could you higher self actually be that old Indian man whom you called "Great Mountain?"

Yes, that could be. I had gotten injured in that lifetime and I was maimed. And I carried that anger – I was very embittered with the injustice of being lame. I strongly felt that in battle I should have survived or died.

So it was a battle wound?

Yeah. I don't know what year it was.

I've found many people can still have access to our memory if we just don't think or judge the answer. So let me ask you know, without trying to judge it, what's the name of the tribe were you with. First name that comes to mind.

Chickataw. (When I looked it up, Chicataw is a derivation of the Chickasaw, native American tribe.)

What year was this?

Like 1768.

Roughly where in the U.S., if it was the U.S.?

Central United States.

What's the first state that comes to mind?

Ohio, Iowa.

Chiqasaw or Chicataw… one of those things I can check out. 1768 would have been in the middle of the expansion of the western frontier from the settlers.[20]

---

[20] I found online that English Trader James Adair reported extensively about the Chickasaw from his travels with them from 1744-68 in "History of American Indians." Originally based in Mississippi, the transfer of Louisiana to Spain in 1762 drove the tribe into the Ohio River valley. They sided with the British, and in 1769 fought the Cherokees on their behalf. Their tribe stretched up into Illinois territory. ("The Chickasaws" Arrel M. Gibson 1971) In 1768, the Chickasaws and Creeks were involved in a "series of war parties." According to Adair the Chickasaw were notorious for deprivations while at war; "the constancy of the savages in mortifying their bodies to gain divine favor is astonishing;" they weren't allowed to eat or sit or in any way comfort themselves while in battle mode. So for a man who lived for deprivation as a spiritual rite, being maimed might be the ultimate difficulty to overcome. (From "History Of American Indians" James Adair pg. 380)

I wanted to go to my ancestors and was quite cranky about it. There was a grand daughter who was supporting me and I didn't appreciate it at all. I was in my own self-centeredness; she was the only one who stayed with me. Everyone else had divorced me because I was so cranky and was not being part of the tribe. She was there to support me until the day I died. I passed while I was in my cabin on a crate. This grand daughter was with me.

Did you recognize her as someone in this lifetime?

I think I did; she's someone I'm not close with now, but we worked together at one point in dialysis at the hospital. We had a great friendship for a period of time and we both went different ways because of work, but I felt very close to her.

Visit to the soul group

I find it interesting to be able to examine that time period in this life as well as to examine the continuation of that story line. Did you get a chance to meet anyone during the between-life portion of your session?

Yes. I got to see my soul family – it was the same group from my NDE.

How did the experience look visually?

It was interesting, the NDE was so rich, so fast, so hyper real, and the between lives journey was like looking through a window. But I could look through a window from different points of view. Looking at my soul family from these different perspectives, to see my soul family in a way that was... I think because I was in such awe during the NDE I missed details. For example during the NDE I only saw their eyes but in the LBL I was able to perceive them more as beings, and more how they wanted to present themselves.

Did you recognize anyone?

Yes, that was freaky thing. During my near death experience, I saw my guardian whose name is Jason. I mean, I recognized Jason in my group, but at the time, he was alive, he was living with me during the time period of the NDE. But when I had the life between-life therapy session over a decade later, Jason had passed on, so I saw him so much clearer during the between-life session.

Did you communicate with anyone?

I was kind of talking with the entire group.... but not with words, you know how it goes; it's more of a mental thing. But I was able to get their names. And some of the names were really weird. But these names rang so true to my heart as I perceived them; this is the name they carry with them.[21]

And I've heard afterlife names described as a sound and instrument might make.

I was able to get about a half dozen of their names.

It's rare to be able to examine an NDE with someone who's had one – I guess you could say it's different, must less salty or wet in your case, but it is looking through a glass, or "through the looking glass."

(Having an LBL) It's a different perspective of looking at the near death experience; I found it really helped me with some of my integration issues. Because after the near death experience, I didn't read any books, I wanted the experience to be pure to me, whatever that means. But then I finally did write it down, and then I felt I could read some books about other people's experiences. And here were these people "in the light" and asking questions! I wished I had asked questions. And so the between-life therapy session allowed me to ask those questions.

The Canyon of Sound

Did you travel anywhere during it?

The hypnotherapist asked me where else I wanted to go and I said I wanted to go to the "Canyon of Sound" or music.

And I went to this place. It was like I had this balcony that was part of these walls of this canyon and I was on this balcony; it was my space, and the sound was just flowing down the canyon. **And in this space, I was given my tone to contribute**

---

[21] In "Flipside" there's a discussion of the names of members of a soul group. A spirit guide observed that sometimes it's easier to give a name that makes the person having the session more comfortable; "Max" or even "Thor." However, when it comes to their real names, one person said that the names were more of a sound that a stringed instrument might make. Very difficult to put into a word.

to this symphony of sound that was flowing down the canyon; that's where I wanted to go. I was like... "Ohhhh!" Because this is not, this isn't something I would ever think of – but it kind of explains parts of my life, as music and sound have always helped me through tough times.

What was the music like?

Tonal, multi-tonal, but it was flowing down this canyon, so it would weave a short melody here, and combine others there. I could contribute my own tone – I had a tone. My tone was very baritone – a resonant, baritone sound.

What does it sound like?

(He makes a deep resonant sound).

That sounds a bit like the multi-tones of the Tuva singers or the Gyuto monks.

Yes, I have a couple of tapes of that because I find that very soothing. That was the tone I could contribute to this canyon of sound.

It terms of tonality, what did it seem like?

It was constantly flowing in one direction... not back and forth... It was flowing right to left, like a river of sound.

Did you see anyone else around?

Yes, there were other balconies with people on the balconies... there were thousands of them. It felt very free form; it was very free will.

What do you think the purpose of that tone canyon is?

I so enjoyed it, I didn't think of a purpose behind it. **I think it's just a flow of our resonance in life and beyond life that is kind of like the underwater energy that holds us altogether, it's always there we may not perceive it with a physical sense, but there's always an underlying current of tone – it's energy, always flowing, not stagnant.**

I was interviewing jazz pianist Deron Johnson about "Where does music come from?" He described being in a pool and said that music is just beneath the surface – that idea of a liquid current we may not see but is always with us. When you talk about being in a canyon – you're no longer on the surface, you're under the surface, the idea of it echoing and resonating. It's also very Native American, the idea of singing your song... you mentioned a song to the Great Spirit, Wakan Tanka in your book. So why did you choose this life of David and why did you choose that Chickasaw life and what do the two have in common?

Both have a large degree of suffering involved, both lives are connected very closely with the way we deal with suffering, hardship and challenges. Because, you see in that life (as a Native American) I didn't deal with it well, whereas in this life, I've spent a considerable amount of time... I do some healing work now, and deal with the challenges ingrained in our life. It's part of the life coaching I'm doing now – the adversity in my life I've been able to channel that into a heart centered way of living life rather than a self-involved mode. It shows me the different ways we can approach the same challenges. I think that's their connection.

The question is to experience the energy so you can learn and then master it and teach it.

Someday I'll get there (laughs).

A Memory from a Life Review

In your book you talk about your battle with cancer and the amazing journey you went on. The combination of using meditative practices that were healing – your description of your cancer meditation is very close to the Tibetan meditation of "tonglen" – where you imagine your loved one sitting across from you, and pull that energy from them and into you and heal with the with "healing light of the Universe." But in your meditation, you mentioned sending that energy through your crown chakra and "into the four winds." The only difference is that in tonglen you breathe that healed energy back into them to heal them. To my mind, there's nothing more healing than a physical meditation of "loving your neighbor as yourself" or in this case "heal your neighbor as your neighbor is yourself."

For me it's about the inner connectedness we all feel. I learned later in life... I did a lot of self-healing with the cancer, and I got to a point where I was as healed as I felt that I could get...

Plus you had the advantage of seeing your battle with cancer in your life review as a future event.

Well, it's one of those scary things; we all hope that something doesn't happen even if we subconsciously know it might. "No, I don't want to look at that." So when the cancer was presenting itself, I had all this pain, numbness in my arm, I thought it was carpal tunnel. And I got some twinges in my back, and I'd go to the chiropractor. I just didn't know that I had a serious form of lung cancer, and that had metastasized in my spine and was eating my bones.

Where do you think it came from?

I was an engineer in the navy and we'd tear apart the asbestos with claw hammers. We didn't know any better. They tested me before I got out and I had the possibility of *asbestoses* – plus smoking a pack a day for 20 years; I had double barrels pointed at me. Being a macho diver type guy, invincibility was my cloak. And like I said, I didn't want to see what had been exposed to me in the NDE so I was making excuses – and then finally my spine collapsed and the cancer was found.

It seems that knowing you were going to recover from it may have been key.

I had one of those déjà vu on steroids moments in the hospital when the intern came in and told me I had cancer – of course he didn't say the C word, he said "You've got tumors**." But when he was doing it, I suddenly knew before he walked in the door what he was going to say. I had worked at the hospital and knew everyone and he was an intern I'd never met. But I recognized him from my life review, I knew the surroundings, I knew what he was going to say.**

I was an assistant director at the hospital, and here's this new intern about to give me the death sentence, hemming and hawing and I'm thinking "I remember this moment from my life review!" I couldn't help myself, but let him suffer a bit with the information. So it really didn't bother me, what he was going to say, because I had already seen that I was going to have cancer and go beyond it.

I knew that I had to go through the cancer so I could experience the suffering, the pain, all of that, and the doctors told me I had six weeks to live, and that they weren't going to treat it. And I said "Yes we are going to treat it, because I'm going to survive this." Of course they thought I was in denial, you know the Kubler-Ross stages of denial; but I was already beyond that and in acceptance. I knew that if I could just follow my spirit guidance that I was going to survive this cancer without a doubt. The funny thing is that everyone else in my life was certain I was dying, and I was convinced I was going to live.

We talk about going down a path of darkness... I mean I know this sounds pretty morbid. Sounds kind of twisted.

You could write a book about that alone. I have a close friend, Dr. Sadeghi, who's gave a lecture about how to treat cancer like anything else that is part of your body. And if you hate something that's in your body, that's not a logical or healing way to treat your body. He uses the example of a foreign entity such as a baby is treated with love, while cancer is treated like the enemy.

Yes, I learned to perceive cancer as overcoming a challenge in your life. So I don't say that I battled or fought, or beat cancer. I had friends who when they heard I was going to try to overcome this, they sent me a set of real boxing gloves. I appreciated the sentiment – but I didn't view it as a battle. But I hung them in my office, to remind me that this is the way all the doctors and clinicians will perceive this path, to allow them to do so. But when the doctors announced that I was a medical miracle, I sold the boxing gloves at a yard sale.

That's a very unusual perspective – contrary on many levels. But just to point out that at the same time chemotherapy, as primitive as it is, still did help with the work to get you to where your health wanted to be.

I have a lot of friends into holistic medicine and everyone was telling me what I needed to do. So I used spirit as guidance for what would work for me. Spirit made it very clear to me that part of my path was to go through traditional therapies and to balance it out with holistic approaches. I've met people who've used both approaches; some survived just from holistic medicine, others from just using western medicine; but because of my path, I can talk to cancer patients because I've gone through it. That's a gift in a lot of ways, to be able to talk to cancer patients and families; sometimes you have to walk down that road so they can see or hear you.

I've heard that as well, the idea that those who want to be healers choose lifetimes where they experience pain in order to understand pain, as you've said. So here you are a triple threat. You're one of the few people on the planet who's had a deeply profound near death experience, relived it through a meditation, and then had an LBL session where you got to re-examine it, and finally you're someone who's gone in to the mouth of the beast of cancer and perhaps conquer is not the word – but to adjust to it.

I'm still that warrior who was maimed, but I don't carry the same anger or embitterment; I no longer perceive my battle as battles. **That's part of my daily gratitude; I'm thankful for the opportunity to live life, all of it, the good bad and the ugly. I'm grateful for all of it, because that's who I am and that's my life experience. If I hadn't gone through it I'd be a different person.**

I really believe we have to embrace what we see as good and bad – I've really wiped "good or bad" out of my consciousness. I just accept. Part of that meditation on acceptance, tolerance and truth makes it so I can very easily accept this is where we are right now. I can be tolerant, I wasn't before – someone else may not be in concordance with how I feel but that's their way of living life...

Did anyone give you advice during your between-life session?

"You're on the right path." It was a lot of confirmation that "you're doing what you're supposed to be doing, to stay connected to spirit." And the spirit connection that I perceived during my near death experience is them (my soul family), my higher consciousness is there communicating with them. Sometimes that spirit connection comes to me in different voices; my perception now is that it's my soul family communicating with me.

Which one of them said "Go into the light?"

That was the light speaking - ... that conglomeration of the fragments of light... It's what I perceive that God is.

So to sum up; what or who is God?

The oneness of everything, this table, this cup of coffee; it's you and me, everyone. I know that ruffles people's feathers, but God is in everything, is a part of everything. I realize now that God is love, the waves of love that we need to embrace. We really don't know how loved we are, we can't perceive that - but all we need to do is open up our heart, and we can feel that love is there always.

Thank you![22]

---

[22] As noted, that brings the total to about six of people I've interviewed out of 25, who remembered a

In my past life meditation I saw a Native American come to me saying; "You must take what you know here (and he pointed to the third eye region) and move it down to here (he pointed to the belly and navel area). Then you must move it back up again. This will help you find patience." From a post in Carol Bowman's "Past Life Forum" from someone who remembered a lifetime as a Native American.

---

past life as a native. That's nearly 25%. Part of the bodhisattva vow, for those familiar with it, is to "reincarnate until all beings are liberated." There's also the Native American tradition of wanting to return in spirit form to "protect the Earth."

Chapter Three – Dr. Bruce Greyson

"Consciousness: Is It Created by the Brain?"

"If our conscious experience depends on the brain, then there can't be an afterlife. When the brain is gone, the mind is gone - but it's not. (It's) that simple. Even when the brain seems to be virtually disabled people are still having these experiences." Dr. Emily Williams Kelly, Psychologist from the University of Virginia, co-author of "Irreducible Mind." [23]

I was having lunch with my friend Richard, former executive Vice President of Paramount Television, talking "Flipside" and he said "You really should have a conversation with Carol."

"Carol" is a pseudonym for a mutual acquaintance who has been involved with a number IANDS chapters (International Association of Near Death Studies).

[23] "Discovering Heaven" by Lisa Miller, Time Magazine

Because of her extensive career in the science community, she prefers to remain anonymous about her work in helping people share their near death experiences.

Carol is an effervescent person who invited me to speak at the Virginia Beach chapter about "Flipside" and arranged for our trip there. Dr. Bruce Greyson is on the board of the association, and Carol is good friends with him. She suggested we might stop and visit him at the University of Virginia in Charlottesville, where he's located.

As mentioned, Dr. Greyson is considered the "father of near death research," so I considered this a really unique opportunity to discuss my book with him. Prior to our trip to Virginia, Carol suggested I send him a copy of "Flipside," and he requested a number of copies for his staff. [24] As I'm fond of saying about this research "I may not be a scientist, but I know one who is."

This was my first trip to Virginia and my first journey to the august halls of the University that Thomas Jefferson helped design, and Edgar Allen Poe attended (they've even preserved his dorm room with a stuffed raven.) It also happens to house the Division of Perceptual Studies that is in the forefront of studies on consciousness.

I was given a tour of their facility, which includes rooms to study people with ESP via EEG[25] (conducted by Dr. Ed Kelly, co-author of "Irreducible Mind"); it houses the vast research done by Ian Stevenson on reincarnation studies that he

---

[24] Bruce Greyson is Professor of Psychiatry at the University of Virginia. He is co-author of Irreducible Mind (2007) and co-editor of The Handbook of Near-Death Experiences (2009). Greyson has written many journal articles, and has given media interviews, on the subject of near death experiences. Greyson is Chester F. Carlson Professor of Psychiatry and the division director of The Division of Perceptual Studies (DOPS), formerly the Division of Personality Studies, at the University of Virginia. He is also a Professor of Psychiatric Medicine in the Department of Psychiatric Medicine, Division of Outpatient Psychiatry, at the University of Virginia. Greyson is a researcher in the field of near-death studies and has been called the father of research in near-death experiences. Greyson, along with Kenneth Ring, Michael Sabom, and others, built on the research of Raymond Moody, Russell Noyes Jr and Elisabeth Kübler-Ross. Greyson's scale to measure the aspects of near-death experiences has been widely used, being cited 95 times as of early 2010. He also devised a 19-item scale to assess experience of Kundalini, the Physio-Kundalini Scale. Greyson wrote the overview of Near Death Experiences for the Encyclopedia Britannica and was the Editor-in-Chief of the Journal of Near-Death Studies from 1982 through 2007. Greyson has been interviewed or consulted many times in the press on the subject of near-death experiences. (Wikipedia)

[25] An electroencephalogram (EEG) is a test that detects electrical activity in your brain using small, flat metal discs (electrodes) attached to your scalp.

conducted worldwide for over 30 years, which is now carried on by Dr. Greyson and Dr. Jim Tucker. Dr. Greyson showed me some of the *thousands* of verified NDE cases the institute has not yet been able to research in depth.

In my first email to Dr. Greyson, I presented him with a bit of what I'd learned about hypnosis while writing "Flipside." He replied:

> We agree that accurate personal memories can be retrieved through hypnosis. The difficulty for researchers is that fantasies (or accurate memories of things you've read or seen) can be retrieved as well, and it is very difficult to sort out the source of the information retrieved.
>
> But if the information elicited through hypnosis can be shown to be both accurate and not readily available (like the case corroborated by the American Indian tribal historian that I mentioned in my email), it can't be dismissed easily. You make a good case for Michael Newton's work. We look forward to meeting you and learning more.

I had to reflect on the odd reality that yours truly, a filmmaker on his way to his first large scale public book talk, was given this rare opportunity to address some of the foremost authorities in this field.

The meeting was held in a conference room at the Division of Perceptual Studies, with me on one side, and five or six scientists on the other. Dr. Greyson, a handsome man with a touch of gray hair, smiled and said *"Well, Rich, the problem we have with this work you've done in "Flipside" is that science doesn't consider hypnosis a valid scientific tool."* He mentioned the various reasons why that was the case.

My answer? "I whole heartedly agree."

I pointed out that hypnosis as it's been traditionally practiced since Freud, could not be categorized as science for a number of reasons. Having a client come in with a problem they want to cure could skew the results, and the hypnotist's desire to cure the patient could equally alter the results. Further, by limiting the hypnosis sessions to one hour increments guaranteed that the patient would only achieve a shallow depth of hypnosis at best. The clock would always be ticking.

However there are numerous cases where *cryptomnesia* could not be an issue, as some people under deep hypnosis recall family details, names, or dates they could not possible have heard, seen or read about in their lifetime, including reporting meeting dead relatives they weren't aware existed.

Further, that Michael Newton's method offered a pathway for scientific research; sessions last typically 4 to 6 hours, sometimes over days. The questions asked are neutral by design; "Where are we?" "Where would you like to go now?" "Is there anyone around who can help us answer some questions?" There's always the ability for the person to say "I don't see or sense anyone around me" or "I have no idea what you mean" or simply "I'm not getting anywhere."

Newton's work uses past life memories as a jumping off place for between-life realm, where the reports have been consistent over his thousands of cases across many continents. Now that Newton is retired, his associates and students have been asking the same questions and getting the same results with people who never heard of his method or research, who haven't read his books or who live in other countries. The results are reportedly consistent across the globe.

Dr. Greyson offered an alternate theory; that science considers those remembering a previous lifetime they may be tapping into someone else's lifetime memory - as referred to by Carl Jung's "collective unconscious." That somehow the energy of our lifetime moves after death to a pool of everyone else's memories, and under hypnosis, a person merely taps into someone else's lifetime of memories.[26]

As my friend and Professor Julian Baird used to say "I'd agree with you but then we'd both be wrong." I pointed out I had a unique case in "Flipside" that showed that couldn't be the case.

When beginning my path into this research, I met an Oxford Professor, Robert "B." In his session he remembered a past life in Boston in the 1840's, being a banker and married to a particular woman whom he knows from his current lifetime.

During his past life memory, he saw the two of them living in Boston, a city Robert has never been to, but described accurately. And when she died prematurely in that lifetime, it took the light out of his life, and he died soon

---

[26] Important to note the Dr. Greyson is a classic "skeptic" in the true definition of the term, someone who doesn't believe in any prevailing school of thought. "Science is my game. I can understand that there are philosophical or theological ways of approaching this, but that's not my interest. My interest is in the scientific understanding of it." "Altered States" by Lee Graves, UVA archives 2007

after. I asked Robert if he was still friends with this particular woman; he was. I suggested we perform an experiment. I asked that he not reveal anything about his session to her, and if she was willing, I would find a Newton trained hypnotherapist in the States to do a session with her to see if she had any past life memories of her own.

And we did that. He did not reveal any of his session to her, I supplied the hypnotherapist in New York City, who knew nothing about Robert or his between-life session. And she had the *identical past life memory* Robert did – of being married to him back in the 1840's in Boston.

What are the odds of that happening?

Well, there aren't any, really.

A person could not remember a previous lifetime married to someone else, and then have their former spouse independently recall the same life – without it actually being the case. I've heard of a number of instances from therapists where subjects arrive as a couple, have independent past life and between-life reviews, and observe that they've been together for many lifetimes. But in this case, these two sessions were completely independent of each other by design.

Dr. Jim Tucker was also in the meeting, he replaced Ian Stevenson in the department to study cases of reincarnation at the Department of Perceptual Studies.[27] Dr. Tucker's recent book "Return to Life: Extraordinary Cases of Children Who Remember Past Lives" covers a number of amazing cases.

We discussed the protocols he uses with regard to Ian Stevenson's work in reincarnation, and I told him the story of my son's claim that he had been a monk in Nepal in a previous life ("My Son the Monk" a chapter from "Flipside" that is revisited later in this book) and the number of unusual events that pointed to that actually being the case.

---

[27] Jim Tucker is the medical director of the Child and Family Psychiatry Clinic, and Associate Professor of Psychiatry and Neurobehavioral Sciences at the University of Virginia School of Medicine. His main research interests are children who claim to remember previous lives, and natal and prenatal memories. He is the author of Life Before Life: A Scientific Investigation of Children's Memories of Previous Lives, which presents an overview of over four decades of reincarnation research at the Division of Perceptual Studies. Tucker, a board-certified child psychiatrist, worked for several years on this research with Ian Stevenson before taking over upon Stevenson's retirement in 2002. Wikipedia

Dr. Ed Kelly and I discussed how the institute has measured people while having a psychic experience using EEG. I asked what kinds of experiences they looked for, he mentioned they'd had at least one yogi in to study the energy created by a "Kundalini" experience. Another of life's odd coincidences, I have a close friend who can help them with that; he claims he can create that kind of energy at will, something he stumbled upon by accident.

My friend was an athletic coach, did an amazing amount of daily stretching; preferred cold showers in the morning. These are also rituals yogis do to achieve this kind of mind/body experience over decades; perhaps he'd triggered something or it was from a previous lifetime. Dr. Kelly suggested he'd love to be able to measure him in their lab.

Finally, Dr. Greyson noted that a study of hypnotherapy would be a costly undertaking. The problem for any research facility is there are scarce funds to do scientific research. The vast majority of funds are provided by corporations that are invested in the idea we have only one lifetime; spending money on studying the afterlife begs the question, how can one monetize the results?

I suggested an alternative idea. They shouldn't fund a study. They should bring in one person and test them, and if under deep hypnosis they say the things the rest have said – then it would be up to the scientists to find out how that could be. "I'm a filmmaker; my job is to report what people say, but it's up to you guys, the scientists, to find out why."

As the Dalai Lama has said so eloquently about Buddhist philosophy; if science proves Buddhism is inaccurate, then the philosophy must be changed. I humbly submit, the same goes for science.

Dr. Greyson also happens to be part of the Dalai Lama's "Mind Science Group," and he's been to a number of events and given talks about the nature of consciousness.

The following interview is adapted from his talk on behalf of the "Cosmology and Consciousness Conference - Mind and Matter" which he gave in Dharamsala, India in 2011. I've transcribed the talk, added my questions, and sent it to Dr. Greyson for his notes and review.

Dr. Bruce Greyson

RM: The question everyone wants to know; does consciousness exist outside the brain, and is there any scientific evidence that's the case?[28]

Dr. Greyson: Most western scientists assume consciousness is produced in some way by the brain. There is, of course, a lot of evidence for that position, common sense evidence from our everyday lives. When you drink too much alcohol or get knocked on your head, you don't think very clearly. We also have more sophisticated evidence from science of the link between the brain and consciousness; we can measure electricity in the brain during certain kinds of mental tasks. We can stimulate parts of the brain and record what experiences result and we can remove parts of the brain and observe the effects on behavior.

All this evidence suggests the brain is indeed involved in thinking, perception and memory, but it doesn't necessary suggest the brain *causes* those thoughts or memories. As you listen to me speak, there's electric activity in the temporal lobe of your brain, but does that mean your brain, or suggest that your temporal lobe is producing the sound of my voice? Not at all – all the studies showing brain areas associated with different mental functions only show correlation, not causation.

Are you saying it's possible that thoughts aren't created by the brain?

Thoughts, perception and memories could take place in a consciousness somewhere separate from the brain, but are then received and processed by the brain. Much like a phone, radio or television; the signal, the message, is created somewhere else, but your cell phone is necessary to receive and process the message. **If we were to measure the electrical activity inside your cell phone, we could show certain parts of the cellphone were involved in your hearing the message, but we would not be proving that the message is coming from your cell phone, any more than we can prove thoughts originate within our brains.**

How does that square with Western materialist science?

---

[28] This interview is excerpted and edited from Dr. Greyson's remarks with his input. Greyson, B. (2013). Is consciousness produced by the brain? In Johnson, B. (ed.), Cosmology and consciousness: Exchanges between Buddhist scholars and Western scientists on mind and matter (pp. 59-87). Dharamsala, India: Library of Tibetan Works and Archives.

Western science breaks everything down to its component parts, which makes it easier to study the whole. But the component parts sometimes do not act like the whole. **The brain is composed of millions of neurons - but a single neuron cannot formulate a thought, a single neuron cannot feel angry or cold. It seems that brains can think and feel, but brain cells cannot.**

We don't know how many neurons you need to collectively formulate a thought and we don't know how that collection of neurons can think when a single neuron can't. Scientists get around this problem by saying the mind is an "emergent property;" when a large enough mass of brain cells get together it creates thought. What does that mean?

We have no idea what that means. Saying something is an "emergent property" is a way of saying that it is a mystery we can't explain. There is in fact no known mechanism by which physical processes in the brain (or anywhere else) demonstrate the brain can produce experiences, thoughts, perceptions or memories.

The materialist view of the world fails to deal with how the brain can produce a thought or feeling or indeed anything that the mind does. **And yet despite having no idea how it could work, most neuroscientists continue to maintain this 19th century materialist view that the brain, in some miraculous way we don't understand, produces consciousness.** And they discount, or ignore the evidence that consciousness in extreme circumstances can function very well without our brain.

How did we come to believe that the brain was the source of thought?

In the 19th century in the west, beginning with Darwin, people started to explore the notion the physical brain might be the source of our emotions. For the past century, our materialist scientists have been moving toward - based on classical Newtonian mechanics - that consciousness is nothing more than a byproduct of the working brain. Watson, the psychologist who created "Behaviorism," wrote that the brain needs consciousness as little as do the sciences of chemistry and physics. [29]

---

[29] John B Watson was an American psychologist who established the psychological school of behaviorism. Through his behaviorist approach, Watson conducted research on animal behavior, child rearing, and advertising. In his book "Behaviorism" Watson argued that any existence of a mental life is false. Wikipedia

How has quantum theory affected this field of study?

While Watson was doing this in psychology, ironically, physicists were moving away from that to quantum physics, which could not be formulated without consciousness having a role in the universe. As Yale scientist Harold J. Morowitz wrote "It is as if the two disciplines were on two fast-moving trains, going in opposite directions and not noticing what is happening across the tracks." [30]

Classical Newtonian physics was a good model for everyday objects moving at everyday speeds. Involving objects approaching the speed of light, it was only 100 years ago that we saw the limitations of the classical Newton model and a need for new paradigms. The result was quantum physics which explained the world which Newtonian physics could not. But the price scientists paid was to say that consciousness was independent of matter. So too the mind/brain relationship; it's only when we experience events such as what happens when we approach death, that we find the need for a different paradigm.

How did you get involved in the work you're doing now?

In the mid 1960's, Chester Carlson, who invented Xerography, which became Xerox, started giving away his fortune. He told his wife his one remaining ambition was to die a poor man; his wife introduced him to Buddhism, and he went on to fund a number of Buddhist centers in New York. But Carlson was also a scientist, and he searched for a western neuroscientist who was interested in investigating accounts of reincarnation. He found Ian Stevenson, donated to the University of Virginia the funds to establish the research division, and Professor Stevenson devoted himself full time to study reincarnation.

I worked with Professor Stevenson since the early 1970's, training to be a psychiatrist at UVA. Under his mentorship I studied a variety of human experiences that suggested consciousness functioning separate from the brain, but I focused primarily on near death experiences (NDE), the complex experiences people have on the threshold of death when the brain is shutting

---

[30] "Physicists, faced with compelling experimental evidence, have been moving away from strictly mechanical models of the universe to a view that sees the mind as playing an integral role in all physical events. It is as if the two disciplines were on two fast-moving trains, going in opposite directions and not noticing what is happening across the tracks. "Rediscovered the Mind," by Harold J. Morowitz. From Psychology Today, August 1980.

down. Ten years ago, Dr. Stevenson retired and I succeeded him as director of our research division.

In "Irreducible Mind" you argue that there are a number of ways consciousness exists outside a functioning brain. Can you elaborate?

There are four lines of evidence to explore. Number one is the unexplained recovery of consciousness for people who've been unconscious for prolonged periods of time, moments or days before their death. Number two is complex consciousness in people with minimal brain tissue. Number three is surprisingly complex consciousness in near death experiencers when the brain is not functioning or functioning at a diminished level, and number four; young children who can recall details of a past life.

The first challenging phenomenon is the surprising recovery on the deathbed of patients whose mental functions had long been lost. They experience an unexpected return of brain function shortly before death. This has been reported in medical literature over the past 250 years but has received little attention. There are cases published of people suffering from tumors, strokes, meningitis, Alzheimer's, other dementias, Schizophrenia and mood disorders; all of whom had long ago lost the ability to think or communicate.

In many of these patients, there was evidence from brain scans or autopsies that their brains had deteriorated, yet in all these cases, mental clarity returned in the last minutes, hours or days before the patient's death.

We have identified 83 cases in western medical literature – and have collected additional unpublished accounts. Complete recovery of consciousness just before death is an uncommon experience. In 1884 a scientist established that it occurred in 13% of his patients who died. However in a recent investigation into end of life cases in the United Kingdom, 70% of caregivers observed patients with dementia becoming completely lucid in their last hours before death.

There is no known physiological mechanism for this happening – it is indeed rare, but the fact that it happened at all, suggests the link between consciousness and the brain is more complex than we usually think. **It's as if the damaged brain prevents the person from consciousness, but then as the brain finally begins to die, consciousness is released from the grasp of the degenerating brain.**

What about those cases you mention where people have little or no brain tissue?

John Lorber, who specialized in children with hydrocephalus, or "water on the brain" (which usually leads to blindness and other problems) described dozens of people with severe hydrocephalus who seemed to lead normal lives. In a sample of children in whom the cerebral spinal fluid was in 95% of their skull, half of them had IQs greater than a hundred. Thirty years ago Roger Lewin published an article about Lorber's work in "Science" magazine entitled "Is Your Brain Really Necessary?" [31]

What about your research into near death experiences?

Some of the best evidence of the consciousness functioning independently of the brain comes from NDE's. These are profound experiences that some report on the threshold of death. NDE accounts are people who are clinically dead and are resuscitated or revived after a brief interval with memories of what they experience after that period. They typically report exceptional mental clarity, vivid sensory imagery, a clear memory of their experience, and an experience more real than their everyday life; **all of this occurring under conditions of drastically altered brain function under which the materialist model would say that consciousness is impossible.**

Roughly how many of these cases have you examined?

NDEs are reported between 10-20% of people revived from clinical death; I've investigated almost 1000 of these cases. The average age is 31, there's a very wide range; one young girl reported an experience she had at 8 months undergoing kidney surgery – the oldest NDE was 81. About a third occur during surgery, a quarter during serious illness, and a quarter during life threatening accidents.

What are the common features of an NDE?

Changes in thinking, changes in emotional state, paranormal features and other worldly features are the common features of NDEs. Changes in thinking during the NDE include a sense of time being altered; often people reported that time

---

[31] John Lorber was a professor of pediatrics at the University of Sheffield from 1979 until his retirement in 1981. He worked at the Children's Hospital of Sheffield, where he specialized in work on spina bifida. In 1980, Roger Lewin published an article in Science, "Is Your Brain Really Necessary?" about Lorber's studies on cerebral cortex losses. He reports the case of a Sheffield University student who had a measured IQ of 126 and passed a Mathematics Degree but who had hardly any discernible brain matter at all since his cortex was extremely reduced by hydrocephalus. (Wikipedia)

stopped or ceased to exist during the experience. **It also includes a sense of revelation or understanding where everything in the universe becomes crystal clear. There's a sense of the person's thoughts being much faster and clearer than usual, and finally there was a life review or panoramic memory where their entire life seemed to flash before them.**

Typical emotions reported during the NDE include an overwhelming sense of peace and well-being, a sense of cosmic unity or being one with everything, a feeling of complete joy and a sense of being loved unconditionally.

The paranormal features often reported in the NDE include a sense of leaving the physical body, sometimes called an out of body experience (OBE), where a person's physical senses, such as hearing or visual experience become more vivid than ever before. **Some experience hearing sounds that don't exist in this life, and a sense of ESP; knowing things beyond the range of physical senses such as things happening at a remote location.**

And finally, they may report visions of the future. Many report in their NDEs they entered some other or unearthly world or realm of existence; many report they came to a border they could not cross, or a point of no return that if they had crossed, they wouldn't be allowed to return to life. **Many report encountering or seeing a mystical being, and some report seeing deceased spirits, often loved ones, welcoming them into another realm, or in some cases sending them back to another life.**

Do people retain the emotions of the experience once they return to consciousness?

One of the things about NDE that interests me as a psychiatrist are the profound after-effects that people report, is a consistent change in values that don't fade over time. **Near death experiencers report overwhelmingly that they're "more spiritual" after the experience, they have more compassion for others, and a greater desire to help others, a greater appreciation for life, and a stronger sense of meaning or purpose in life. An overwhelming majority of NDErs report they have a stronger belief we survive death of the body, and just as many report they no longer have any fear of death.**

About half lose interest in material possessions, and many report they have no longer any interest in prestige or competition. Some become less attached to material possessions and become more compassionate.

If you could walk us through; how does the NDE experience suggest consciousness is not produced by the brain?

Among several hundred NDErs I've studied; 47% report that their thinking is clearer than it is in their normal waking state, 38% say it's faster than usual, 29% say it it's more logical than usual, and 17% say they have more control over their thoughts. An analysis of their medical records shows that mental functioning is significantly better in those people who come closest to death. Many NDErs experience a panoramic life review, not just visual images, but elaborate events, sometimes the entirety of that person's life.

There was a 25 year old nurse who became depressed and overdosed; he took medication from the hospital where he worked, became quite ill, then decided to phone for help. He tried to walk to the phone, but had difficulty standing and walking. He hallucinated there were many small people in his apartment stopping him from getting to the phone. In that confused state, he found himself leave his body, standing ten feet above himself – he watched his body sway unsteadily, and saw himself looking around in confusion at the imaginary people. He was thinking very clearly from that above perspective and could not see the tiny people; so the center of his consciousness had left his body and could see what was happening to him down below.

Professor Kenneth Ring did a study of 31 blind near death experiencers who were able to describe the scene around them, including accurate descriptions of colors of a number of objects. In a recent review of 93 published reports, a study showed that 92 were completely accurate, 6% had a minor error and 1% were wrong – but even in the case where someone reported it to someone else first, they were 90% correct.

A 56 year old van driver had emergency heart bypass, and during the procedure, while fully anesthetized, he left his body and was able to look down and see his body. To his surprise, he saw the surgeon appear to flap his arms as if trying to fly; not something you'd expect a surgeon to be doing. The day after the operation, he asked the doctor why he was "flapping his arms."

The surgeon was embarrassed and asked the patient "Who told you that?" No one had told him; he saw it himself from above, during the operation. When he got over his embarrassment, the surgeon explained he was supervising his assistants, and in order to ensure his hands remained in sterilized gloves, he put them on his chest, and used his elbows to instruct his nurses where to cut, which caused him to look like he was trying to fly.

Have you had any accounts of seeing other people or family relatives during an NDE?

Among several hundred NDE's I've studied, 42% reported seeing people during the NDE's.

An American pediatrician treated a 9 year old boy with meningitis. During the 36 hours the boy was surrounded by his anxious parents who never left his bed, and during the vigil, when his fever broke, he described seeing several of his deceased relatives, including his sister Theresa, who told him he had to go back to his body. The father got very upset because Theresa was away in college in another state and very healthy; but the boy insisted that Theresa told him she had to stay there and he had to go back. The father learned later that Theresa had in fact been killed in an automobile accident.

Sometimes the deceased person in the NDE is a person the near death experiencers didn't know existed. Elisabeth Kubler-Ross reported a case of a woman who saw her brother during heart surgery and the parents revealed she had a brother who had passed away they had never mentioned to her before. **Of course if consciousness is produced by the brain, then when the brain dies, consciousness ends – it cannot continue into another incarnation – so if some of us do remember our past lives, then those memories cannot reside solely in the brain.**

Eben Alexander reports the same kind of story; while he was in his NDE he says his sister was his guide. He didn't know he had a sister until his parents revealed she'd died before he was born. How about Ian Stevenson's work in reincarnation? Did he find scientific proof of reincarnation?

Dr. Stevenson did much of his research in Asia where reincarnation is an accepted part of the societal norms. Children mentioned names, names of relatives, details of how their past life ended. In many cases we could take the child to the remote village and the child was able to identify people and places never seen before in this life. They may exhibit qualities of the previous life; sometimes remembering a past life as another gender, or a child will remember being a Muslim and reject certain types of food, or they were Japanese pilots shot down during WWII in

Burma, and they reject food their parents offer and want traditional Japanese food.

Some exhibit unusual skills they've not been taught, play a musical instrument they've not being taught, or have skills related to their occupation in a past life. We've also examined children who can converse in languages not of their current country. 335 of them had birthmarks or birth defects matching wounds from past life, 18% of cases match confirmed medical records or autopsy reports that death wounds correspond to marks in current life.

Are there many cases in the United States?

James Leininger, born in Louisiana, as a toddler, seemed to remember being shot down during WWII. He would often play with planes and wake up screaming from a nightmare of being trapped on a plane. James gave many details of his past life including the name of his airplane and details of the plane, the aircraft carrier he flew from, and the details of his death. The deceased pilot's sister, who is still alive, confirmed the boy's accounts of her brother's friends and the boy identified several objects in her home that used to belong to him in his previous life. She's convinced this little boy is indeed the rebirth of her dead brother.

In terms of the research, it sounds a bit like you're saying that in some cases, consciousness functions better in spite of the brain.

There's a lot of evidence from scientific research that the brain, under extraordinary circumstances, seems to come unlinked from consciousness, and consciousness can in fact, function better without the mediation of the physical brain. Again this evidence is not accepted or known by most American scientists; nevertheless it is there, it is reliable and reproducible evidence.

We have cases of people whose brains have been deteriorating for years suddenly think clearly on their deathbeds, people who function normally sometimes with high intelligence who have virtually no brain tissue, we have people who during a near death experience think more clearly than ever, when their brains are not functioning. And we have very young children who can barely speak, who talk about their past lives with accurate details.

These phenomena - all well investigated by modern scientific methodologies, and building upon decades or centuries of prior research - strongly suggest that

under extraordinary circumstances, consciousness can be produced and can function without the intercession of the physical brain.

Thank you.

———————

As to the question of how this research has personally affected Dr. Greyson, he's said: "I don't think I was uncompassionate before this (research). But before I started in this field, I saw things like the Golden Rule as things we were supposed to try to live up to. People come back from near-death experiences and say, 'It's not a guideline for you. This is the way the universe works. **We're all in this together. If I hurt you, I'm hurting myself. There's no distinction between you and me.**' That sense tends to rub off after you hear it week after week, year after year, that we are all in this together. ... It becomes not a matter of following a rule, but living your life according to these principles." [32]

"The evidence that I have found most promising has been that provided by children who claim to remember past lives." -- Professor Ian Stevenson

———————————————

[32] "Altered States: Scientists analyze the near-death experience" by Lee Graves. UVA archives 2007.

Chapter Four - "Live Long and Prosper"

Interview with an Afterlife Teacher

"Coincidence is God's way of remaining anonymous." Einstein

After "Flipside" appeared in print, a couple of friends contacted me about having a between-life session and allowing me to film it.

In this case, a friend I've known since grade school called me about doing a session. She wanted to explore some unusual dreams she'd had her whole life, and felt safe allowing me to film her session.

I picked up "Ivy"[33] at the airport, and drove her to Michael Newton trained hypnotherapist Scott De Tamble's office in Claremont, California, a sleepy college town about an hour outside of LA. On the way, my friend talked about how she had called Scott to express her fears of "not being able to be hypnotized."

---

[33] In all of these sessions I used a pseudonym for each participant.

Scott had sent her to a colleague in Manhattan to see if she could be hypnotized, as he didn't want her to fly all the way to California if they weren't going to get anywhere. (By the way, I've yet to see Scott not "get anywhere" with a client.) The following are excerpts from her first session with another hypnotherapist in Manhattan that Scott recommended.

Ivy's Earlier Session

Therapist: Let's go back to a previous lifetime... floating to a place and time and you are there at the number one. First impression, daytime or nighttime?

Ivy: I feel nauseous. Like I'm vomiting, like I can't stop vomiting.

Allow that to be experienced.

I think I've been poisoned. (Gasps.)

Are you a man or woman?

I don't know (coughs).

What do you notice around you?

(Chokes.) I don't know.

I want you to go backward in time before you felt this way. What do you notice?

I don't know, it doesn't make sense, but I've got like, men's shoes from the time of Louis 16th. Pale blue, made of gold, very pointed and they're... I think I'm in Versailles somewhere. It feels like that time. I'm a man. And I have a child. The child is on my lap.

Notice the child's eyes. Remind you of anyone?

It's a boy. I'm not sure if I know this person. I want to say it's my sister but I don't know. We're walking through a yard at Versailles, together. He's a boy and his hand is in mine. I feel the sun beating down on me. And he's a very cute baby. And his name is Henry. I think my name is Louis. I'm not the King.

Who are you?

I'm someone in the King's court. My name is Louis also. Did I say the boy's name is Henry? His name is Henri. And he's about two. And he has the most beautiful cheeks.

Where's his mother?

I was just thinking about that. I don't know. I'm getting the feeling that she passed away. And it's just me and him.

How old are you?

34.

What's your last name?

Marchant (or Marchand).

What's your role?

I'm an advisor to the King.[34]

How old is Henri?

Two. We're walking through the gardens and he's playing with this thing, it's like a ball but it has a stick with it, that's like he's... the stick has a hole and I'm throwing the ball through the whole and he's laughing.[35]

How do you feel?

---

[34] In researching this, I found the term "Prevot de Marchand" as a member of Louis XVI's court. Translated, it means "Provost of Merchants" and was an influential position in the court until it was abolished after Louis XVI's execution. As it turns out the name of the last Prevost of Merchants was indeed named Louis: Louis Le Peletier de Morfontaine, Marquis of Montmélian (1730-1799) the penultimate provost of Paris. He was Secretary of State and wrote a number of letters to Thomas Jefferson on behalf of the King. His name is now a street in the 9th arrondissement, the rue Le Peletier and metro station Le Peletier. (Wikipedia) Also, the records show his mother was Marie-Louise of Feydeau Calende, daughter of Henri Feydeau, who was "President of the House of Investigations." So if indeed this is the Louis in question, naming a son Henri may have been after the paternal grandfather who was also part of the royal court.

[35] I found this toy through an extensive online search. It's called a "Bilboquet" a French game played as early as the 16th century. "The game was popular in the royal courts of Europe, where players caught a swinging ball in a cup at the end of the handle." The "Kendama" version has a point, which goes through a ball, as described above. (Wikipedia)

Really nice. I love this child. But I know we're going to die. I think things are falling apart. The French revolution is happening.

Your days are numbered?

Yeah. I poisoned myself, because I didn't want my neck cut off. I gave a lot of money to a peasant family to take care of Henri. I'm trying to enjoy the day as much as possible because I know it's one of my last. I don't know if it's my last, but I know it's close.

Anyone else in your life?

Um... there's the King... and the Queen. I don't like the Queen. She's very conniving. She's manipulating people. She's also... is she Austrian? I don't trust her. I don't like her eyes. The queen was having an affair.[36]

What's your relationship with the king?

He trusts me. I tell him he's got to leave and he can't. And I have a plan to get him out of the country, but he refuses to go.

Describe the king to me.

He's not very tall. He's funny and flamboyant. Kind of looks a little too inbred. Like sharp strong features, sharp nose, big lower lip, kind of a funny chin, he's wearing a white wig. He's not thin; there's something kind of paunchy about him but he's not fat. He's kind of got a belly. And he's making jokes all the time. He likes to party and have fun. And he likes to be waited on. [37]

How do you feel?

I feel tired. I feel like could it all be true? -- I'm feeling like it is true."

---

[36] Marie Antoinette was notorious for a number of reasons, including her affair to Swedish soldier Hans Axel von Fersen. "Judging from the correspondence between the two of them, they had a very intimate relationship. Some claim there's no way to tell if her children were Louis' or Fersen's. But Louis accepted the children as his own, and Marie Antoinette and her lover were careful to avoid any unwanted pregnancies." ("How Stuff Works" "Top 5 Marie Antoinette Scandals")

[37] This is an accurate, if not unflattering, portrait of the real King of France.

Needless to say, having known Ivy for most of my life, I found it pretty amusing that she would have this past life memory of living in the court in Versailles. Many people complain that "everyone under hypnosis remembers being famous, like Cleopatra") – that may be true for people doing stage hypnosis, or some other event that is monetary based – but in this case, I know for a fact that Ivy had no delusions of being someone in the French Court who had to sell his son and commit suicide to avoid the guillotine.

It was a powerful session for Ivy that didn't answer some of her deeper questions, but demonstrated at the least that she had no problem being "under hypnosis."

So as we were driving to Claremont to see Scott De Tamble, Ivy turned to me and said; "By the way, a couple of things might come up in the session today. One is that my dad molested me and the other is that my brother OD'd using drugs. They're two things that I've had a lot of therapy over, and I'm still working on them, but they might come up." I expressed sorrow to her, as best as a friend could hearing something that they had never known about their friend.

She and I had driven to and from Chicago and the East Coast a number of times during college – we'd spent days in the car, literally, drive all the way from Brooklyn where she was going to college, we'd spend an evening in our home town of Northbrook, and then pile back into the car and drive back. So we had a lot of time to talk about everything – and somehow neither of these topics came up.

She also expressed the same to Scott, and he deals with them in the session – but as a "command" during her induction process, where she remembers things from her childhood, he asked her to "only remember happier times" during that childhood, so the session wouldn't just be about the traumas of her youth. And what transpired is below.

Ivy's Session with Scott

Moving back to the stairway... 9 months, 8 months etc... one week... and before birth and in the womb now, before birth and in the womb, feel the protection of this dark warm environment, where you drift and float inside of your mom... how does it feel?

Um. I don't feel protected.

What are you feeling?

Scared. Frightened. Feel frightened. Feel hot.[38]

About how many months of gestation are you?

I want to say six.

Ok. Do you know the source of that feeling? That fright? Is it something inside of you?

I think it's in my mother. She's very unsure of herself.

Her emotions are affecting you?

Yeah, she's very erratic. Although it feels light in here – I can fell white light – I feel it shining on me. I feel like you're shining a light in my eyes right now.

Is the light pleasant?

Yeah, it's very comforting, makes me forget about my mother.

But you're given comfort from another quarter?

Yeah, but it's not there all the time. Maybe when I get really scared it comes, I don't feel scared right now.

Let's imagine talking to that light for a moment. Who are you? And what is your relation to this baby here?

I'm here as protection. I protect Ivy.

Are you a personality? Like someone with a name?

I'm healing energy.

Call the light to you right now.

---

[38] During a session I'm filming, especially with a friend whom I've brought to the process, I get concerned when they begin saying things like "I'm not comfortable" or "I don't see anything." Despite a 100% record with everyone I've brought to him for hypnosis, I'm not as confident as Scott De Tamble is that we'll get anywhere. But we always do.

Okay it's on me. When I want to protect stuff I surround it with white light. I'm feeling really nice and peaceful and protected. I'm bathed in white light. It's very energizing.

Soak that light up, soak it in. While you're bathing in that white light, I'm going to ask you some questions. Is that okay? First impressions now, what month did you join the fetus? What number comes to your mind?

Four.

And what was your initial impression of this brain and body?

That I didn't want to be here. But they made me.

Why didn't you want to be here?

I didn't feel really safe.

Let's go back to the time when they are telling you to do this. Let's go back to that that moment. What's being said?

I'm trying to figure it out – um... I'm being sent, to help people. And it's not my first choice.

What would your first choice be?

I don't think I was given a lot of choices, I didn't like any of the choices, I uh, I don't think I wanted to come back this time.

Let me ask you this – you didn't want to come back, yet you did – what was the determining factor?

To help people.

What's your impression of this body and brain? How does it compare to others?

It's not as nimble.

Are you usually female or male?

Uh, both. I don't really care.

What are some of the positive things about this body or brain?

It's smart. It's street smart. It can figure things out. It can heal. I can help people heal but I'm impatient.

How can you help people heal?

The energy. I can tune in. I know how to do it.

You have an intuitive empathy thing going on?

More like a thermometer up their butt. I don't think I'm empathetic.

You can just sense what they're going through? How does this enable you to heal them?

Because I can show them the way, I don't want to do it though.

What is the way?

Everyone is different.

But yet you're not wanting to do this? Why?

I'm impatient. Because I want them to do it now, it's not that linear. It's a process. Frustrates me, it irritates me. That's not healing.

What about the emotional system of this body here? What's that like?

It's very sensitive and um, very hot tempered. But… um… fun and jovial.

Your soul mind has a personality, this body has one – do they mesh?

My soul mind has accepted the assignment. It's part of my learning.

Do you know why you accepted this particular assignment?

I think there are people I'm supposed to help.

A Ship's Captain

So let's move away, disengage, float up and away (to a previous lifetime that has some influence on this one...), etc. Be there now. First thing that comes to you... Is it daytime or nighttime?

I have a stomach ache.

Let's go back in time, ten minutes, half an hour, maybe an hour, from three down to one, let's go back in time, three, two one... so what's happening now? Still have the stomach ache?

Yeah. It feels stronger. It's stabbing me a little bit... it's stabbing.

Does it feel like something from inside or outside?

I think it's inside.

So let's go back in time before, before this stomach ache started, three, two and one, be there now. No stomach ache.

I was stabbed.

So let's go back in time, I know it may be uncomfortable, you don't have to experience it, you can observe from a higher perspective, but let's go back, three two one, be there now.

Oh. (Sighs.) I'm fighting. I have a foil, I'm fighting another man. I'm a man.

It's a duel?

Yeah, but, I'm on a big boat.

Like a big melee?

It's a fight. It's a lot of people.

Is this a war battle?

Yeah, they came on our boat, the pirates. I want to say we were surprised.

Ok, let's go back in time before this attack, when everything's relatively calm, going back in time to a calm moment, three, two and one... all is well. Tell me about your boat here. What's the purpose of this voyage?

We're transporting goods. I feel like we're coming from the Middle East, like China or something. I'm a Caucasian man with dark brown hair and blues eyes. I'm British.

What's the year, the number that pops into your mind?

I keep seeing 1610.

What kind of goods are you transporting?

We're transporting fabrics, silks and spice. Spice is in barrels. I don't think we have boxes, I only see barrels and rolls of fabric.[39]

About how many men are on this boat?

There's 37 of us. [40]

What's your name, what do they call you?

Phillip Martin.

How old are you? In this moment on this boat?

25. Dark brown hair, blues eyes. I'm about five eight and I'm lean. I grew up on boats; my father owns the boat. We pick up goods and deliver them.

Does the boat have a name?

I'm looking. I see it on the front. It's something with a C A.. I want to say P.. Cap.. can't make out the rest. Cap.. I can't make it out.

So Phillip, you've grown up on boats. Do you like the boat life?

I like the sea, but I spend time on land too. My dad's a merchant and I'm picking up goods for him and delivering them.

Do you have a home base in England or some other European state? Like a warehouse or a dock. Tell me about it.

It's the outskirts of London. We have a big building where we store goods.

---

[39] The British East India company was created in the late 1500's in London. By 1610 they had begun their trade with the East Indies. I think it's interesting to note the detail she observes; bolts of fabric is not something people put into films or books about this era, but it is what they transported.

[40] That's an accurate number for a ship of this size and purpose. In Henry Hudson's voyage in 1610, he had a crew of 25. According to the East Indian records from 1600, smaller East India ships in the 17th century had a crew from 35-50. I'm convinced it's not a detail that Ivy is consciously aware of.

Do you live nearby?

We have a house; I live with my dad and my mom and my two sisters. The boat is my sister's name Catherine, the boat's named for my little sister. Or maybe we named my little sister after the boat. [41]

What's the other sister's name?

Margaret; she's not well. She limps. A birth defect - we have to take care of her. It looks like one leg is shorter than the other. She has a walking stick.

How does mom spend her time?

She cooks and cleans and takes care of the house.

How do you spend your days?

I work, and I go to the pubs. I work for my dad. I do different things; sometimes sell the stuff that he brings in, that he imports and exports.

Where is the place where you have your warehouse?

The street is named Bright, Brighton.[42]

What are the main goods your dad deals with?

Spice. Pepper. Salt. We go to many places.

Tell me about some of the places you've been.

India.

What's it like there?

Very busy. Very dirty. Different than London. The buildings are different. It's more flat.

---

[41] There was a ship named "The Catherine" sailed by the Courteen Association Fleet in the East Indies. From "The travels of Peter Mundy in Europe and Asia, 1608-1667" Wellesley College online catalog.

[42] In the online records of the Old Bailey, which contains all the records of the British Court, I found a court case filed by a Phillip Martin in 1610, his address listed was Brighton. (www.oldbaileyonline.org/)

What other places do you go?

Go to islands. They're small, I just remember stopping on an island. I think we had to stop because we had a problem with the boat. We hit something.

Any other places you remember you've been to?

I will say... Africa.

You've been all over the place then. Ok. Let's go back to the time when you're on the boat and all of a sudden, bang you're hit by some attackers. Tell me.

It's night. And they board the ship. We're all asleep, there were two boats. We're all inside.

Are there swords or firearms?

There are cannons on the boat, but the watchman fell asleep – and one of the guys.. Jonathan didn't see the boats coming. He's was driving the boat, but why didn't he see? How could he call him a pilot - he was in charge of... the sails?

What do you call him?

I want to say first mate.[43]

So what happens to you? Do you wake up?

I'm asleep and I hear fighting. And I got my sword.

Tell me about your sword.

I love my sword. It's silver. It's thick and it has one of those handles, like a cup. I can feel my thumb in it, feels really good. My dad gave it to me – it's long, it's very long, about three and half feet – its single edge, it's straight.

My Dad's Going to be Upset

---

[43] These are accurate terms for a sailing vessel of this era. Henry Hudson's manifest includes his "pilot, William Baffin" as well. Maritime law of the era refers to Pilot, Master and Crew.

Etch this sword in your mind so you can draw it later. What do you do? You pick up your sword?

I run up to the deck and I start fighting; I'm very good with the sword. I kill several of them. And then, two guys start fighting me at once and we're outnumbered, like three to one. One of them stabs me. My dad's going to be so upset.[44]

So do you feel this is a death wound? Or something you can survive?

I don't survive. They take our goods and leave us all wounded on the boat. They stabbed me right here, but I can't move anymore. I'm alive, but I can't move and it hurts.

What are you seeing?

The stars. I'm trying to get up but I can't. Everyone's moving. One of the pirates turns me over and kicks me in the head.[45]

Let's move ahead and forward to the moment just after death. Died and crossed over, leaving the pain, rising above, it's okay now, it's okay. You'll be able to continue to talk to me, rising about that, feel your awareness expanding... etc. So where are you? Above off to the side?

I'm above it.

How are you feeling?

Like I failed my mission. Because we didn't get the goods home and my dad's gonna be mad. He's at home, working.

What does it feel like to cross over?

---

[44] It's interesting that the first thought that comes to mind here is "My father is going to be upset about this" rather than a fear for a person's own life. If a person was creating this scenario, you'd think there might be some other motivation to consider rather than how their father would feel.

[45] Pirates were a constant topic of discussion in the English archives. From a letter in 1603: "Henry Middleton succeeded with as many four ships but the Dutch represented the English as pirates, that they came with a design to plunder his country (India), the King commanded them to leave it, the Governor confessed the Dutch (had) offered the natives 12,000 dollars not to trade with the English." [East Ind Corresp., March 23, 1613.]

Um... feels like a relief. Cause it really hurt. It's still kind of there, like I feel a remnant from it.

Tell me about your dad. What's he like?

He's hard, but he's kind too.

What's your father's first name?

Phillip.

Phillip Martin?

Yeah, I'm junior. He's going to be upset about losing me.

What's your relationship?

Very good.

I understand you feel bummed about failing to complete the mission – what else is going through your mind.

That my dad is also my dad in this lifetime. Only we... We were really close. I was his son. He took care of me (in the Phillip life).

As Ivy you got to be with him again.

Yeah, but that wasn't so good.

Okay. Is there anything you need to do as Phillip?

I want to say goodbye to my sister Margaret. It's my brother Larry, oh my god, my sister Margaret is (my brother from this lifetime) Larry. Oh God.

Spend some time with Margaret.

Oh, I feel so bad... (She starts to cry.) Um, that there's not going to be anyone to... I told Margaret I would take care of her in her old age, and now I'm going, 'cause no one's going to marry her.

Because of her deformity?

Yeah.

But for now, why don't you visit with her in spirit and you can feel bad about that. Give her a hug or do whatever you need to do. Just to tell her that you love her and that you're sorry. Obviously you have a bond with her.

(Wipes away tears). She tells me she's going to be okay. My dad's going to buy her a husband.

What about Catherine?

She's going to be okay, she's a real beauty.

What about mom and dad? You want to stop by your dad?

Yeah. He says "Its ok, he'll miss me." I was his pride and joy (wipes away tears).

We can now move away and explore your eternal existence as a timeless being... we'll be able to know incredible details about your life between-lifetimes... in a few moments, we'll be going to a place of expanded awareness...

I see London; I don't know if they're burning coal, but it's very polluted; the sky is like black, smoky, grey, and its overcast.

Do you feel any sense of pulling or floating?

Floating. I felt cold. I'm floating up. Now I see everything's getting smaller.

As you travel all the emotions and cares and worries fall away... bit by bit... If you wish call that white light to guide you... protect you... how are you feeling now?

Relaxed. Light. Free. Happy. Very happy. Kinda giddy. It's nice to feel weightless. Feel like I can zoom around.

All right, let's skip forward in time to a time when you have some sort of encounter or arrive somewhere. Be there now. What's happening?

I run into my dad (from the London lifetime).

What is he communicating to you?

That I did a good job. He's uh... just giving me a big hug. He wanted me to know that I was very brave and that's why that I was supposed to learn about bravery.

How does that make you feel?

Really good.

Anything else he wants you to know?

That he loves me.

I wonder if he would like to direct you to some place or some person... maybe he would like to take you somewhere or escort you somewhere.

He said that I'm supposed to go that way (points) there's this path... it's like really beautiful, trees on both sides and I'm over there. He's happy to see me. He said I have to go by myself.

So let's go through that path. What's the surface of that path like?

It's like... carved, not carved but a limestone path. Trees on both sides and its near water.

A Field Trip from Class

What does it feel like on this path?

Feels kind of confusing because it's like there are things that don't match. Palm trees with the smell of pine. So moving on this path. All right.. I'm just giving him a hug. Kind of walking and waving goodbye. I'm walking down the path.

What are you noticing?

There's a clearing and a cover. Over the water. There are people. I'm counting... looks like 23.

Are they familiar to you?

They seem to know me, they're waving for me to come over.

Let's go over and greet them. What are they saying to you?

"We missed you." (Laughs.) I seem happy to see them. They're sitting in a circle like an Indian circle with their legs crossed. "Come join the circle."

What's going on in this circle?

They're doing some kind of... looks like they're lifting this thing with their... they're going like this (lifts her arms) and holding this thing up but they're not touching it.

Like levitating?

A piece of limestone, a big piece, but they have one hand and they're waving with another – kind of funny. That I should come sit with them.

Let's go ahead and do that; sit down.

Ah. There's a place for me.

You know how to lift that rock too?

I do.. I don't know if it's them or if it's me. I mean they were doing it before I sat down. Yeah, now it's going higher.

What's that feel like?

It feels like child's play. It feels like very basic.

Levitation is Very Basic

What's the purpose of this?

To move things with your mind.

Is this a practice?

Yeah. Moving things. I have this flashback of like turning light bulbs on and off with my mind... back here on Earth. And making them explode and laughing (laughs.)

So you're learning to project energy?

Yeah.

Is this group your friends?

I think it's a class. And I'm the teacher – but I wasn't here (laughs). How could they be learning if I'm not there?

Let's go to a time forward or back when you are instructing them in this activity. Be there at a time when you're instructing them; what are you telling them?

That they can move mountains with their minds. I'm talking to them about focus; you have to have focus. And you have to put all your energy in – that levitation is very basic. But handy for moving things.

If levitation is basic, what would be more advanced?

I don't know what's basic.

Walk me through this as if I was one of your students – "Teacher, what do I focus on to lift this thing?"

You focus on the energy of the rock. And realize all is made up of energy – and that all is capable of levitation. And I'm having them do it in a group. Because it's easier in a group, doing it by yourself is harder, it's more advanced, because you have the group to help you – it's a lesson in working in groups – that's the lesson – it's not about the levitation; it's about working together as a team.

Because together we can do things that one alone can't. People in groups are more powerful. The group is moving it, I'm having them try it each by themselves and they can't move it, I'm having two people try it and they can't... not three. Not four. They still can't... not five... (Laughs) – Okay, eight; they can do it now (she's moves her hand). I can do it by myself –

Demonstrate that for them.

I am. I focus on the energy of the rock and I have energy that comes from my solar plexus that I make stronger and stronger and stronger and I focus on moving the rock. I put out my hand for show but I don't need my hand.

So I get this straight – the energy comes from your solar plexus; you increase that energy. How do you project it to the object?

Focus on the object. I just focus on it, this energy becomes more and more powerful, bigger and bigger, and I focus it there and I move it.

Are you telling the object to rise? Or are you picturing what you want it to do?

I picture what I want it to do, I visualize it doing it, and then I can do it, but I have to use my solar plexus. That's the key to the energy.

Tell me more about that.

Well your solar plexus feels like it's the energy source. It's smaller and bigger and when you make it bigger it gets more intense and it glows and it can do things. Kind of cool (hands are floating in front of her, imaginary shapes).

Who taught you about this energy stuff? Where did you learn this stuff?

(Her hands slowly moving). From Marnanda. Marnanda is one of my teachers. Oh my god Marnanda is (my friend in this life) Julia. Huh. Hi Julia (pause). She just said "It's Marnanda up here."

So she is teaching you about energy? You want to spend some private moments together?

Yeah. She told me she had to let me go so that I could grow more.

She had to let you find your way?

I needed to experience more. She was there just to help me when I needed it. Had to teach me astrology here (on Earth). So good to see her, I've missed her. She's my teacher.

I would like to speak to Marnanda directly and she can answer through your voice is that ok? What advice do you have for Ivy today?

She says to "Continue on the path that I'm on" (laughs). What path is that? She says that it will unfold; she can't really tell me, but that I'm doing what I'm supposed to be doing.

What do you call Ivy up there?

Lily. So many people down here call me Ivy Lily – they pronounce my name wrong when reading it. Ivy Lily.

Ivy has brought many questions to this session. Can you direct us to a teacher or wise one to get these answered?

She said "Up the hill."

Let's do this. Give her another embrace, thank her for her help today, it's time to go up that hill... Lily. Let's go up the hill and find what we need to find.

Looks like a limestone kind of, almost looks like a castle. Going up the hill. A lot of water; it's very beautiful.

Other Spirit Guides

So let's be there now. What is this place?

It's where we all live. And work. And learn.

Let's go to the place where we can get the questions addressed. Let's do that now.

Okay I'm there. I see a being; it's a being... with light - light around... looks like a collar of white light – standing up, going all the way around. That person is – it's about protection and this will protect me. I don't know if it's male or female.

What's the name that comes to mind?

Katar.

I want to speak directly with Katar – and would ask Katar to answer in the mind of Lily – or just through the mouth of Ivy. Would that be okay? What's your relationship?

I am her mentor (hands frozen apart).

How do you think she performed in her life as Philip?

Very well, she did a good job.

Was it about bravery?

And selflessness.

She performed well?

Very well.

What advice do you have for Lily as Ivy today?

Lighten up (laughs). Dial down the intensity. Things will happen. Whether or not she's intense.

"What is the significance of 2056?" She thinks it's the year she will pass on.

Yes, it's when she's going to pass.

Is there a reason why she's being made aware of that?

So she'll pace herself. She needs to pace herself.

What is the soul purpose of Lily in this Ivy life? Why is she here?

It's something about excess. **Extremes and excess.** I feel extremes and excesses; overcoming excess. There's more but I can't get it.

If you step to the side, Katar can come through more and more clearly. So she needs to experience these extremes in order to overcome? What is the main mission of Lily in the Ivy life?

Healing excess. Too much excess on Earth – (struggling, gasping) evolving, excess.

Thank you Katar, can you make your energy a little more smooth for Ivy – we want you to come through, but we want you to finesse this.. so let her body handle this high energy. What is this about excess? Healing excess? What does she need to do?

Let go. Let go of over consumption. Of everything. Not just food.

So you're saying Lily has a tendency to over-consume?

Everything.

Knowing your own Power

So the purpose of this lifetime is to moderate that?

She wants to feel what it felt like to be excessive, it was her idea.

And now she has done that – what has she gained from this?

It's another form of energy control (gasping, struggling, speaking as Katar).

She says that Ivy says she has the chart of a healer, but she fears the responsibility of that. Can you talk about that?

She needs to heal herself first, then take on responsibility. (Her body begins to convulse while trying to speak.)[46]

I'm feeling a sense your energy is so high that Ivy is having a hard time... would it help if I touched Ivy to help smooth this out? Would that be okay?

Yeah.

Let some of the energy come through me so we can sort of calm this body down. Because Katar you are a powerful being – your vibration is so high. It's causing a lot of shivering and such. So let's just take a few moments to allow the body to assimilate and balance. Using me as a help. As a heat sink. And just breathe. Ivy Lily just breathe deeply. And let the body be calm.

I don't know my own power.. I mean I know my own power. Oh. I understand something. **My father and brother came here to experience excess. In my group we're all experiencing excess together.** I had second thoughts about it. I made an agreement with them that I would do it to.

So you honored that agreement? Are you glad you did it?

I am glad. I guess my brother didn't fail; he died of excess.

Let's go through more of these questions. Ivy asks "Why did I choose gluttony during this lifetime?"

Excess. Extreme energy.

"What else do I have to do to put this obsessions to bed?"

It's not about the food. It's obsessive energy – to lower your energy level.

---

[46] When Scott asked her guide a question, she convulsed and shook when answering it – to such a degree that Scott asks if Ivy is okay. But when he asked Ivy a direct question, she didn't shake at all. This occurred often in sessions as if to differentiate the answers from the spirit guide from those of the subject.

(Scott reacts to Ivy's shaking) Can you help Ivy-Lily dial herself down a little bit? The excess class, tell us about that.

(Becoming calmer) They want to feel what it's like to come and use energy to heal these excesses. All excesses. Food, drugs, alcohol, sex, gambling, people, excess takes many forms.

Is there anything else Ivy needs to know to complete her lesson?

It's never completed. It's always there. (Again speaking in a halting manner) But talking about it is not necessary. It's a choice. A spiritual choice (shaking, convulsing).

One of a Kind

Is Ivy's shaking a concern?

She's fine.

Ivy, can you get through this ok?

(Normal voice) I'm fine.

Ivy wants to know... why do I turn everything into a business?

(Shaking voice) It's fun. She likes it. She finds it entertaining. It's like child's play to her.

Question "Why do I feel like I don't fit in anywhere?"

Because she doesn't; she's one of a kind – unique (convulsing).

Is Lily an Earth sort of person, or does she come from somewhere else? Has she lived on another stars?

Many, yes.

Is Earth sort of her – her Earth lives are they – how can I ask – as a percentage, how many other lives?

About 40% here.

She wants to know about her session with the therapist in New York – "Was I Louis Marchand?"[47]

Yes she was.

It was in the time of Louis 16th?

Yes, she was an advisor in charge of a kind of espionage. He walked among the people and reported to the King. She was his man on the ground.

So as Louis Marchand she picked up the feeling of the populace?

She was a master of disguise, travelled back and forth between different worlds for the king.

What sort of worlds?

The nobility and the people. And the public, I think that's what you call it.

Yes. How did Louis Marchand know they were going to die?

He knew of the public unrest because it was his job. He was very good.

Like Turning on a Switch

"Who did I give my son Henri to?"

His mother's parents. They moved to Nancy. [48]

Ivy wants to know "Did I die giving birth to a child in a previous lifetime?"

Yes, she did.

---

[47] As cited above, inside of Louis XVI's court was the "Prevot de Marchand" or the royal "Provost of Merchants" or a Secretary of Commerce. Louis Le Peletier de Morfontaine was the Provost at this time period, he had been Secretary of State, and his grandfather was in charge of the "House of Investigations" a version of today's FBI. Louis' maternal grandfather's name was Henri, and perhaps Louis named his son after him.

[48] If this is the Louis in question, his third wife was Catherine Adelaide Leconte de Nonant Raray, married in 1791. The mother Madame Catherine Le Pelletier survived the revolution, and died in Ribecourt in 1814 at age 57. Her family roots are not far from Nancy, France. (Comptes rendus & mémoires lus aux séances, Volumes 4-5 By Société archéologique et historique de Noyon)

Is that affecting Ivy in some way now?

Fear.

"Why did Ivy freak out both times when she was pregnant?" (In this lifetime)

Because she died giving birth to that child (in a previous life).

Show Ivy when and where that was or tell her.

(Normal voice) I was on a farm, very rural – it looks like Kansas. I was a young girl. It was flat lands.

So Katar, how can we help her release this?

(Starts to shiver and shake as she answers as Katar) – Yeah... I'll do it.

Experiencing Excess

Thank you (after a long pause, she stops shaking). Feeling better?

(Back to being Ivy, with no shaking). I was on a table, and it was like turning on a switch and all this light was coming through me. It penetrated my body. Made me feel warm, comfy and cozy and good.

Etch that in your mind. You can meditate on that and be there and receive more of your treatment.

My guide doesn't want to come closer to the table and I can't understand what he's saying. I feel better, I think I can get off the table. He talks very fast. He's saying I can't be on the table, the table is just... can't do two things at once. I'll get off the table now. Okay, I want to give the table a hug. The table has energy too. Okay. All right I'm off the table.

What was the purpose of dad sexually abusing Ivy? Was there a purpose to that? Can Katar shed light on this? Why did her brother get into drugs and waste their lives?

Excess. They were supposed to.

You mean they went too far?

I mean they succeeded.

In experiencing excess?

Yes.

Find Me In The Light

Someone else I want to ask about – your mutual friend Paul Tracey.

Oh Paul. He lived down the street from me.

Any messages from Paul; can he send a message?

Something about that he's going to see Rich next time around. I don't know what that means. He says "Next time around."

All right, I want to bring Katar back in... What are Ivy's gifts as a soul or spirit? What are her talents, strengths and gifts?

She can move energy (haltingly). She can change room energy. Energy in a room. She's got a great laugh; she likes to laugh.

We know she's a teacher of energy. Any other specialties she aspires to?

She likes to learn everything. She likes to be undercover.

Like Louis Marchand?

Yeah. She likes to change her form.

Why was Ivy brought to this session today? What does she need to get out of this experience?

Lighten up. Not to take herself so seriously. Be a conduit to see if we're real.

What practical way could she do that?

Market masses.

Tell the masses that spirit is real?

Yeah.

If she wants to contact you, how can she do that outside of a session like this, can she do this on her own?

Meditation. Quiet the mind. Stress free. Relax. And bathe in the light. White light (gasps, struggling). She can find me there in the light.

The Lily Pond

Thank you Katar. What do you suggest we do; is there something you'd like to show Lily?

(Normal voice) He's taking my hand and he's said that he wants me to see my favorite place. He said I'll have to come here and meditate.

Let's go to your favorite place.

It's really... he showed me it's a Lily pond – he named it after me.

There's a place to sit?

Yes, I love this... place!

Be there in the pond of your own name and be there in your favorite place. Let me know when you're ready to move on.

(She laughs). (A look of ecstasy) It's so beautiful here! Why would we ever leave? I feel so light and free. It's so beautiful it's making me cry, it's just - the beauty is unbelievable (cries).

That's okay, you can cry, you can feel it. Let it move through you, all around you. I have a question for Katar – "If it's so beautiful in spirit back there, why would we ever leave? Why do we leave?"

He's saying that you need to experience everything to learn; joy, sorrow, love, hate, greed, poverty, you need to try what we learn here.

So etch this pond in your mind as well. To feel peaceful, sacred, free, light.

Oh yeah. I see why people come back (to this realm). Because it's so beautiful here; the air is so fresh. Love is so strong. I don't feel angry up here. **I feel a heart to heart connection with everyone.** Maybe it's soul to soul but it feels like heart to heart. **There's an umbilical cord between all of our hearts that are attached to one another, and it glows and shines and lifts us, never felt anything so wonderful.** [49]

Does he have a final word for you today?

(Laughs.) It's ridiculous. **He said "Live long and prosper."**

(Both laugh.) All right is there anything you Lily or Ivy, anything you want to experience before we wrap up?

I think I just want to be here longer; it feels so good.

You just be there as long as you want. Are you still in your Lily pond?

Mm-hm. My class is coming to say goodbye. They're showing me that they've got the ability to levitate as a group down to six people - they can do the levitation with six people or souls or beings or whatever we'll call them. I want to hug each one.

I think you should tell them to keep trying until they do it with just three.

I was thinking one.

You're a task master.

They have lifetimes to do it. Many lifetimes.

Let's let all those people come forward to say goodbye, Katar and your family, your excess group, all the students, let them all come forward in a big massive hug.

Oh, I like heart hugs. Have never had a heart hug.

So as we begin now to leave the high realm of the spirit world, I want you to remember this world is always with you, inside of you all the time... see all the

---

[49] Here's another reference to an "umbilical cord" that connects all of us as referred to in Volume One.

*colors your friends radiate – if they were to look at you, what color are you
radiating at your core?*

Deep wine. Maybe a little darker. It's got some, like a pink quartz color.

What's that signify?

Glaze in it, a lot of pink, like marble – it feels like its energy flow.

*Beautiful. So everything we've talked about will be retained in your memory to
help empower you… as you complete the remainder of your current life, which is
slated to be a long time, you've got to pace yourself. Thanking everyone for being
here… etc…. I'm going to count to three and you can be back in the here and
now… number one…. etc. How are you feeling?*

(After a pause) God that was kind of strange."

Ivy is someone I've known since my early teens, someone I've stayed in touch
with for the past 30 years. Her session revealed some pretty unusual memories.
In terms of her memories of a life in Versailles, I was able to find the toy she said
she was playing with (the Bobiquet) as well as a likely candidate for this person
she claimed to be. I was able to track this person's family to the towns that she
claimed they were from.

In terms of her lifetime as a British sailor, I was able to look up the name of the
family in England. In the online records from the "Old Bailey" – the court in
London, which has all of its records posted online, I found the name "Phillip
Martin" from Brighton Street who filed a lawsuit in 1610. Could have been his
father who had the same name. I was able to find a ship "The Catherine" sailing
in the East Indies in the early part of the same 17th century.

But then when she finds herself in the life between lives, a number of unusual
events; it turns out she's a teacher of a class. For those familiar with "Flipside"
this was an area that was of interest to me – as my friend Luana had repeated
dreams before she died of "being in a classroom." In each of my sessions, I've
gone to visit classrooms, and Galen Stoller also mentions attending classes in the
afterlife in the chapter on his book in Volume Two.

And now, here is my friend, describing her outdoor class of energy transformation. Wow. Where is this University? Where is this energy class is taking place – is it on another planet? Is gravity in this classroom? Is it a classroom that's been created in the minds of the students, and it includes all the laws of the universe - because they've agreed to create it that way?

Remains to be seen.

"We have no evidence whatsoever that the soul perishes with the body." - Mahatma Gandhi

Chapter Five - "Apotheosis"

Neuroscience & Consciousness

Christopher Hitchens hovered above me tonight and said, "There is no afterlife."
Steve Martin (Photo: Perseus with Medusa's head by Cellini)

I've slept with Steve Martin.

It was in Santa Barbara staying in his amazing architectural home he lived in near Montecito. The walls were curved concrete, and the entire building was like being in a large elegant bunker built during World War II. Ignoring the wonderful antiques and artwork on the walls, I pointed up to the ceiling and said "There are cracks in your ceiling."

It is one of those things that an architect's son notices. My father, raised in the Chicago Prairie School of design, a former architect from the Chicago firm of

Holabird & Root, former Assistant City architect for Chicago, pointed out to me that concrete doesn't "breathe" the way that wood or other materials do. "The Earth is always moving" my dad said, and pointed out why cracks will always appear in concrete structures like the Guggenheim Museum in New York, which is one giant curved slab of concrete. As Frank Gehry once pointed out to me discussing cracks I'd seen in one of his structures; "They don't crack when they're sitting as a model on the client's desk."[50]

I forget what Steve said when I pointed it the cracks in his ceiling. Perhaps a withering stare that meant either "I heard you" or "And you are...?" I was with Luana, our mutual friend who came back from the dead to visit me in "Flipside" and Charles Grodin, who was Steve's pal and co-star in "The Lonely Guy." I've run into Steve on other occasions – like a restaurant in West Hollywood where I said "It's good to see you" and he said something like "Oh, right, like you remember all the other good times you saw me."

Steve is a contrarian of the highest order – meaning he has crafted his comedic responses in such a way that you cannot repost, or reply – well, you can repost them on twitter – but it's too hard to say a witty reply, because he's crafted them in such a way that allows very few to turn a phrase in a different fashion.

One can argue that I'm not even in the same universe as Steve Martin – a multi-talented, multi-faceted actor, writer, and musician – but we do share the same derivation of a name. Mars was the God of War in Roman times, and those who worked for him were "Martins" – blacksmiths. My name is from a family of those smiths who settled after their service to the Empire in the mountains in northern Italy, and Steve's family name comes from... somewhere. I don't know. He's a wordsmith of the highest order. Me; from a lesser guild.

But just as staying in the same structure as Steve Martin doesn't constitute "knowing" him, living on the same planet as everyone else doesn't really give us any insight into what they're doing, or why they're doing it. Neuroscience is a field that explores what the brain does under certain circumstances – by putting a series of receptors on a person's skull, the electroencephalogram (EEG) is a

---

[50] When I worked on the film "Salt," one of Phillip Noyce's assistants was Adam Haggiag, a tall lanky filmmaker. We were chatting about my dad one day and he said "That's funny. My grandfather is John Holabird." My dad had met him on a train to Chicago in 1949 on his honeymoon, and went to work for him. What are the odds?

noninvasive test that observes the electrical signals happening in the brain. It's a way of studying what's happening with the brain while it's doing its thing.

The following interview was conducted via Skype with the renowned neuroscientist Dr. Mario Beauregard. Mario's book "Brain Wars" details his research using EEGs with a variety of different patients, during a near death experience, or in his noted study of Carmelite nuns. The nuns showed that while they were having "spiritual experiences" there was no particular locus in the brain for that experience – hence the idea that there is a "God spot" or some part of the brain that creates near death experiences, or out of body experiences, or some other blissful like state is proven to be inaccurate. Mario was at his home in Montreal, I was at my home in Santa Monica - the only thing that put us together was the internet.

One can find clips of Dr. Beauregard interviewed in the feature film "What the Bleep Do We Know?" and in the sequel which will be coming out soon as well various clips of him speaking on Youtube.

Mario Beauregard

What's your educational background?

I have a Bachelor degree in psychology and a Ph.D. in neuroscience. I consider myself a neuroscientist.[51]

Me: In layman's terms, if you can, what is neuroscience and why is it important?

---

[51] Mario Beauregard, Ph.D., is a neuroscientist currently affiliated with the Department of Psychology, University of Arizona. He has received a bachelor degree in psychology and a doctorate degree in neuroscience from the University of Montreal. He has also undergone postdoctoral fellowships at the University Of Texas Medical School (Houston) and the Montreal Neurological Institute (MNI), McGill University. Dr. Beauregard is the author of more than 100 publications (articles, essays, book chapters) in neuroscience, psychology, and psychiatry. He was the first neuroscientist to use neuroimaging to investigate the neural underpinnings of voluntary control in relation to emotion. Because of his research into the neuroscience of consciousness, he was selected (2000) by the World Media Net to be one of the "One Hundred Pioneers of the 21st Century." In addition, his groundbreaking research on the neurobiology of spiritual experiences ("Brain Wars") has received international media coverage, and a documentary film has been produced about his work ("The Mystical Brain")

MB: It's the study of the nervous system; the central nervous system including the brain and all the related aspects -- can include the anatomy, the structure of the brain, the physiology, how the nerve cells connect between themselves electrically or chemically. When we speak of chemistry there's a sub-discipline, neuro-chemistry - we also now have neuro-genetics, how genes impact the brain and the nervous system. Why is it important? Because all the mental functions are mediated through the brain, and when I say mediated, I mean not necessarily produced by, associated with; it's a big distinction.

Is that the essential distinction between materialist science and -- what would you call it, non-materialist science?

Post materialist science. Yes, it is the main contention, exactly.

Where do you think that began? Can you point to a particular scientist who really was the founder of post materialist science?

The father of American psychology, William James, said basically that 100 years ago; to be careful to not find a correlation or an association or causality. For example, just because you observe a lesion or deficit in a specific portion of your brain doesn't mean that lesion produced the function (that you're observing), but that it may be associated with the function. It's a fairly large distinction.

And we can date Materialist science to when?

The end of the 19th century.

Then post materialist science picks up with James; do quantum physics dovetail from that?

Yes, quantum physics is post materialist science; it was the starting point and about the same time. But William James[52] was rejected by his peers, and the materialist framework won the argument so to speak. So in Psychology, the behaviorists now control the field of psychology; theirs is idea that everything is physical and everything is determined by the brain.

We have the same kind of vision in various fields, in philosophy, psychology, etc. It's true that in physics they had a big revolution 100 years ago, when they

---

[52] A William James quote: "I believe there is no source of deception in the investigation of nature which can compare with a fixed belief that certain kinds of phenomena are impossible."

showed that you can reduce the world to physical matter, they dematerialized the world. But in other fields of research, scientists have not realized that because they are not really familiar with quantum physics. So that's another problem.

I like to ask people when their first conscious thought happened that they would be doing the work they're now doing for their work. I asked an FBI agent this question and she said it was in preschool, and I asked "Why preschool?" And she said "Because I kept lists on everyone and what they were doing." When was your first conscious thought you'd be doing what you're doing now?

I had several spiritual experiences when I was young. When I was 8 years old I had the sort of vision or insight that I would later on become a scientist – I didn't then know the words for the field - but to study the brain. And not to just study, but to demonstrate that the brain does not produce what we call "mind" or "consciousness in the soul" or the essence of the human being.

That was at 8 years old. And my parents were not in that field at all, they were farmers. They were normal Roman Catholics in the living in Canada in the 1960's.

What town did you grow up in?

A town called Granby, it's near the border with Vermont.

So, how did it manifest itself when you were 8, and did you tell anyone about it?

No, I didn't tell anyone. I simply took the decision to become a scientist. That was the starting point.

What happened?

We had a small farm and there was a forest near the farm, so I was walking in the woods where I walked very often. It was summertime, summer vacation, and one day, as I walked in the woods, I was tired and decided to sit on a big rock and then I saw that (vision). But at first, I sensed that there was a sort of union with the trees and the rock and myself -- that we were all included in some sort of wholeness, I didn't use these words of course, I was a young child.

But, it started by this experience. A mild altering state of consciousness, and then I saw; it was not in the form of images, it was a feeling, an insight, a certainty... it lasted for perhaps a few minutes, I don't know, it was a long time ago, but that was the starting point. I felt like I was in contact, and I knew that this was my mission in life; very clear.

To become a scientist or to explain what that feeling was?

To become not only a scientist but to become sort of a revolutionary, a "Che Guevara of science" or something like that. I always knew I would have trouble and problems with colleagues through this whole process, but it was part of the deal, I accept this. I never underwent a regression, but I supposed I would find information related to this. I met a hypnotherapist in Montreal last week.

Jean Charles Chabot. I interviewed him for this book.

I'm very interested in his work, so I've decided to learn how to induce hypnosis myself, and I will train under him next year.

Have you run into any accounts that were similar to what you experienced?

From other scientists? No. Not really.

I've gathered maybe a dozen of these accounts, the only word that I can come up close to it is the Greek word apotheosis; "suddenly knowing." It's like you're remembering something; it's not a new thought.

Yes, I would say it was almost like a remembering.

I've been studying LBL sessions and how that involves consciousness, one thing I'll ask people when considering this research is for them to remember when they met your significant other, think of that moment and try to recall it in detail. In almost every case I've examined, I hear a version of "I had this feeling after we kissed, our third date, once he held my hand; I just knew that I was going to marry (or be with) this person." It's always told in past tense. If you meet someone for the first time and they seem familiar, or you have a deep feeling of knowing them, how could that be unless you encountered them before? Here's the question everyone wants to know from you. Does consciousness exists outside the body and is there any scientific research to back that up?

I would say "yes" to both questions. And my answer is based on one instance of near death experience, in this case one of the experiences triggered by cardiac arrest. During cardiac arrest, if you're measuring the electrical activity of the brain with an electro-encephalogram (EEG) system, you'll see that when the blood flow to the brain freezes during cardiac arrest, after a few seconds the EEG will become flat.

So in that kind of state, according to main stream science, consciousness is not possible. Yet during the past 12 years there have been five separate studies conducted in the US, UK, the Netherlands; these studies have documented over 100 cases of patients who were able to remember mental experiences, who were conscious during cardiac arrest. How do we know that? Because they've been able to provide accurate information, for example during the re-animation procedure or physical , the patient gives accurate details about the physical characteristics of doctors, and even what was happening in the next room in **certain cases. I would say "Yes" now.**

To me now the brain does two things. It acts like a filter, meaning that under normal circumstances, it restricts the access to other realms of reality. But this filter function can be deactivated, or affected under various conditions. For instance; with sensory deprivation, psychotropic drugs, near death experience, or a clinical death; it's a filter and it's also an interface for mind and consciousness. It's like a television set, for instance; it receives information, it processes information, so if you alter, for instance, the electronic components within in the TV set, you're going to affect the reception of information. You will experience disturbance in terms of color, sound. But that doesn't mean the program itself is created within your set; in fact it's not. And that's the analogy I'm using to help people understand this mind/brain connection.

Another example I've heard is that the brain is like an FM receiver, even if your receiver is unplugged you sometimes get radio signals to the speakers; it's not like there's a little band in there making that music. The receiver can be completely unplugged but it's still picking up music from somewhere else. Are there any other filtering systems we have in the brain that we can deliberately shut on or off?

Visual spectrum. If you take visual perception for instance, we are able to decode information but it represents only a minute fraction of the entire electromagnetic spectrum. It's not the same for other species - some species are able to see within infra-red or ultraviolet, we're not. But that doesn't mean what they're perceiving doesn't exist. So the materialist (scientists) are in the same situation; they don't see it, so it doesn't exist for them, but there are so many things that exist in nature that now we're are able to detect because of technology. Where it was not possible 50 or 100 years ago, and it will be the same 400 years from now. And so forth.

Which adds to the sub-question, why is it a big deal? Why do you think people get so upset when you posit that consciousness might exist outside the brain?

Classical physics are what they call "modern science," which became what it is around 400 years ago; it's based on a number of physical assumptions about the nature of reality and knowledge. One of them is materialism, it is one of the core assumptions, one of them is reductionism so you can reduce complex organisms to very simple phenomenon; that was valid three or four hundred years ago, but it's not anymore. However it's become like a religion within science, so these assumptions are like central dogmas of this scientific religion, and if you dare to openly challenge the dogmas, you're going to be excommunicated.

Has that happened to you?

I've been told that by other people in my career.

I'm sorry to hear that but at the age of 8 you knew you'd become a revolutionary and decide to take upon this mantle. Perhaps in the long run it's a benefit on your path and your career.

Yes, I can see that now. It's just hard on the salary.

Tell me about the research you did of the imaging of Carmelite nuns and how your study showed that there was not a single God spot in the brain as some of the materialists were saying. The God spot being that there is one specific place in the brain where materialists claimed "spiritual experiences" exist. You're quoted as saying "spiritual experiences are complex, like intense experiences with other human beings."

Yes, they involve many mental functions like perceptions. You can have sensory images, visual images even if you have your eyes closed; you can have thoughts, you have feelings, so it makes sense that the regions of the brain and the networks that are mediating this kind of experience... well, they are very complex and involve several regions of the brain; it's not a single point like some neurologist proposed thirty years ago. But they were materialists; they said that because in some cases when you have an epileptic seizure within the temporal lobe it can trigger a religious or spiritual experience – very rarely by the way, it occurs in 1% of the cases, very rare, but based on that, they believe the reason must mean that these experiences are "delusions created by a dysfunctional brain."

Just recently there was a story about rats passing fear through DNA; the conclusion was that rats pass it along to their offspring. I would argue that's one possibility – there are other possibilities – if mice are afraid of a type of human for many lifetimes, if only for the simple reason that's the most logical thing a mouse could learn it doesn't necessarily mean it's through the DNA.

Right.

If you could design an experiment to prove that consciousness exists outside the brain, as opposed to just taking data, what do you think that would entail?

I have designed something like that, it's called "The Aware Project." Dr. Sam Parnia of the UK is leading the study; there are hidden probes in the surgical room, and they're working with people suffering from heart disease, or people that they are expecting may have cardiac arrest while in the operating room. They're hoping when the patients have an out of body experience, that they'll remember and identify the hidden targets and symbols. It's very interesting project - problem with that is I've talked with several near death experiencers who are fascinated by their own physical body, and they don't care too much of the details, so it's a long shot.[53] (The report, cited below, notes "Widely used yet scientifically imprecise terms such as near-death and out-of-body experiences may not be sufficient to describe the actual experience of death.")

You've met with Dr. Greyson, he mentioned something about it as well - is that his project?

Yes, they participate in this global project. [54]

---

[53] "Near-death experiences? Results of the world's largest medical study of the human mind and consciousness at time of death" University of Southampton: Summary: *The results of a four-year international study of 2060 cardiac arrest cases across 15 hospitals concludes the following. The themes relating to the experience of death appear far broader than what has been understood so far, or what has been described as so called near-death experiences. In some cases of cardiac arrest, memories of visual awareness compatible with so called out-of-body experiences may correspond with actual events. A higher proportion of people may have vivid death experiences, but do not recall them due to the effects of brain injury or sedative drugs on memory circuits. Widely used yet scientifically imprecise terms such as near-death and out-of-body experiences may not be sufficient to describe the actual experience of death. The recalled experience surrounding death merits a genuine investigation without prejudice.* Science Daily Magazine. October 7, 2014.

If you were asked what or who is God, how would you answer that question?

To me it's not a matter of belief. I've had many spiritual experiences. In this kind of experience, you experience another level of reality or something else. And after that you don't need to believe, you know. It becomes a certainty – so I've had an experience, I've had deep experiences, transcendent - where you become one with everything that exists, and with the source of everything. I would say based on my experience, I would simply say it's the ground of being; the source.

One of the people I filmed asked that question "what or who is God?" He said "God is beyond the capacity of the human brain to comprehend, it's just not physically possible to do so. However you can experience God." I was thinking like you can experience water, hard to describe what it is, or being drunk, until you have a glass a wine or jump in the water, but you can experience water, so to experience God you need to open your heart to everyone and all things. So that oneness you describe seems to be the definition of God.

Yes, and you find that in all the books of mystical descriptions.

"God is love" – should be "love is God."

Yes, it's Unity or oneness; they're saying the same thing basically.

Okay, I have a question about – why you consider materialist science – in 'Brain Wars," you suggest non-locality and quantum entanglement suggest the universe is an undivided whole?[55]

I'm no expert in quantum physics, I'm saying that from the various lines of research in the book, take for instance, the so called phenomena; the influence

---

[54] During the AWARE study, physicians will use the latest technologies to study the brain and consciousness during cardiac arrest. At the same time, they will also be testing the validity of out of body experiences and claims of being able to see and hear during cardiac arrest through the use of randomly generated hidden images that are not visible unless viewed from specific vantage points above. - See more at: http://www.nourfoundation.com/

[55] In layman's terms, quantum entanglement refers to the discovery that two ions created at the same time will react simultaneously to an outside influence no matter where they are in the universe. Einstein referred to this as "spooky action at a distance." In physics, non-locality or action at a distance is the direct interaction of two objects that are separated in space with no perceivable intermediate agency or mechanism. Wikipedia In other words "some invisible thread" connects everything.

of mental intension of random number generators, biological systems, plants, animals, other human beings, it means that all the various levels of what we consider reality are interacting and they are constituting a whole. So in that sense, it's in line with what spiritual traditions have been saying for millennia. But it's a new kind of science – it's a Post materialist. Science.

Any opinion or thoughts about Michael Newton or his work? Or the idea that the "veil is thinning?"

Well I read your book, I saw your movie "Flipside" and read more and more about that after that and I think it's very important work. Because like you said, "The veil is thinning." It means that this work is opening portals, other realms of reality, so it's major.... it's paramount - this is why in my new book, the first title was "Expanding Reality." So we're very close – I'm going to talk about this work.

I've read about the effect of showing someone with a speech defect, or having a tantrum, film of them having the event. So they can see how it looks. Or sometimes a child with severe autism; by showing them a video of their behavior, it helps the brain to make or alter pathways. Perhaps on a small level talking in public and sharing information with people may affect their perceptions. Have you heard of the "Overview Effect?" They interviewed astronauts when they returned from being outside the planet and they say they've begun to see the Earth as an ecosystem. They began to lose the "us vs. them" perspective. The same way as Carl Sagan's "Pale Blue Dot" – has altered people's point of view. Perhaps discussing this research will help thin the veil. Functioning like scissors.

I'm aware of that film ("The Overview Effect.") Yes, it's a feeling I have; I think doing this kind of work (altering people's perspective on how the planet is interconnected) is exactly why I'm doing it. It's an insight I've had, but I didn't know the term. Yes. (It's also) what you're doing. It's the same thing.

Thank you!

_____

I received an email from hypnotherapist Jean-Charles Chabot (interviewed in Volume Two), who is working with Dr. Beauregard in Montreal; they're using EEG equipment during the LBL sessions that Jean-Charles Chabot is conducting.

Jean-Charles writes, we "have decided to officially start research on EEG brainwaves with clients in LBL states. We did a pilot (session) where we measured a client with the 19 electrode helmet. The client showed a huge amount of gamma brainwaves during the "connection with Guides" (phase) and when experiencing "unconditional love," which according to Mario's hunch, seems to be a brainwave related to the connection with "inter-dimensional frequencies."

Promising results; if Mario can show that the brain experiences gamma waves during an LBL, and that they occur during a particular experience of the brain, then he will prove beyond a shadow of a doubt that hypnosis is not, nor could it be *cryptomnesia*.

Knock on wood.

"I would love to believe that when I die I will live again, that some thinking, feeling, remembering part of me will continue. But as much as I want to believe that, and despite the ancient and worldwide cultural traditions that assert an afterlife, I know of nothing to suggest that it is more than wishful thinking." — Carl Sagan

Chapter Six – Interview with Hypnotherapist

Scott De Tamble – "Light between lives"

"Life is a great sunrise. I do not see why death should not be an even greater one."
- Vladimir Nabokov

Some years ago, I asked the former President of the Newton Institute Paul Aurand who he would recommend in the Los Angeles area that I could speak with about the research, perhaps to film sessions of deep hypnosis. He recommended Scott De Tamble (LightBetweenLives.com). I called Scott, and we spoke on the phone for about three hours. It's rare to find those people on the planet where you feel you've just left off a conversation, but Scott is someone like that.

Recently I filmed Scott giving a talk to the International Association of Near Death Studies (iands.org) in Orange County, CA. The following is an adapted transcript of that talk. Michael Newton's fourth book "Memories of the Afterlife" is comprised of case studies from many Newton-trained therapists who discuss memorable clients or sessions; Scott contributed a case study to the book.

Scott De Tamble

"I'm a clinical hypnotherapist in Claremont, California, and have been doing this work for 12 years. I'm a Southern California guy, born and raised here. I was lucky enough that my grandmother taught me to read when I was 4 years old, so I had a jump on school. I became a reading fool after that, read everything I could get my hands on. I loved history, was always interested in the past... archaeology, ancient cultures and civilizations; and as I became older I became more interested in metaphysics and spirituality or what's beyond this 3-dimensional reality. I was probably too young to understand the concept of reincarnation but I always had a feeling for that.

Past Life Regression was always a fascinating interest of mine, because I felt like I'd lived in other times and other places. I felt there was a lot more to this world than what meets the eye, so at a certain point I decided to learn about Past Life Regression; how to do it, and really, I wanted to experience it myself. I went to a hypnosis school in Anaheim. My teacher was a lady named Dr. Jeanne Neher-Schurz. She has since passed away, but Dr. Jeanne was an experienced teacher who pretty much knew everyone who was anyone in the hypnosis world. She gave me a really wonderful and broad foundation in hypnosis, from the 'old masters' of the 1950s and 60s on up to the newest modern cutting-edge techniques.

I started practicing hypnotherapy, and studied Past Life Regression with Dick Sutphen, a spiritual hypnotherapist, author, and researcher who'd written some intense past life books in the 70's that I'd read as a teenager. In my practice I focused on past lives, and then a couple of years in, I heard that Dr. Michael Newton was training people in this thing called "Life Between Lives." I'd read his book "Journey of Souls" some years back when I was in the library studying. I'd be haunting the bookshelves near the astrology and the occult sections, and so I had found his book, and I was pretty blown away. I'd read quite a lot of esoteric and metaphysical books, but Newton's went beyond what I had read, what I had known.

I found out that Dr. Newton was giving a training in hypnotherapy and his 'Life Between Lives' process in nearby Studio City, CA. At the time, I wasn't sure if I was going to able to afford it, but my friend Lani helped convince me. She was familiar with Dr. Newton's book 'Journey of Souls,' and she called it "The Book," as if it was the Bible. Her belief helped me take the leap. So anyway I went to that training, and my life was changed.

So today I'd like to talk about Dr. Newton's 'Life Between Lives' hypnotic process. Generally, we start with a guided meditation with the client, taking them back into earlier times of their current life; then we travel through a past life and through its end; and finally we'll go into what we call the spirit realm or the spirit world – our life between lives.

'LBL' work is a very deep hypnotic process that takes you into the spiritual existence between-lifetimes, between our Earthly incarnations. As spirits we live a long, long time -- if not forever -- and there's a lot going on up there in those higher dimensions. This technique opens the doors of soul memory. A session lasts 3-4 hours, sometimes longer. I had one the other day that was about 5 hours; it's a deep and lengthy process.

Before we begin, I talk with the client -- 'What are you looking for in this session?,' 'What is it you want to find out?' I'll have them bring a list of personal questions, i.e., "Why did I marry Joe? Why did I get hit by a car when I was 11? Am I on the right path? What should be my next move?" In our LBL session we can usually receive direct spiritual guidance from spirit guides, loved ones who have crossed over, and/or higher beings that we call a Council of Elders.

Whatever wise and loving beings we encounter in these sessions, we can direct the client's personal questions to these beings, and the answers come into the client's mind and through their own voice. It's very cool. My favorite part of this work is getting my clients to channel this higher wisdom, and conversing with higher spiritual beings through them. It's something like modern day shamanism. But instead of a shaman taking the journey for you and then reporting back, we're guiding you on your very own journey.

So how do we start? We'll talk with the client, explain about the process, light some candles, turn out the lights, play some nice quiet music, and start the session.

Generally, we begin with a slow, measured hypnotic induction, going into a deeper state of awareness. We have a pretty good framework that Dr. Newton developed, so we use his methodology. We'll go backwards through childhood, do a bit of age regression. We'll stop at a few points in childhood, looking at happy or pleasant or neutral scenes or situations. We're not really looking at doing therapy at that point, just kind of doing memory warm-ups. So we'll move back in time, and then we'll regress them all the way back to the womb, to the time before they were born.

There's some really interesting information to be found in the womb, such as "When did your soul energy actually enter this fetus?" We get some pretty interesting answers; the average month of gestation the soul actually comes into the fetus is around the 3rd month, but sometimes we seem to move in and out. Our soul will come and check out the baby to see how it's developing, saying "Yeah, wow, this is who I'm going to be." Sometimes the soul can actually make physical or other modifications to that child, using telepathy or sending energy, doing energy healing, or even working with the mother in some way. Sometimes the mother is anxious or worried, and we find that the soul energy of the child can do energy healing and send her love to calm her down. So it's a very interesting part of the session, the visit to the womb.

From the womb we go back into a past life. We'll sort of rise out of that situation and go into a past lifetime, then we'll move through the life, exploring some of the milestones and interesting points, and find out what was the primary mission of that life. Every life has lessons, layers and layers of lessons and missions and things that we're working on. The whole point of this thing seems to be to grow and develop – to develop as spirits, to grow more compassionate, to grow in our capacity to love, to grow in our awareness, knowledge and wisdom – this is why we take these human incarnations, to experience these things and grow and evolve as souls. So we'll look at some of the important events and relationships, and we'll go through the last day and the death, and then through the crossing over into spirit. So this point is where it ties into the NDE's that you've all been researching.

In these hypnosis sessions we can go back and remember different ways that we cross over, what happens when we die; we can remember what we did and felt, how that was for us, and just as in NDEs there are lots of different types of experiences. The surprising thing for me is that the vast majority of clients re-experiencing their death in a past life say they feel free or 'I feel wonderful', or 'What a relief!' It's not a scary thing, or painful; once they leave the body behind, all the pain is gone and they're just expanding their energy and remembering who they really are... that they are vast and they are connected to the entire cosmos.

In the crossing-over, crossing from the human side to the spiritual side, sort of making that shift into the spiritual dimensions, it's a shift of energy, a shift of consciousness, a shift of awareness. There are many different paths and journeys people take in this crossing-over… it's very interesting. Some people just go right up – *whoosh* -- "It's over, I'm done with that, I've got to meet with my buddies; I'm working on this project, I can't believe I forgot about that for 80 Earth years!" And they go rushing back to this meeting place where they're working on some project with their soul group friends and advisors.

Then, I have other clients with whom it may take a long time to leave the Earth behind. We may have to stop at a cloud for a while and chill out. There are way stations where a person may need to spend time, as the person's vibration is changing, their frequency is changing, it's a transition… so I just go with them and see what happens. Some folks need time to adjust from the dense, heaviness of the physical to the higher, finer vibration of spirit.

Then there's another class of people -- and I was one of these in my first LBL session -- where, after I died, I didn't really want to go anywhere. I just wanted to sit against this oak tree for a while. I went to some meadow and sat in this oak tree for what seemed like a year… I just wanted to be in Earth's natural environment because it felt good. I certainly wasn't in a rush to immerse back Into the "business" of the spirit world at all. I had a client recently who did that; she sat in a tree for a while, she was one with the tree. She flew with the birds for a while; she could have played all day, and I guess she did; but I had to move her along! We only have so much time and energy in these sessions.

I have some brief excerpts from clients illustrating various experiences or 'station stops' during their sessions. This one fellow was in a war in his past life: "I'm just above the battlefield, a bullet went into my eye; I'm a mess. But I'm glad this life was over… **I feel like I'm moving now, being sucked through a straw - the grey turns into bright light, it's brighter and brighter… I'm home."**

A pretty common experience is to be met by some person or energy, a spirit guide or a loved one who's preceded you in death. Sometimes it's a messenger or escort, nobody special to you personally. Most often, you're met by your spirit guide and you may want a bit of orientation. You may still be thinking about the lifetime you just left, when someone comes to meet you and takes you by the hand to escort you into this realm.

Meeting your spirit guide is probably one of the most profound experiences you can have in these LBL sessions. We all have spirit guides, at least one primary guide assigned to watch and teach us for eons and eons. There may come a time when our guide will pass us on to another guide because we've graduated to a higher level. But usually, after death, and in these sessions, we're met by a primary spirit guide. They may be flanked by affiliated spirit guides, because we have lots of interests and projects, and lots of help.

Here's another excerpt from one of my client's sessions: "I have a spiritual guide here; he dresses in robes of green silk, white hair, kind, compassionate, wise, very, very old. He's pleased with what took place in my last life." Our spirit guides will talk to us about what we've just been through, and we're debriefed: "How do you think you did in that life?" You might say "I guess I could have done a little better." They usually point out; "We're proud of how you did."

I'd like to take a moment to say to everyone here in this room: you are the brave ones. You had the courage to incarnate. In case you haven't noticed, Earth can be a very intense place. It's a place of conflict and of testing. We come from the spirit world into this place of conflict and chaos... it's a rough ride being here and just living in a human body. We have physical needs, hunger, thirst, survival instincts, hormones racing through us. Physical existence is a place to work and experience and grow. So I salute every one of you for being here today, you truly are the courageous ones.

Now in our session the client's spirit guide will talk to us about these things, and we'll get the client's personal questions addressed. The client's spirit guide can also help me guide the session, because he or she may have things planned for the client to experience. So I'll ask him or her, "Ok, where do you think she needs to go next?"

A beautiful thing is that there are places of healing in the spirit world. These places of restoration and healing can take many forms, as varied as we are individuals. Very common is a healing chamber with what appears to be light energy. So we'll go there and I'll ask the client "How are you feeling?" and they'll say "Oh my God, I'm filling up with light energy!" So we'll give them some time for that, saying "Take your time there and just let me know when you're done." You should see their faces while they're re-experiencing this healing treatment; it seems they're also receiving it now. Their face lights up, they get this beatific look, the years roll away.

The healings can take many forms. I've seen people describe being in a cave; "Oh, they're shining all this light on me." Or "A shower of light and the light just cleans me." Or "I'm in a field with the daisies and I just soak up the sun." Here's one client's excerpt: "I think I'll go to the purple light; it's like bliss. It disintegrates your fear, your worries, it's like taking a shower after you've rolled in the mud." So after we've rolled in the mud of Earth we get to clean this off. We're in the spirit world and we're doing this restoration.

At some point your spirit guide might say "Do you want to see your friends?" We have Soul Groups in spirit that that are like our families here; and we learn and play with these souls up there, and we incarnate with them down here, over and over. These are souls that we feel very close to. When incarnating, we take different roles, so who is your mother today could have been your daughter in a previous life; or your friend or lover or maybe even your enemy. We tend to have five or six close members; and as many as 15 or 30 total in our soul groups. The people in the front row here (gesturing to the crowd) might be your tightest friends, spouses and siblings and children; or the gentleman back there might be a grandpa or neighbor. It's very touching during our sessions to visit with these soul friends. If we have the time and inclination, we'll talk to each of those souls. Perhaps a person is currently incarnated as your brother, but as a soul in these sessions, from his higher-self perspective, he can tell you "Man, you are taking things way too seriously, you gotta lighten up!" So meeting with a person's Soul Group is a beautiful thing.

On the question of soul mates, or what Dr. Newton calls 'primary soul mates,' most of us do indeed have a particular special soul that we are closest with, and will tend to incarnate as lovers and mates. Meeting with that soul mate during a session can be a lovely interlude. It's an intense bond and a feeling of wholeness. And sometimes we can learn important things in these reunions.

Another adventure in the LBL experience is what Dr. Newton terms the Council of Elders. We each have a council of very wise beings, maybe two or three rungs above spirit guides in knowledge and evolution, and we'll go before this panel between our lifetimes. These wise souls analyze you to see how you're doing, take a look at your progress, see what you might need to work on next, and pass that information on to your guides, or sometimes directly to you in certain ways.

The Council chambers can take many forms. People sometimes go into what appears to be a dome, or a Greek temple, or a Cathedral. It definitely has a

sacred quality; these beings are very wise, very advanced, and clients feel awestruck going to meet them. These beings will give us advice about the most recent past life, the present life, our soul's progress in all our lives, speak about our gifts, and advise us about our current lives and situations. A very good question to ask at the end of the Council meeting is "Why was Mary brought to this session today?" Because Mary was brought for certain reasons, and the answer to that can be very profound.

Here's an excerpt of a client's meeting with his Elders: "The Elders appear radiant... an all-wise, all-knowing feeling of omnipotence. They are far beyond me. Divinity, joy, ecstasy... the essence is love. One is in a green robe, a Master Healer. The one in the middle is in purple, the spokesperson. The others are experts in different areas of development."

As you grow as a soul, the number of Council members tends to grow as well. For example, maybe you develop a keen interest in archery that has far-reaching benefits, and you'll gain a Council expert to help you: "I'll teach you how to hit that target." Your Council will continue to grow as you do.

By this time it's been 3 hours or more into the session; the client may be getting fatigued. But if we can, we'll go to the Place of Life and Body Selection and ask "Why did you choose this life? Why did you choose to become Mary?" And we'll go back and visit the planning session in spirit when that choice was made. You might be sitting around a table in a library talking with a soul group, there may be library archivists or advisors, along with your personal spirit guide; "We've got this life for you, or we've got this one for you." A bit like a car salesman: "You want to be a person in Southern California where you can go surfing? You want to be an Eskimo and have close family ties?" And you choose, you each chose your life, believe it or not – (laughs) I don't know what you were thinking! But you chose your life, so you've got no one to blame but yourself!

Friends, the LBL experience and the message I bring today is of hope and of love. Hope because through these sessions we see the whole pageant of our soul; we see the tapestry of our soul's journey throughout history. We see that each life is very precious, yet it's just a drop in the ocean of your soul's evolution, your soul's journey. And you see that you are indeed making progress as a soul, a being of intelligent light. You are expanding and you are advancing.

The message is also one of love. We all sense the existence of the Divine in some way, and the emissaries of that Divine Source are all around us. Beings of light, spirit guides, Elders, we are surrounded by love. Someone once said "Ask and you shall receive," and if you just ask for guidance and support, it will come... maybe even today!

Some members of the IANDS had questions for Scott.

Question: "What about the concept of "vacation lives?"

Scott: We take all different sorts of lives, and from time to time we may take a life that is a bit easier than most. Yet even during a "vacation life," you're going to be working on some kinds of lessons. Does anyone go through a life without a challenge? Maybe you're a young guy in WWII, you see your friends all get blown up, maybe you get blown up. After going through that, you might like to take an easier road for a while. Maybe become a rural postman with a quiet route; but you're still going to have family and struggles and all of those challenges."

"What about angels, what are they?"

I get the sense that angelic beings are spirits that don't incarnate. They are our brothers and sisters, they love us, they help us, these beings of light, but they don't choose to incarnate. They navigate other realms. Our spirit guides, however, have incarnated... how could they give us advice without having "been there and done that?" So we have a large team assisting us, we have spirit guides, Elders, and angelic beings of light as well.

"What about dreams?"

It's very common for souls to communicate to us with dreams... doesn't mean that every dream is that way, we have many types. But yes we do have dreams that are seeded from other realms.

"What about abuse? What happens when two souls meet (in spirit), who have been abusive to each other?"

(He smiles) You mean when you get back into spirit and see that person, you might ask the question: "Was I cruel enough for you?" And your soul friend might answer "Yes, I think you over-did it!" But these things are pre-planned in spirit before even incarnating. A question along these lines might be, "Why would I or anyone want to be hurt, or to suffer?" In our LBL sessions, a lot of people say they choose to go through a lot of pain because they are on the path of becoming healers. In order to become the most empathic healer, they feel they need to suffer themselves, to truly understand what it feels like.

"So if I see someone being abused, I should just walk on by and say, 'Hey, that's their plan?"'

Maybe that's an opportunity for you to be courageous. There are no easy answers here; it's so complicated I can't figure it all out. How do I know what to do when I see someone being hurt? Just follow my heart. If you see someone being hurt, just follow your heart. Maybe it's an opportunity for you to help.

Thank you. I want to mention that we have over 200 hypnotherapists worldwide trained in Dr. Newton's techniques. To find an LBL therapist near you, please go to newtoninstitute.org."

"You live on Earth only for a few short years which you call an incarnation, and then you leave your body as an outworn dress and go for refreshment to your true home in the spirit." - White Eagle

Chapter Seven – "Purify the Tragedy"

"Did you know that trees talk? Well they do. They talk to each other, and they'll talk to you if you listen. Trouble is, white people don't listen. They never learned to listen to the Indians so I don't suppose they'll listen to other voices in nature. But I have learned a lot from trees: sometimes about the weather, sometimes about animals, sometimes about the Great Spirit." - Tatanka Mani 'Walking Buffalo'

I gave a book talk at a nearby bookstore in Venice, California.

Scott De Tamble said he might be able to make an appearance; I warned him I had no idea how many people would show up. As it turned out, about a dozen folks showed up for my talk at Mystic River books, including an old friend of mine whom I met while teaching film. I mention these details because the following sessions was not planned by anyone involved.

During my book talk, I told the story of how during my LBL session, I remembered the lifetime of being a Lakota medicine man. I wasn't getting anywhere during the session, when the hypnotherapist Jimmy Quast[56] told me to "just look down." In my mind's eye, I looked down and saw my bare feet in a stream. From there I

[56] Eastonhypnosis.com

saw that I was wearing buckskin and had long hair. When he asked me who I was, I said "I'm a Lakota medicine man."

My conscious mind chuckled, as I'd seen "Dances With Wolves," a film about the Lakota, and I'm a screenwriter. When asked for my name, I claimed it was "Watanka" and when Jimmy asked about my village, I said "I don't want to go there right now." When he asked why, I saw a village that had just been attacked – bodies were lying everywhere, with teepees afire.

When he asked who had done this, I said it was the "Damned Huron." But even while I said these things, my conscious mind was amused; I know "Tatanka" means buffalo in Lakota, so why was I pretending to hear "Watanka?" And everyone knows the Huron are from Eastern Canada – how could their tribe fight the Sioux if they're in Montana?

Part of the process during these sessions is to allow your subconscious to say whatever it is you're experiencing or sensing, without judging it. My experience with hypnosis is that I was never "under" – rather, I was relaxed, calm, and had the ability to allow my subconscious to run wherever it wanted to. But as you can see, that didn't stop my conscious mind from criticizing what I was saying.

As recounted in "Flipside," some months after the session, I ran into a cousin of mine at a funeral in Wisconsin. He casually mentioned he'd befriended some members of the Lakota tribe and knew their history. I had looked online and found nothing about the Sioux fighting the Huron, or what the word "Watanka" meant.

So I told him about this session where I had a past life memory of being Lakota. He said "Wait, don't tell me anything. What were you wearing?" I said "Buckskin." He said "How many feathers did you have?" I said "two." He asked "Were they up or down?" I said "Down." He said "That means you were a medicine man."

He said "What was your name?" I said "It sounded like Watanka." He said, "Well, the Great Spirit is called Wakan Tanka; that was likely your nickname." I said, "Okay, but why did I say that the Huron had wiped out my tribe?" He said "Because you're sitting in the place where they fought for sixty years; Eau Claire, Wisconsin."

These were details I initially tried to look up but could not find on line. Only after doing extensive research, did I learn that his definition of "Wakan Tanka" was correct and that indeed, the Sioux had tribes along the Mississippi who fought the Huron in and around Wisconsin centuries ago.

Oddly enough, now that I'm familiar with this past life, when I look these details up, they are vivid to me. However, none of this was accessible to me in any movie, book or casual search of the internet. I tried to find these details but could not. So in the classic sense of the term, my past life memory could not have been *cryptomnesia.*[57]

During my book talk, I recalled how it felt when I had walked through my village filled with freshly murdered friends, their blood everywhere. How I had come to my teepee, felt the leather of the flap as I opened it and saw a woman with long black hair lying in a pool of blood. I said, as if experiencing it for the first time; "They've killed my wife and taken my son."

During that memory, I had began to sob. My conscious mind said "Wow, if you're making this up, this is an incredibly difficult and painful feeling you've created." I've never felt such pain or loss in any lifetime I'm aware of.

So at this moment during my book talk, when I recounted this experience, my friend burst into tears.

After the book talk, Scott noted she was still distraught and asked what triggered the emotion she felt that moved her so. She said when I described the massacre of the village she felt as if she had experienced the same thing.

Scott asked if she wanted to try a bit of hypnotherapy to see if he could help her. The following is an edited transcript of what occurred. Again, she had not come for a session, and none had been planned, and this is the first time Scott has done a past life regression in public. I'll call her "April."

---

[57] Cryptomnesia: "the reappearance of a suppressed or forgotten memory which is mistaken for a new experience." Collins Dictionary. "Cryptomnesia is, literally, hidden memory. The term was coined by psychology professor. Théodore Flournoy (1854-1921) and is used to explain the origin of experiences that people believe to be original but which are actually based on memories of events they've forgotten." The Skeptic's Dictionary

April and Scott

April: I was having a reaction to a past life while Rich was talking, when he was talking about his past life as an Indian – it triggered a deep emotion response in me. I don't know what it was, but it was a huge upheaval in me. I feel I'm here tonight to have that experience.

Scott: *What was the emotion you felt?*

April: Just really, really sad.

Scott: *Would you like to – I don't do (hypnosis) demonstrations - but would you like to examine this? I usually take longer to hypnotize someone but I can do it quickly.*

Scott quickly brings her under hypnosis in this noisy bookstore.

Native Americans

Scott: *As I count from five to one, we're going to the origin of this feeling.... number five, like a bridge to the past, number four, three, two one, be there now. Use your voice. Are you inside or outside?*

April: I'm outside.

What are you experiencing?

Just a feeling of sadness.

A certain part of your body?

My chest. In my throat. I'm scared of feeling it.

Let's do this, allow you to rise above and out of the body so you don't have to feel it, yet you can observe it, and understand it. Are you above that feeling?

I think I'm kind of in it. I think I'm crawling and there's ash all over my face.

Male or female?

I'm a Female. 12 maybe 16. I'm outside. I'm crawling into someplace, looking.

What are you looking for?

My family. (Cries).

Go ahead and feel that and let it out. It's ok.

I feel I'm hurting...

Tell me about your family.

It's a picture of what Rich was describing (in the book talk, a memory of a massacred tribe), a picture of people strewn about - being dead. Native Americans.

What year is this?

1843 or 1834.[58]

What's the location?

Western Virginia.[59]

What do they call you?

Wei-le – (*Wi-he* means little sister in the Omaha tribe)

Go back to before this happened. Tell me where you lived, before anything bad happened. Do you have a family? A mother or father?

It's a great mountain.

Where do you sleep?

On white beds, in a teepee

[58] "Andrew Jackson's removal of Native Americans from the South began in 1839, known as "the Trail of Tears." In 1831, the Cherokee, Chickasaw, Choctaw, Muscogee Creek, and Seminole (sometimes collectively referred to as the Five Civilized Tribes) were living as autonomous nations in what would be called the American Deep South. In the winter of 1838 the Cherokee began the thousand-mile march with scant clothing and most on foot without shoes or moccasins." (Wikipedia)

[59] A second group of Siouan tribes, embracing the Catawba, Sara or Cheraw, Saponi, Tutelo, and several others occupied the Piedmont region of Virginia. (Siouan Tribes of the East, Bull. B. A. E., 1894)) "April" later said over dinner, she felt it was from a place further north. West Virginia became a state in 1863.

Anything else in the room with the beds?

I see myself with a baby on my shoulder; I don't know if I'm the baby or the mother.

When I count to three you'll know.

I'm the baby.

Sioux Comes to Mind

So when you're a little baby. On your mother's back? Tell me about her.

She's beautiful.

Etch this picture in your mind of your mother's face and her beauty. Tell me about her. Do you have a father?

She's singing. And my father is a great man (sighs and cries). He has a lot of feathers on his headdress. He's a very profound man and people listen to him.

A wise man, a warrior?

He leads the people.

If you were to know in English, what's the name?

Sioux comes to mind. [60]

Let's go to a happy scene when you're a little girl.

I'm picking flowers, purple ones. Some have red lips on them. [61]

What do you do with the flowers?

[60] This is of further interest, as most Indian lore and most American history books put the Sioux in central or northern states. When I first posted this online, someone wrote "the Sioux were never in Virginia." The Monacan tribe is part of the Sioux nation: "The Monacan Indian Nation is located near Bear Mountain in Amherst County, Virginia. (She mentions living near a "big mountain") One of the oldest groups of indigenous people still existing in its ancestral homeland, and the only group in the state whose culture descends from Eastern Siouan speakers...." http://virginiaindians.pwnet.org

[61] "Bittersweet Nightshade" a flower found in Virginia with purple petals and red lips when ripe.

I'm trained to heal people with the flowers. I'm learning medicine.

Who's teaching you?

My spirit guides – they teach me when I'm by myself. My mother's there too, but they come to me. [62]

How do they communicate with you?

I just know. And the breezes, they guide me.

Purify the Tragedy

Ok, let's move to the scene where we began... be there now. You're crawling through the ashes. And what else do you notice?

There's babies. They're all dead.

Any adult people around?

(She shakes her head.)

Anyone alive?

There may be.... last gasps.

Let's skip forward, what do you do?

I prepare something.... a campfire. I must burn their clothes. To purify.

(Sobs) I don't want to do it. But I've been taught to do it.

Why don't you want to?

Because I have to gather the clothes.

Let's skip forward, see what you actually do.

---

[62] Turns out these purple flowers with red lips not only grow in Virginia as stated in her session, but are used in herbal remedies. The subject assured me she has no conscious knowledge of this information. http://www.botanical.com/botanical/mgmh/n/nighwo06.html#med

(Nods.) I do it. [63]

Let's go to the moment when things are burning, what's going through you?

(She lifts her hands and moves them to point in four directions) I'm going to the four points; east, north, west and south... and it's to the great sun - so that I can help them rest (moves her hand to indicate) and I'm transitioning them.[64]

Let's let that fade away. Let's skip forward to a time when you're older.

I'm older. Maybe 32.

What are your living arrangements?

I live by a lake. There are families there.

So you've found yourself a new home. A new tribe?

They're displaced. (In 1832, the Trail of Tears began where vast amounts of Native Americans were displaced and sent to live on reservations in Oklahoma.)

What's your role?

They want me to free them. Their land needs to be purified.

How do you purify the land?

It looks like I'm building another fire but with houses. I don't know if that's what I use - to put in the fire. Because it's like – huts or something. (She later said they looked like miniature or models of straw sweat lodges in a field that would purify land by being burned.)[65]

---

[63] E. Curtis' 1908 book "North American Indian" recounts tribes burning clothes after death to free spirits. Vol 15 Pg 14 "After the rite of cremation... the ceremonial washing of the clothing of the dead person... (some time later) the clothing of the dead person was brought to the fire... and burned." The purpose of the burning ceremony was "to terminate period of mourning and efface all feeling of sorrow." This is not a rite or ritual easy to find online, nor is it in any other books I could find, other than this 1908 version of a *Luiseno* ritual.

[64] Most Native American cultures use the four Cardinal directions, including the Sioux: "The Medicine Wheel symbolizes great spiritual significance for the Sioux... Within the (medicine wheel) is a cross shape, it symbolizes the four directions, North – (Red) wisdom, place where the ancient ones passed over, South – (White) youth, friendships, East - (Yellow) beginnings, family, West – (Black) solitude, adulthood. http://siouxpoet.tripod.com.

Like a piece of straw?

It looks like it symbolizes a hut, like a home (the hut representing the home). That's what the fire consumes, the building. We're using wood pieces and we're building them like the hut…and then burning them.

How do you feel about what happened when you were a little girl? Have you recovered from how you felt as a little girl?

I feel I'm always needing to purge and purify – purify the tragedy – by performing the rituals for others. ("Purge and purify" are actions and words often associated with Native American traditions like the sweat lodge)

So you perform this ritual for others - to help them purge and purify?

And I had a feeling before asking me the questions that I help other people transition, but I can't help transition on my own.

Let's move to the last day of this life, the final day. Before you've passed over. You have not crossed yet, but your very last day. Inside or outside?

I'm inside. I'm lying down. I'm with some people. With my daughter. I'm pretty old. I'm hundreds of years old (She later said she was "over a hundred years old.")

You have a daughter? So do you know this is going to be your last day?

I know. I'm making peace with my maker. (She casually lifts her hand, palm open, to her shoulder when she says the word "Peace" – a symbol of peace, or "sign language" used by many tribes including Arapaho and Cheyenne)

What do you think about this life you just lived…. as you look back on it?

I lived such an… amazing life. All these things that I've seen, things that I've lived through. I can see it in my face. (Over 100 would be circa 1918 to the 1930's)

---

[65] Smudging, or burning incense in a new home or lodge is a common Sioux practice, however usually sweet grass is burned inside the structure, and the smoke purifies it. I wasn't able to find any reference to this ritual of burning a "straw man" structure, in order to purify the land.

As I count to three, die and cross over into spirit (her head drops back, Scott catches her). Rise above, feel the freedom and beauty and letting go of her feelings. Tell me what you're experiencing.

Um... I'm circling. Something's circling around me.

Something circling around you? What do you sense that is?

I think it's just motion... flight.

Let's skip forward in time to when you're talking to a guide or arrived somewhere (In order to shorten the session, Scott skips ahead to ask if she has anyone to speak to – normally he'd wait for her to find someone in her own time). Be there now. What are you noticing?

I'm noticing a very light haired person with blue eyes. It's a male.

Look into those eyes, what do you feel about this person?

I feel surprised.

What's the relationship? Is this a stranger?

I personally don't feel like (I know this person), but my person who is there feels it and says his name is Paul. I don't know this person.

So in your conscious life as April you don't know him. What are you feeling?

(Bursts into tears) This person has such a deep recognition of me.

Can you let this person, this Paul embrace you?

Ok but it doesn't feel like it's me.

What does this feel like?

I think the color of his eyes is so strong and magnificent, it's um... amazing power, amazing energy – that I can't even comprehend.

You sense the power in him?

(I feel it) by his eyes.

Ground Yourself in that Power

I'm going to ask Paul a few questions. And he can answer through you. Paul why was April shown through this Indian life today?

(Holds up her hands). It's really to let go. Any fear of self-undoing, that she feels that she doesn't want it to be transparent.

That's cryptic, can you explain that?

Any fears of transparency that she feels uncomfortable with. To let herself be known and see herself be known and be seen for who she really is.

To let the fear go of being seen? Doesn't have to be invisible anymore?

(She cries.) Yes.

So Paul what advice do you have for April in her life?

To hold the power within and to ground yourself in that power.

How can she do that?

(Smiles.) Her health.

Tell me about that.

To have her stop doing things that take her out of her energy pattern that's negating her power.

Paul anything else you want to tell her today?

She feels there's a vast difference between who she is and who Paul is.

Like he's more advanced?

(Nods). She has to recognize herself in him.

So Paul, when April wants to connect with you, what does she need to do?

Water...[66]

Anything we need to give her?

He's giving me a necklace. It's this necklace I've been wanting for a long time. It's a crystal cross with a blue green stone. I feels that it calms me.

If Wei-le could give a gift to you, what would it be?

To fully transform myself before I can go and transform others.

And if you could give a gift to her what would it be?

I would clean her up; I would hold her. (Cries, sighs)

All right, in a few moments we're going to close that window – I want you to let these different selves be integrated with your soul, all melting into one person who is living as April now... deep breath... and relaxing. Count to three and back to the here and now... etc.

As mentioned, I know the person who did the session; we've been friends for many years. I drove her home after the event, and she confirmed that she had never had a past life regression before, and had never had any conscious memory of being a Native American. However, when I started to discuss my past life memory, where I saw and felt the emotion of seeing a tribe of my friends and family wiped out, massacred, she began to cry in the front row of my book talk.

It was Scott who asked her if she wanted to explore that, examine it through the benefit of hypnotherapy. (And he did so live in front of a crowd of people in a book store in Venice, CA, something he's never done in public before.) No money changed hands here, there was no "stage hypnosis" done, and there was no planning or discussing prior to the event what may or may not happen. It occurred just as I've recounted it, entirely unplanned.

She recounted a number of details about a previous lifetime of an American Indian that are counter to what the average person might know or even look up about American history. There is no common reference to burning clothes in

---

[66] In a later session, when a woman was asked how to stay in touch with her guide, he recommended "going for a walk near water every day." Why water would have a different energetic pattern, or perhaps a soothing effect, or some effect on a person's energy is interesting to note.

order to purify them, nor is it easy and simple to find purple flowers with red lips that happen to grow in the Virginia highlands that have medicinal qualities.

As I've spoken with therapists about examining or exploring forensic details of a past life session – and by and large they say they aren't really interested in the forensic details of a past life regression, as they're purpose in doing one is to help people with an issue or problem. In this case, the woman had not come to the book talk with a presenting problem, but while listening to the account of someone else's past life memory, she found herself overcome with emotion.

And then, in a few minutes, she was recounting her own memory of being a Native American and witnessing the death of her loved ones, family and friends in a massacre, and being tasked with burning their clothes to release their spirits. Finally, she was able to connect with someone who appears to be like a spirit guide to her, who she names "Paul," and he tries to let her know that he's always with her. As we'll see in the rest of the book, this is an abbreviated session done in public, the longer, more intense sessions allow for a deeper and more resonate examination of events.

One can argue it's not important to know that we had a past life because it's not consciously affecting us on a daily basis. On the other hand, someone might argue that repressed memory affects us the same way that past life memory does. We may not be aware of the details but we are aware or emotionally familiar with what happened. And when doing forensic research into past life memories, I've found there's always small inconsistencies to the reports, just as there would be in eye witness reports. But when you take the hallmarks of these sessions – the guides, the soul group, the libraries, etc, then we can compare them to NDEs and other LBLs in general. There are three descriptions from people in my books who remember previous lifetimes as an American Indians (myself included), but I think it's that we have these specific memories at all which deserves further investigation.

I find the ensuing quote (below) from scientist Carl Sagan worth commenting on; Sagan said he heard his deceased father and mother calling to him often. Like any materialist scientist, he assumed that it was a random event – a neuron being stimulated, like in the mind of schizophrenics - for no particular reason. But as we'll see in this research, the source of the sound that he hears isn't necessarily being created by his brain.

It's possible that his mom or dad have found this way to communicate with him, by sending an etheric stimulus to the part of the brain that retains the memory of their voices. When you hear someone speaking to you from the great beyond we can't always assume its wishful thinking.

When my father spoke to me clearly on the night of his death and said in my ear "I'm experiencing indescribable joy" – I assumed I had made that sentence up until my mother confirmed that on rare occasions, that's how he would express himself about seeing something "beyond beauty." It was news to me. But worth repeating.

"Probably a dozen times since their death I've heard my mother or father, in an ordinary conversational tone of voice, call my name. They had called my name often during my life with them... It doesn't seem strange to me." - Carl Sagan

Chapter Eight – "Stairway To Heaven"

*"And as we wind on down the road, Our shadows taller than our soul.
There walks a lady we all know, Who shines white light and wants to show
How everything still turns to gold. And if you listen very hard
The tune will come to you at last. When all are one and one is all
To be a rock and not to roll."* From "Stairway to Heaven" by Jimmy Page and
Robert Plant (and according to legend; "Taurus" songwriter Randy California)

*"Jimmy Page was strumming the chords and Robert Plant had a pencil and paper.
Plant said suddenly his hand started writing; "My hand was writing out the words,
"There's a lady is sure, all that glitters is gold, and she's buying a stairway to
heaven." I just sat there and looked at them and almost leapt out of my seat."*
(Wikipedia on the writing of Rock & Roll's most requested song)

Some folks consider events that appear to come from someone in the afterlife as
coincidence. But when you add up the many cases of reports of "other worldly
events" that occur at key moments in our lives, it becomes apparent that terms
we use to define these events; ESP, coincidence, or kismet, need broader, better
definitions.

The following story is from Arlo Guthrie, the singer, songwriter and son of
American Icon Woody Guthrie, as excerpted from his Facebook post.[67]

My mother, Marjorie had a school in Brooklyn... one of her closest friends who helped her run it was a woman named Shirley who had a son, Frankie who was the same age as me. Whenever the family took a vacation or did something together Shirley & Frankie were there. They were as much part of my immediate family as anyone... And although we were separated eventually by time, distance and work, we still kept in touch.

...Frankie went on to become a song-writer and produced a number of wonderful recordings, some of which were collaborations of my father's material. We worked together on many things, and you've seen his name especially on the recordings we did for children. A few months ago I'd heard from him that he was battling cancer. I hadn't heard anything since then until a few days ago when something very odd and wonderful happened.

That evening I had left my cell phone on my desk to charge it up. It had been there for hours, and eventually I fell off to sleep. At some point later that night I got a call from Frankie. It was great to hear his voice but sorry to learn that he was in a hospice in Santa Barbara and that he didn't expect to be around for much longer. Then he told me that he was sorry he hadn't answered my call, but happy I had called him, and that he was calling me back.

I said "Wait a minute, Frankster! I didn't call you. My phone must have called you on its own." We laughed at that, but it was obviously meant to be that we talk and catch up on things.

Last night, I got a call from Frankie's closest friend & partner who had been taking care of him in the hospice. She told me he had passed away a couple of hours earlier. She wanted me to know that my conversation with him was the last lucid talk he'd had with anyone, and that he felt really good that I'd called. They both had been very surprised that I even knew where to call because they hadn't informed the family of their whereabouts, and to see my name come up on the caller ID on the land-line at the hospice was quite a surprise.

I said "Sue. I've never had the number to the hospice, and I didn't initiate the call." The conversation stopped for a pause. Eventually we

---

resumed talking. She had other calls to make, other friends to inform, all the usual things you have to do to finish up a life.

I'm left here this morning doing what she'd asked which is to get the word out to friends all over with the news. I'm also left with a jaw-dropping, "wow." All I can say is, "Frankster, everyone you ever met, left knowing you with a smile on their face. And that, my friend, has never changed. Farewell and say hi to everyone for me."

Recently, CNN marked the anniversary of the TWA flight 800 disaster – the plane somehow exploded in mid-flight and all the passengers were lost. In the recent broadcast, they interviewed Donald Nibert, who had lost his 16 year old daughter Cheryl aboard the ill-fated flight. [68]

At about 8:30 p.m., my mother, who had been dead for two years, said to me in her Southern Ohio Kentucky accent that I can never misplace, she said, "Don, Cheryl is OK. She's with me." She did not say "heaven" (but it) was implied. I turned around expecting to see my mother, but I saw nothing. (Later) I received the telephone call from the mother of one of Cheryl's friends' (who) was on the trip. She said, "Don, (there's been a) plane crash out of JFK at 8:30." And I turned the TV on… My wife (Donna) and I both realized (no one could have survived)…

In this case, the man was getting a message from his mother, prior to getting the word that his daughter had died. He wasn't aware the plane had already fallen out of the sky, or that his daughter was dead. But his mother sent him a pre-emptive message of solace.

My uncle from Niagara Falls, NY spent the last few years of his life in a hospital with a debilitating illness. My aunt told me that the night he died, he appeared at the end of her bed and woke her up. "I'm okay," he said. "I love you." She said he appeared as a younger, healthier version of himself. And moments after she heard him say that to her, the phone rang and the hospital called to say he had passed away. She had never told anyone this story, including members of her family.

My grandfather Valentino Martini had a favorite leather chair he sat in and smoked his favorite cigars. After he passed away in his late 80's, the chair went to my cousin, and he put the chair in his family's basement. One day while my cousin was downstairs in the basement working in his dark room for photography, he emerged to find our grandfather sitting in the chair, smiling at him. My cousin says he was startled by the vision, thought he was "seeing

[68] CNN SPECIAL REPORTS "Witnessed: The Crash of TWA Flight 800" transcript July 15 2014

things" and went back into the darkroom. He said he then slowly opened the door again and peeked out at the chair. Our grandfather was still sitting there as if to say "Hi! I'm still here!" Terrified, my cousin ran past the chair and went up the stairs.

The argument would be, just because something doesn't make sense, doesn't mean it doesn't make sense in a quantum universe. We don't really have an agreed upon language to describe these kinds of other worldly events. As Richard Feynman said of quantum theory, *"If you think you understand quantum mechanics, you don't understand quantum mechanics."*

The odds of someone coming into Arlo Guthrie's house and dialing the number that Arlo was not aware of are astronomical. The odds of Arlo making a mistaken call to a random number so his number would appear on the phone, coincidentally owned by one of his oldest pals, is also astronomical. The simplest, most logical answer in light of this research, is that someone in his soul group made that call; someone who isn't physically on the planet placed that call, or someone who was aware that this call was an important one, for whatever reason.

Some might argue that there's coincidence involved. But they'd be forced to admit people being contacted by others prior to their death, about someone else's death prior to there being any public knowledge of it, would equally be astronomical. Coincidence is defined as *a remarkable concurrence of events or circumstances without apparent causal connection.*[69] But there seems to be a clear connection between remarkable concurrence and this research. Perhaps the meaning of the word itself needs to be expanded, the way Indigenous tribes of the North have so many different words for "snow" or the Bushmen of South Africa have so many different words for "water." We need to be able to increase the definition of "coincidence."

My brother recounts the story of a close friend of his who called him one night to express his profound thanks for their friendship. It was an odd call, his friend was a tall athlete with an easy smile, and not prone to sharing his feelings publically. But in this call, he thanked my brother for a lifetime of friendship and how much it meant to him.

And the following day, after a freak accident at the ballpark, this friend had a heart attack and died. At his funeral, his wife pulled my brother aside and said how unusual she found it that the night before his passing, he had called my brother out of the blue and expressed so many tender feelings of love for their friendship. She too had never heard him speak in that manner before.

[69] Oxford Dictionary

Is it possible that we may know somewhere in our subconscious mind what's about to happen to us? And our spiritual selves help us find resolution with our loved ones?

Another "remarkable concurrence of events" involves a friend of mine who lived in Phoenix. As I mentioned in Flipside, Paul Tracey was a dear friend, close-as-a-family-member, whom I grew up with back in Northbrook, a suburb outside of Chicago. If you're friends with someone, you're "friends forever," but it wasn't until Paul's death and a number of unusual "visitations" I had from him, that I connected the dots to how Paul and I had known each other for a few lifetimes. During my between-life sessions in "Flipside" I claimed to recognize my friend as being a monk with me in Tibet at one point.

And when I was physically walking around Mt. Kailash in Western Tibet, making a documentary for Tibet House about Robert Thurman's trips into Tibet, I heard Paul's voice clear as a bell as I walked the sacred path around the mountain. I was reflecting how difficult it was to walk at high altitude carrying camera equipment and said to myself, "This is the hardest thing I've ever had to do."

And I heard Paul's voice in my ear say "You think it's hard for you to walk? It was hard for me every day." I was startled to hear his voice – and remembered how he had a football injury in high school that eventually led to hIm having a hip replacement, which caused him no end of pain throughout his life. He went from a sterling athlete and the fastest kid on the football team, to carrying a cane and walking with a limp the rest of his life. So when I heard his words, I knew what he was referencing.

Still, it was odd to hear his voice, as I hadn't heard it since he'd died a few years earlier. I said in my head "Paul, is that you?" He said "Yes." Then he said "You were responsible for the happiest day of my life." I had no idea what he was talking about. I had no recollection of what might have been the happiest day of his life, and I spent a few minutes wondering what the hell he meant – at the same time wondering if it was just the altitude that was making my brain think I was hearing his voice.

And then a memory came into my mind – it was the two of us in Brecksville Ohio in the 1970's – we were in our teens, and staying at my uncle's home. A.J.P. Martini was the head of the Contractor's Union in Ohio, who prided himself in never being part of union labor and all that entailed. He built about half of downtown Cleveland's skyscrapers, and the airport as well, and lived in a massive hunting lodge that overlooked the Cuyahoga Valley.

One summer afternoon Paul and I decided to slide down the hill into the forest behind his house, into a valley that went unimpeded for 200 miles into Pennsylvania. And once down into the leaves we found a creek and followed it, and found a swimming hole complete with a water fall and a giant rock we could jump off of. The two of us spent hours climbing that rock, doing cannon balls into that swimming hole. It was a memory I had completely forgotten about – we had gotten lost, so I was concerned how we were going to find our way home, but we spent most of the day just swimming and laughing and eventually did find our way home.

But it wasn't a memory I was aware of – I had completely forgotten it - and Paul's reminding me put it into my mind. "The happiest day of his life." Wow. He mentioned it to me, I wasn't aware of it, but now that he tells me it was the happiest day of his life, I do remember it as a particularly joyful day.

When I had started this trip to Tibet, I had remembered to bring along some of Luana's ashes – when I asked her where she wanted me to scatter them, Luana said "wherever you go" and have been doing so for the past 17 years. A bit here and there, and in this instance, Luana came with me to India where I was producing and wrote a Bollywood movie, and then to Tibet where I was shooting the documentary "Journey Into Tibet with Robert Thurman."

But I also decided to bring along Paul's hip. He had been cremated as per his request, and his mother had sent me a small little Tupperware jar full of his ashes with a note that said "Paul would have wanted you to have this." I got out a spoon and a baggie, and opened the little Tupperware jar to extract a spoonful of Paul.

And I felt something hard in the bottom of the container. A clunk. I moved the spoon around and pulled out a small ball bearing, about two inches in diameter – a melted piece of metal. I recognized that this must be his titanium hip, or what was left of it. As our mutual friend Dave Patlak said "the thing that Paul hated most in his life he willed to you."

So I took the titanium ball and put it in my suitcase. I spent six weeks in a hot sound stage in Delhi's Juhu district making "My Bollywood Bride" when I got an email from Robert Thurman inviting me to join his trip around Mt. Kailash. So I packed up my things and sped to Katmandu, where I joined Robert's traveling group that was going to cross Tibet from Lhasa to Kailash. And the titanium ball had slipped my mind, until Paul's voice startled me on that mountain pass at 16,000 feet altitude.

When I got around to the area where people leave clothing and artifacts of loved ones, I found a perfect spot for Paul's hip. There was a 20 foot stupa standing on the east side of the mountain, facing Mt. Kailash, stones that had been deposited by pilgrims who had made the sacred journey over the centuries, and had left a stone to commemorate their trip. Smack dab in the center of the stupa, I shoved my hand in and placed Paul's hip. He's now holding up a stupa in western Tibet.

I picked up my phone messages one day and a familiar voice said "Richard, call me, I have a message for you." The caller was a dear friend from Chicago, someone with whom I went to high school and have had more laughs with than I can count. She was an early advocate of "Flipside" and it's always good to hear her voice. When I got her on the phone she told me the following story.

"I was asleep the other night and Paul came to visit me." I had recently scheduled book talk in Phoenix where he had passed away, and so he'd been on my mind as well. "What did he say, what did he look like?" I asked. She said he was older, as if it was a memory of him that was more recent, and not from her memory of him in our college years. She said the odd thing was that "It wasn't a dream, because I was awake. I had been asleep, but awoke and I could clearly see him sitting across from me."

She said he reminded her of a weekend they had spent together in college. It was his freshman year, and she had gone out to the university to meet up with a new boyfriend and ran into Paul. She and Paul had flirted in high school, and occasionally dated, but this weekend turned into an accumulation of all those flirtations. They spent the weekend together.

She said that weekend, Paul had shown her a side of himself he rarely showed anyone; she said he'd been open and sweet and endearing to her instead of his usual jovial and comical self. And as he was showing her this memory, he said to her "That was a very powerful and meaningful time in my life. I'm sorry I wasn't more open to you when we were in high school."

She said that during this vision, Paul reminded her of the last moment they saw each other – saying goodbye on that Monday morning, she was looking over her shoulder, and the sad look on his face showing how much that experience had affected him.

Then he said to her, "Tell Richard I'm sorry I called him."

When she said that to me, and odd high pitched laugh escaped from me – something between a sob and laughter, as only I know the meaning of that sentence.

Because Paul had called me late one Sunday evening. We'd spoken on a number of Sunday evenings – often he'd had too much to drink. It was an affliction he fought the last years of his life, and though I didn't support or condone his drinking – he had been in and out of rehab a dozen times; so many times the medical care system refused to admit him anymore, I always had fun talking to him.

But this particular evening when I saw his phone number pop up on the telephone, I assumed he was loaded and answered the phone with an annoyed "What?" He hung up the phone. I figured I would talk to him the next day or whenever he sobered up.

But that wasn't the case. It turned out to be his last phone call. Later, I learned from his autopsy there was no discernible reason for his death – it was not caused by alcohol, it was not caused by anything anyone could easily figure out. As it turns out, the doctors had begun giving him a powerful anti-hallucinogen called Zyprexa and one of the "side effects" is listed as "sudden death."

I was distraught because if I had called him back – or even simply called his folks to alert them that Paul couldn't be reached – he might still be on the planet. That's a pretty powerful kick to the rear to realize answering the phone with a sarcastic "What?" might have contributed to the death of one of your closest friends on the planet.

But this dream for our mutual friend was an indirect message to me. "Tell Richard I'm sorry I made that call." There's no one else on the planet who could have understood what he meant by those words.

Sometimes friends will get messages from loved ones who've passed on but they dismiss the message as an unusual dream.

I spent my Junior Year in college abroad in Rome, through Loyola of Chicago Rome Center and made a number of friends who are still close. Melinda from Santa Cruz, was a blue eyed California beauty who we all fell in love with. She and her boyfriend and I remained pals, and after college I spent time with them in San Francisco. Later I heard Melinda had accompanied a friend on his test flight for his final flight exam from flight school and the plane hit some wires. They both died in the crash.

Some decades later I was giving a "Flipside" book talk in Santa Monica. Four friends I hadn't seen in forever showed up; Larry, a friend I knew in St. Norbert's Grade school; Peter Bill, a pal from Venice, California, Debbie, a girl I met at the Rome Center, and her pal Patrice, who came with Debbie. I remembered Patrice was Melinda's best friend in college; someone I'd never met, but had heard about. Later, Patrice sent me some photographs of Melinda from that era, and it was great to see my old friend alive again.

Then Patrice had a dramatic dream which included a conversation with our friend Melinda. And because of this research, she shared her memory of what Melinda said to her:

> Hi Patrice. I'm here. I've been waiting to see you again. Don't worry about this job stuff. It's just a trick and it doesn't matter. You need to remember how smart you are, so don't let these guys take that away from you. You are smarter and they are frightened of you, or just plain stupid.
>
> I am so happy here. But I do miss my friends and flowers and trees. Enjoy them now. Not because they will be gone, but you will be different. Don't worry.
>
> It is just a game and I will help protect you. You need to listen when your ears ring. (When that happens) I am talking to you - to tell you something inside that you can't understand.
>
> Your smartness isn't everywhere, so I need to use the ringing (you often hear in your ears) to get to your heart fast. Don't be scared. There are many on your side who are also watching out for you. Pray for others too. Some need it much more than you.

I am fine, please remember that. I get confused and want to talk to you and... lots of others who remember me. Who loved me. **I have sent them to you and it was hard. Don't worry. We are watching. You are loved. You give love. It will all be rewarded but not in the way you think. Keep loving.** Keep laughing. It is what I loved about you.

No, I can't stay now, I know it hurts to say goodbye again. Don't cry. I am here. I am here. I am here.

Just a couple of notes on Melinda's letter: "Enjoy trees and flowers. Not because they will be gone, but *you* will be different." As if you may be able to experience or see trees from that other realm, but that won't be real. Then her comment that "It's just a game" and Patrice's recent loss of her job "is just a trick." Sometimes dreams can allow us to know that our loved ones still exist.

In Michael Newton's research he asked people under hypnosis about the process involved, of being able to communicate from the Flipside during a dream. He was told that dreams are a common way for those who've passed on to communicate with their loved ones; those on the Flipside blend or direct energy into a dream so the loved one wouldn't be frightened, but will be able to understand the message communicated, if only to let the loved one know they aren't gone. They're "Just not here."

They haven't gone anywhere. The fact is, they've merely gone home.

"Sunrise early in the dawn, Slips away, then it's gone, Leaves the night to carry on While it's going home. Once a man he lived and died, What he said death could not hide, Even though it's often tried, But he was going home. Now my friends it's time to go, And this love will live to grow, And I want you all to know, I'm going home." "I'm Going Home" written by Arlo Guthrie

Chapter Nine – Dr. Helen Wambach

"Life Before Life"

"I don't believe in reincarnation — I know it." Dr. Helen Wambach[70] (Photo: The Pantheon in Rome where my film students and I stop for cappuccino. It was the first building I stumbled upon when in college there; felt like I was "home.")

As outlined in the interview he gave me for "Flipside," Michael Newton was a hypnotherapist who did not believe in past life regression. He said he was a psychologist practicing in Los Angeles when a client spontaneously went into a past life where he was a soldier fighting in World War I. Newton was skeptical, so he contacted the British War office, and the details the man gave were accurate; there was as a British officer matching those details who died in the "Battle of the Somme."

---

[70] American licensed psychologist assembled over 1000 subjects in small workshops and using hypnosis, regressed them to periods of past lives. A college psychology professor (Brookdale, NJ), a senior psychologist and a clinical psychologist (Monmouth County NJ), she authored several books, including "Reliving Past Lives," and "The Evidence Under Hypnosis" and "Life Before Life" (Bantam)

That led Newton into opening his practice for past life regressions in the early 1960's; but as he put it, as long as the clients were curing themselves of psychosomatic illnesses, it didn't really matter to him whether they were accurate about past lives or not. Then in the late 60's a client spontaneously went into the "between lives" realm where she described being with her "soul group." Newton took extensive notes, and was so startled by what she was saying that he closed his public practice, and for the next 20 years or so only focused on cases and clients who could take him into that realm. His first book was published in 1994 - "Journey of Souls" – based on 7000 clients who helped him examine the between lives realm.

Newton was assiduous about not going into bookstores to avoid the possibility of his work being influenced by book titles. I interviewed his wife Peggy as well, and she confirmed this detail. When I asked her what she thought of the research that her husband was immersed in during this period she said, "I thought he had gone over the edge. I was worried they'd come and take him away." That is, until he played her tapes from his sessions. How could thousands of clients say the same things about the afterlife if they'd never met, never had access to any material that described this arena? It didn't matter what their background was, their religion or status in life; as soon as they were under deep hypnosis (typically a 4 to 5 hour session) they would say basically the same things about the journey of souls.

From an interview he gave to Wisdom Magazine (2008)

> Dr. Newton: When I first made the discovery that it was possible to reach people's immortal soul and mind through deep hypnosis I did not tell anybody about it. Of course, the people I worked with knew about it and they told friends, many of whom became clients, but I did not go to metaphysical conventions, I did not go to bookstores for metaphysical material - I did not want to be biased or influenced by anything. I simply worked alone trying to put the pieces together. Most of the research was done in the 60's and 70's and I didn't even begin writing "Journey of Souls" until the 80's. It took me quite a few years to write that first book because nothing like it had been written before and I wanted the material to be clearly understood. When I finally did publish and my old colleagues saw this, they thought I had lost my marbles! They couldn't believe it! Some were fascinated, mostly those working with hypnotherapy, but by and large this is not a subject that is appealing to a

very conventional type of psychotherapist. The people who really embraced my work were the general public who wanted information on what life is like on the other side, what their purpose is in being here, why they chose the body they have, etc. [71]

When I first came upon this research I tried to imagine all the possible scenarios for interference; perhaps Michael Newton was influencing them, guiding them, or somehow manipulating their sessions. I found that not to be the case, because I began filming sessions and found that no matter who the person was – especially since I had chosen the subjects for their skepticism or ignorance of this work – they all had the same experience. Despite my attempt to disprove this hypnotic method of investigating the afterlife by filming it, I wound up with the exact same results that Newton had, and then some.

But what of other psychiatrists or psychologist who practiced hypnosis with their clients? Had anyone else come up with the same results?

I was speaking with the painter, great thinker, Oxford professor Robert Beer[72] recently and he turned me on to a talk given by Dr. Helen Wambach about her research into previous lives, in her book "Life Before Life."

One of the criticisms that comes with reports of hypnosis is that very few have done this kind of dedicated research. Newton didn't publish his work as case histories, rather as a book that explained in layman's terms what his patients had said consistently. In Dr. Wambach's case, she took her success with hypnosis to a larger group setting and used her skills as a scientist to document the results. I found it fascinating that Dr. Wambach's research was so similar to the work of Michael Newton.

Dr. Helen Wambach was a psychologist working with hypnosis in the 1970's conducting workshops in group hypnosis, meaning a room full of people would all experience the same questions and be given the same surveys to fill out. Dr. Wambach wrote "Life After Life" for Bantam in 1978 based on her results with 2000 patients.

---

[71] From "Interview with Michael Newton," Wisdom Magazine, Mary Arsenault 2008

[72] TibetanArt.com – some amazing articles about the afterlife and Buddhist philosophy on Robert Beer's blog.

She asked specific questions about the time periods in which people lived and the clothing, footwear, utensils, money, housing, etc. which they used or came in contact with. Dr. Wambach wrote that "fantasy and genetic memory could not account for the patterns that emerged in the results. With the exception of 11 subjects, all descriptions of clothing, footwear, and utensils were consistent with historical records."

In "Life Before Life" she published results of hypnotizing 750 people and taking them to the time between their past and current lives. Her findings corroborate Newton's where people claim they chose whether or not to incarnate. She wrote "The soul usually enters the body near birth, and has a choice of which fetus to enter. If one fetus is aborted, it is possible to choose another. In some cases, the soul who will occupy the fetus, is in contact with the soul of the mother, and can influence her decision regarding abortion."[73]

Dr. Wambach found that 89% of those hypnotized said they did not become part of the fetus until after at least six months of gestation. A large group said they did not join the fetus, or experienced being a part of it, until just before or during the birth process.[74]

She wrote "The soul exists in a quite different environment in the between-life state." Her subjects reported a new-born infant may feel "cut off, diminished, alone compared to the between-life state." These results are consistent with the research of Michael Newton on the same topic as well as many of the sessions which I've filmed.

Here is some of the raw data from Dr. Wambach's sessions in 1978 in Chicago. She had already done 400 of these sessions before she began to ask questions about the "choice" of being born, and whether they were eager or reluctant to come to the planet.

---

[73] KPFA in San Francisco posted a transcript with Dr. Wambach from March 1984 interview. The interview can be found on youtube under "Regressing into the Past and Progressing into the Future."

[74] In Michael Newton's research, he generally found people don't "show up" energetically to meld with the fetus until after the fourth month. I've filmed accounts where people say "there's not much to do" in terms of the human development until after that time. In terms of still births, miscarriages or abortions, these events are said to occur for a variety of spiritual, physical or genetic reasons depending upon the parents and soul that was scheduled to arrive. Every birth is reportedly a sacred choice made by the entering soul, and conversely not arriving would be one as well. As controversial as it sounds, the vast majority of people surveyed under hypnosis claim they didn't arrive until after the fourth month, and in Dr. Wambach's research, until around the sixth month of gestation.

Dr. Wambach: *I want you to go to the time just before you were born into your current lifetime. Are you choosing to be born? Does anyone help you choose? If anyone helps you choose, what is your relationship to the counselor?*

- "Yes, I chose to be born. Someone did help me choose and it seemed to be some voice that I trusted greatly. It was kind, helpful and wise, very wise."

- "I chose this time period to be born because it is a great period of change where people need stability within themselves. I am supposed to help them somehow. I did choose to become a male, because it is good for my work and I enjoy that sex role." (Pg. 28)

This is consistent in the between-life research. Counselors "speak to" or advise souls on their next incarnations. We may not remember all the details of the "life review" but that we were helped in our selection to come here.

- "I chose to be born and a guide or teacher counseled me. It was a big decision and involved a lot of thought and debate with my guide. My purpose for this lifetime was to become free of materialism and to combat negativity..." (Pg. 34)

- "A small group helped me choose. We were about six people in the group. My feelings about the prospect of the coming lifetime was a feeling of excitement." (Case A 372)

- "Advising me was a council of many in a circle. They seemed to be seated in large wooden chairs, and some kind of ancient customs were occurring." (Case A 325)

This is also common in between-life sessions; seeing advisors sitting at a dais, or behind chairs – it doesn't mean that there's a council chamber that's the same for everyone, in fact, almost all of the descriptions are different (and depend upon the person making them).

- "There seemed to be a board or committee – a group of authorities to help me choose... I knew I had something to do on this plane, something to accomplish" (Case A 408)

- "There was a group helping me choose. They listened to what I had planned and made some suggestions. My feeling about living the coming lifetime was that I was not happy, but I knew what I was going to do was important." (A 431)

All of these cases repeat variations of what people say under deep hypnosis; that they chose this lifetime, that sometimes it was with the help of counselors, friends, or others in the afterlife realm. [75]

This is nearly identical to the results Dr. Newton obtained during relatively the same time period, although he didn't publish for over 25 years after his first client took him into a between-lives realm. Dr. Wambach couldn't have been aware of Dr. Newton's work in California, as he didn't share any of his cases with anyone, and didn't publish until after she had passed away. And in his case, he and his wife told me he avoided even going into a book store to avoid being influenced by someone else's work or questions, so he wasn't aware of her case studies.

However, here we have two different sets of people, in two different states, with two different psychologists using hypnosis and they're both hearing pretty much the same things about the soul's journey. In Dr. Wambach's case, she was doing group sessions with clusters of clients, and in Dr. Newton's case he was seeing people individually over the course of his career. And yet both clients say nearly the identical things about the soul's journey.

In my own research, I've filmed over 25 sessions with many who claim they'd never having heard of Michael Newton's work, and yet they too say the same things that Dr. Newton's and Dr. Wambach's clients say.

Just as a matter of logic – if one person describes an event that isn't in popular literature, that is contrary to the prevailing school of thought and that is contrary to medical history and general education, it stands to reason that it wasn't made up by the client in order to fulfill some kind of fantasy. Since what these people were saying is pretty much the opposite of every known religious stance on the spirit world, and is in direct contradiction of all major religions from Christianity to Buddhism, is also in direct conflict with the way that the afterlife is depicted in

---

[75] Michael Newton didn't publish his work until 1994, and as I've verified by others, he avoided going into book stores so that other research on the topic wouldn't influence the questions he asked during his sessions.

popular media, its baffling how people could have inadvertently tapped into this alternate way to view how we choose to come to the planet.

Fortunately, in Dr. Newton's case and in Dr. Wambach's case, they both took assiduous case notes, and published the results verbatim.

In the research I've done filming people under deep hypnosis, I've included people selected at random for their avowed skepticism, or some other compelling reason which didn't have to do with them seeking out the help of a therapist. Some of the subjects were lifelong friends whom I could verify what they were saying about their childhood, some were acquaintances who professed disbelief in the idea of the afterlife altogether, but for some odd reason were willing to be part of a study which included me filming them for up to six hours at a time while they revealed their inner most secrets.

None of my subjects were looking for a hypnotherapist, most had never been "under hypnosis" nor had any desire to "find spiritual answers." They had no "presenting problem" as doctors call it, and therefore, the hypnotherapist had no preconceived ideas about "healing them." The only reason they participated was at my request.

Birth Selection

More cases from Dr. Wambach's research on "Birth selection."

It appears not everyone agrees on coming to Earth, but they all appear to agree that it was a choice.

- "When you asked if I chose to be born; I didn't want to, but I was convinced by a counselor that I needed to "help with enlightenment." The man who helped me choose seemed to have a white beard and a cane and was a kind of spiritual guide." (Case A 434)

- "Yes, I chose to be born, but I kind of hemmed and hawed. It seemed there were friends helping me choose; a lot of them. They wanted me to go... I feel I kind of went along for the ride." (Case A 481)

- **"My brother and some soul guardian seemed to be helping me. When you asked about the prospects of being born, I felt "Oh no, not again!" but I also knew I had to learn more."**

"Oh no, not again!" is a comment that demonstrates the idea of free will. We can say "No thanks, I don't want to play that role again." But usually our loved ones (or our spirit guides) will try to advise us why this would make a good choice. Also, I might add, this may account for those people who feel their entire lives were "a bad choice." We apparently sign up for what we think we can handle, and sometimes, unfortunately, we aren't able to.

- "There was a group talking it over, but the choice was up to me." (Case A 482)

- "Yes, I chose to be born, but very reluctantly. There were several others around me when I was deciding and they seemed to be just like me. They said they'd be around to help me in the coming lifetime. I did not want to leave the beautiful garden and my friends there..." (A 489)

- **"I was offered the chance to be born and I agreed at a sort of important conference. There seemed to be an old bearded man there who was a big boss... I wasn't happy to return as a woman, that sort of put me off, but I still elected to come."** (A 316)

It's reported that we choose what gender we're going to be and what lessons we're going to learn from that choice. But as you can see from the answers above, the choice is not always made with complete enthusiasm. Our loved ones may be the tipping point, arguing that they need our help for their ability to learn life lessons. And out of compassion or love for them, we agree to show up for the lessons to be learned.

Dr. Wambach also points out that people choose their parents sometimes because of unfinished business:

"87% of all the subjects responding to any of the questions about the birth reported that they had known parents, lovers, relatives and friends who were known to them in past lives."

- "I knew my mother and I know I chose her because we had not finished whatever it was we had to work out..." (A 341 pg. 95)

- "I knew my mother had been my mother previously." (A 513)

This is also a common experience in the between-life arena. People often see that they were related to their loved ones in another fashion.

Just prior to my wife's mother's passing, she whispered to Sherry, "I'll be your mother again." Having been raised in the Mormon religion, it's not something she would have said based on her cultural references, and my wife didn't share it with the rest of her family as she knew the idea might disturb them.

But it's something I've heard more than once: "I was your parent this lifetime, and you'll be mine in a future one."

- "I had the feeling I was consulting others whom I would be born with and I had known them in past lives. I knew my brother as a good friend – and I wanted my friend June to come too, but she said "not this time." (A 191)

- "My mother was a nun in a former life and my father was a gambler. **I picked them to experience extremes and help them work out their destiny as well as my own. I felt the purpose of my life was to bring together elements from former lives.**" (A 361)

So why don't people show up to the fetus until after the fourth month, and in this research, more commonly the sixth? Dr. Wambach's research is as follows: "Birth. **Out of 750 cases, 89% of all the subjects responding said they did not become a part of the fetus or involved with the fetus until after 6 months of gestation. Even then, many reported being "in and out" of the fetal body.**"

Dr. Wambach says that they "**viewed themselves as an adult consciousness relating to the fetal body as a less developed form of life. The largest group in the sample, 33%, said they didn't join the fetus until just before the birth process. Nearly all reported being aware of their mother's emotions prior to birth.**" (Pg. 99)

- "I attached to the fetus just before birth. I had the feeling being pregnant was a nuisance to (my mother)." (A 444)

- "I came at the beginning ... while the fetus was developing, but I split when it got too squishy, and didn't come back until just before it was time for me to be born... I felt (my mother) was unaware of me when I was born because she had been sedated." (A 313)

People report that they don't have to stay in the womb when they arrive – apparently they're free to move "in and out" up until birth. When asked "where do you go?" sometimes people respond with "I have other work to attend to" or "I fly around to see others and help them."

But according to a number of reports, even if the spirit does decide to travel "we are always attached by an umbilical like cord to the baby." There are a number of instances reported of this "thin wispy string" that keeps our energy always connected to our body even during NDE's or out of body experiences.

- "I wasn't attached to the fetus until I heard some voices (I think they were my guides who helped me choose to be born) warn me that the birth would be premature and they urged me to "hurry up and get in there" at about seven months." (A 98)

- "I did not enter the fetus until the last minute. I was too happy and too busy elsewhere. I wasn't interested at all in spending time in the fetus." (A 490)

- **"My twin wanted to come into life at this time and talked me into going along with her. She seemed to have more karma to work out than I did, or at least was more eager to go. I agreed to come with her and we chose twin fetuses. I was not in the fetus until just before birth, nor was my twin. Then I had the impression we were arguing about which twin we would choose – one would be brown haired (and the other) blonde. ... I hung back and was reluctant to enter the world. I became aware that she was urging me to come along and to hurry up."** (Pg. 154)

Dr. Wambach reports "86% of all the subjects said they became aware of the feelings, emotions and even thoughts of their mother before they were born. Many of the subjects said that they were aware of the mother's feelings because they themselves were not locked into the fetus, but instead seemed to be hovering around it." (Pg. 120)

In "Flipside" there were a number of cases cited where people under deep hypnosis saw that they had been with their adopted child in a previous lifetime.

Dr. Wambach finds the same results:

- "I chose my parents only for the genetic material they could give me. I chose my adoptive parents and I know (sic) ahead of time that I will be adopted by them, because I needed the environment they could provide for me. I had a job to do in this life and I wanted to plan it as carefully as possible. I chose one set of parents for the genetic background and another for the environment." (Pg. 164)

These cases serve to bolster the point that even though we all may experience relatively the same thing – a life selection process, guidance on our choice, help on choosing when and where to be born, help with our birth, the joint experience of physical death of the body - the details of the experience appears to be different for each individual, and tailored to each of us. In other words, each of us is the star of our own movie, and we experience it as such.

For example, this research demonstrates that when a person dies, they may not make a quick journey back to the between lives realm. They may, for various reasons, choose to stick around on the Earth plane for a certain amount of time. Or perhaps they find themselves in a realm where there are other people who have died suddenly and haven't reconciled being in this other realm. They may remain here, as a choice, for some time - a year, ten years, one hundred years – the concept of time is reported as completely different to someone no longer on the Earth plane. But eventually, everyone returns "home."

As discussed, one person described their time on Earth, away from their class in the between lives realm, as the time it would takes to have "a cigarette break." In this case, the lifetime this person remembered lasted 25 years. Is it possible that the five or six minutes it takes is equivalent to 25 Earth years?

It's that's accurate, a jumping off place to understand the difference between time back there versus time here on Earth, is to say a lifetime here might last as long as a stage play. Some plays are longer than others, but most last are about two hours long. And they all have a beginning, middle and end.

I offer this only by way of metaphor – but thinking of a lifetime being the length we experience a play or a movie might be how living a difficult or stressful life might be something the stronger of us could handle. "Two hours? I can handle that."

I worked on the film "Cowboy Up," about championship bull riding, and filmed a number of rodeos up and down the California coast. Personally, I could never volunteer to ride a three thousand pound bull for any amount of seconds, let alone eight of them. Settling into the chute, wrapping my legs around a snorting bull – and then nodding for them to let the gate open so the bull could stomp me to smithereens - I just can't wrap my head around me agreeing to do that.

Nor can I imagine volunteering to go into the ring with a professional boxer. Just learning how to hold gloves over my face to defend myself is hard when you're being smacked in the head repeatedly. I can't imagine signing up for a lifetime where I'd spend time in a foxhole watching bullets and hellfire screaming overhead. And yet, people have the courage to do these things, and apparently have the courage to choose these lives.

But if we consider for a moment they're own experience might be something akin to a brilliant performance on stage, it gives some solace to realize those who've left the stage early are merely backstage, and not suffering from any part of their journey onstage.

Here are more of Dr. Wambach's case studies about choosing our roles to play:

- "I was sort of reluctant, others were around me when I was choosing. It was my sister and some other person, and my brother from a past life and my boyfriend in this life." (A 354)

- "I felt that my soul-mate who was my husband in this life helped me choose... but I had a sense of sadness in returning to this plane." (A 361)

- "I felt it was going to be a hassle. Someone helped me choose, someone more knowledgeable than me. My feelings about living the coming lifetime were that it was something that had to be done, like washing the floor when it's dirty." (A 285)[76]

In each of the above cases, someone steps up to help the person decide to choose that particular lifetime.

---

[76] Dr. Wambach: "81 percent of my subjects said that they themselves chose to be born. 19% reported that either they were unaware of the choice, or got no clear answer to the question... of those reporting counselors in the time before birth, 59% mentioned more than one counselor, 105 reported people in their current lifetime "as their counselors.""

Again, Newton's work notes that we have free will, and there is always the possibility for a person to say, "No thanks, sorry, I don't want to play that role this time around. We've already done the whole Viking, pillaging life full of angst. It's not for me. Have fun. I'll sit this one out." But then loved ones from the soul group insist. "But you're so good at playing the pillaging Viking. I don't think I can learn the lessons I need to learn unless you play that role for me. Pleeeeze?" Sometimes, it appears, we're *nudged* into our roles.

Gender Selection

I think it's important to note Dr. Wambach's questions with regard to gender. It's a topic that's been hotly debated in our culture, about one's "choice" of sexuality. But if we really examine the question, not only do we choose who we're going to be attracted to on a personal level, we also choose what our gender is going to be so we can learn from that choice:

- "I chose to be a male because I felt I had sexual problems as a male to work out." (Case A2)

- "At first I wanted to be a male, but I changed to a female because I could be gentler." (A 17)

In many of the LBL sessions I've filmed, and in countless ones that Michael Newton cataloged, there are reports of being different sexes in different lifetimes. Sometimes people say they "for the most part" incarnate as one sex – they feel they can advance or learn the most from that experience. However, many subjects say something akin to "I wanted to see what it was like" and choose a different sex for a different lifetime.

- "I chose to be a woman because my mate wanted us to be the same sex we were in (a past life)." (A 15)

- "I chose to be a female because my parents would accept that more easily than if I were a male." (A 387 Pg. 77)

- "I chose to be male because of my wife – to help her solve a problem, and she had chosen to be female." (A 27)

- "I was male in my last life and I wanted to continue where I left off. I wanted to become a scientist because in my last life I had the same but died as a soldier." (A 35)

Councils of Elders

Dr. Wambach also explores reports of visiting with a council for advice on a future life. In Michael Newton's work he uses various terms from his clients such as "Council of Elders" or "the wisdom makers." According to the research, we all have them, and they help us choose our next lifetimes.

- "Before my birth there was a conference and I had a feeling of deep love from one of my advisors. He talked of my learning to reach my life plane." (A 341)

- "I died not too long before and I was very anxious to get back into a body. I thought this time and date would give me the opportunity to lead a much different life than before." (A 494)

This is also a common experience – people dying before they had the opportunity to learn the lesson they'd signed up for and are in a hurry to get incarnated again. It really depends on the individual.

- "I got the impression that there were almost too many units of learning this time around, I became aware that I was given an option to leave if I got too tired, but I had already passed this up to finish the last two units, one I am doing and one still to go. I don't know quite what these are." (A 437 Pg. 88)

I like this last one, because in Newton's research, and in my own case examples, there are those who speak of classrooms and traveling to them. And in this case, the person even refers to them as "units" in the same way a student might refer to how many units they're taking in college (even if that's not the intent.)

And finally, it's fairly universal that people choose to come here to help others while they're here. We don't often remember the reasons we chose to come here, or the details, but under hypnosis some do:

- "I knew that I was here because it's important for me to help others overcome their programming and learn to love." (A 143)

- "My purpose is to work with others to develop higher consciousness in this time period." B 56

- "I am here to learn, but also to teach and to help in this period of a transition in history from the religious to the scientific to the spiritual life." (B 88)

Pretty unusual to see our current era as a transition in history from the religious to the scientific to one that focuses on the spiritual life. Well, I guess that's a relative reply, as not everyone wants to see history transition from the scientific to the spiritual life, do they?

- "My purpose (in coming here) is to overcome fear." (A 353)

- "My purpose is to learn humility." (A 46)

- "My purpose for this lifetime is contact with space brothers, bringing together ideas of western medicine and eastern healing." (B 5 Pg. 91)

I'm not sure what "space brothers" means. It's possible we're all brothers traveling through space, or perhaps the meaning is related to the case in "Flipside" (Chapter "Over the Rainbow" pg. 207) where a person remembers that he normally incarnates on another planet, and the reason he came to Earth was to help the humanity "raise its consciousness."

One therapist told me about her client who had been "outed" by his church. He felt humiliated and scorned, as he lost all of his friends and family when they learned he was secretly gay. But during his hypnotherapy session, he learned that the man who outed him was one of his spirit guides.

And this man said something to the effect of "Don't you remember? You've had many lifetimes within the church and about the church. But you wanted to get a full experience of living a life outside of that. And this is what you came up with." In that moment the young man was able to forgive his church and his family for participating in a journey that he had crafted for himself. It didn't make his Thanksgiving dinners any less lonely – but it gave him the context for why his family had behaved the way they did and he was able to drop his anger towards them.

Why Incarnate Now?

When Dr. Wambach asked her clients about why they chose to be born in this time period, their answers are equally interesting:

- "Because it is the time of Earth changes and the raising of levels of consciousness." (Case B5)

- "This century is the dawning of a new age of awareness, and many souls are going to transcend to another plane of oneness." (A 379)

This concept of our century being one of change and consciousness shifting is popular in new age literature, as well as in many of these sessions.

- "I chose the last half of the 20th century to be alive because more advanced spirits are being born and we are close to obtaining world peace and a sense of the total self of mankind." (A 384)

- "The last half of the 20th century is the time of enlightenment I have been waiting for, to live another lifetime." (B 91 – Pg. 76)

What does Dr. Wambach's research point to?

It echoes the same research another psychologist Michael Newton did which shows that we choose our lifetimes. Sometimes reluctantly, sometimes with the loving help and guidance of our loved ones, sometimes because we're in a hurry to get back here. We each have our own reasons for choosing a lifetime, none are exactly the same, but the idea that we choose them is consistent.

Reportedly we choose our gender. We may normally incarnate as a man or woman, but depending on the upcoming adventure it appears that we'll choose our role accordingly. And finally it appears that we appear to be fully conscious between lives.

Most of these reports from people under deep hypnosis, or during an NDE, report being fully conscious of, or aware of, many, if not all of our previous lifetimes. And then as the process to incarnation begins, we seem to put the mental blocks back in place to keep this information from being accessible. That could be a consequence of choosing the human body – it could be the brain is naturally equipped with these blocks or filters to prevent overload – it could be because we don't want to "spoil the ending," or "know what's going to happen at the end of the book" so we can fully experience what we've set out to learn.

But for those who wonder why there hasn't been more scientific research done in this field of hypnosis and a discussion of past lives, they're overlooking Dr. Wambach's earlier work which dovetails with Michael Newton's later, equally extensive work.[77] Interviews with the late Doctor Wambach (she passed away in 1986) can be found on youtube, and I recommend listening to her speak about her ground breaking research.

"I still feel his presence every day and often find him in my dreams at night."
Nancy Reagan on the 10th anniversary of Ronald's death. (NY Daily News, June 5th, 2014)

---

[77] All excerpts are from "Life Before Life" by Helen Wambach PH.D. Bantam Books 1979.

Chapter Ten– "Celestial Music"

"When in the evening I contemplate the sky in wonder and the host of luminous bodies continually revolving within their orbits, suns or earths by name, then my spirit rises beyond these constellations . . . to the primeval source from which all creation flows and from which new creations shall flow eternally. . . . The spirit must rise from the earth, in which for a time the divine spark is confined, and much like the field to which the ploughman entrusts precious seed, it must flower and bear many fruits, and, thus multiplied, rise again towards the source from which it has flown." -- Ludwig Van Beethoven, *Letters, Journals*

How does music fit into these visions of the afterlife?

During LBLs and NDEs people often report "hearing" music that's not of an Earthly nature. In a number of LBLs I've heard people report that music and healing come from "related" places in the universe. But there are many musicians who claim to hear music when composing.

When we study the great composers, like Beethoven, we find that they spoke often of "hearing celestial music." Oliver Sachs, the renowned scientist, considers this "hallucinatory music." As he notes:

True musical hallucinations are experienced by those who have them as unprecedented and deeply disquieting. There is insufficient awareness among physicians of musical hallucinations, in part because patients are reluctant to report them, fearing that they will be dismissed or seen as 'crazy'. But musical hallucinations are surprisingly common, affecting at least 2% of those who are losing their hearing, as well as patients with a variety of other conditions. Working with a population of elderly patients (though I have seen it in younger people as well), I am often given vivid descriptions of musical hallucinosis, and I think it is by far the most common form of non-psychotic hallucination. I related two stories of musical hallucination in my 1985 book "The Man Who Mistook his Wife for a Hat," and since then have received hundreds of letters from people with this condition. With musical hallucinations it is common for several voices or instruments to be heard simultaneously, and such experiences are almost always attributed, initially, to an external source. Thus in 1995 I received a vivid letter from June M., a charming and creative woman of 70, telling me of her musical hallucinations:

> "…Most of the music I hear is from my past—many of the songs are hymns, some are folk music, some pop up from the forties and fifties, some classical and some show tunes. All the selections are sung by a chorus—there is never a solo performance or any orchestration. This first started last November when I was visiting my sister and brother in law in Cape Hatteras, NC, one night. After turning off the TV and preparing to retire, I started hearing 'Amazing Grace.' It was being sung by a choir, over and over again. I checked with my sister to see if they had some church service on TV, but they had Monday night football, or some such. So I went onto the deck overlooking Pamlico Sound. The music followed me. I looked down on the quiet coastline and the few houses with lights and realized that the music couldn't possibly be coming from anywhere in that area. It had to be in my head."

It was not clear why June M. started to have musical hallucinations, or why she still has them, 11 years later. She has excellent hearing, is not epileptic, has no known medical problems and is intellectually quite intact. With her, as with many other patients, the most searching examination may fail to pinpoint the cause of musical hallucinations..." [78]

There is another possible explanation for the source of her music that Dr. Sach's hasn't explored: that it is not created by her mind.

A speaker can sometimes pick up the vibrations from other sound waves and reproduce them, but the sound is not being created by the speaker. Sometimes our radio picks up bursts of short wave radios from police scanners, but it's not that the announcement is created by our stereo.

In Eben Alexander's NDE he heard "celestial music." "I heard... the richest, most complex, most beautiful piece of music (I've) ever heard." It's also one of the hallmarks of NDE's according to Bruce Greyson's research.

> "As a high school student, Burt Bacharach always had trouble getting to school on time: he couldn't sleep at night because he kept hearing music in his head. Throughout his life, Bacharach would never stop hearing music, because for him music would always be about sounds rather than ideas." [79]

In David Bennett's interview ("Voyage of Purpose") he talks about hearing a "canyon of sound" during his NDE. He gives specific details on what that music sounds like.

Pete Townshend, legendary member of the band, The Who, heard celestial music as an 11 year old boy. "Townshend tells of hearing the music while on a boat with his Sea Scout troop. "I heard violins, cellos, horns, harps and voices, which increased in number until I could hear the threads of an angelic choir. It was a sublime experience. I have never heard such music since and my personal music ambition has always been to rediscover that sound and relive its effect on me."[80]

Stuart Sharp heard celestial music when he was a young man. The experience was similar to Townshend's: he first heard the angelic orchestra in a dream as a boy in 1956. Years later he heard it again after his baby son Ben died at birth. He explains: "In my dream I was back at Ben's graveside staring down at his tiny white coffin. I heard distant angelic music with choirs, violins, cellos, horns and harps that grew in intensity and I gasped as Ben's spirit rose slowly through the

---

[78] "The Power of Music" by Oliver Sachs. Oxford Journals *Brain* Volume 129.

[79] "Self Portrait of an Experimental Songwriter" David Galenson, Huffington Post 2-19-14

[80] "Who I am: a Memoir" by Pete Townshend Harper, 2013

coffin. I couldn't bring myself to see him in the mortuary. I didn't have the courage."

He was so haunted by the music he quit his job as cook in a Leicestershire country pub, left his wife and two daughters and moved to London and into a homeless shelter. He taught himself to play music after he bought a battered guitar from a second-hand shop which, by an amazing co-incidence, happened to be owned by Townshend's parents. Eventually Stuart Sharp met someone who was moved by his story and helped him record with the London symphony – the result is an orchestral piece called "Angeli Symphony."[81]

I've found other accounts, just from searching them out on the internet. From the NDE of "Jeanette Mitchell-Meadows": "When I went for surgery the operation took nine hours. During the operation my spirit left my body, in the time it takes to blink an eye, I was in Heaven and saw the light of Heaven... There were musical notes I have never heard on Earth. They were so clear and flawless, and the tone was so beautiful. It is the most wonderful place to be. [82]

Or the account of an NDE from Canadian musician Gilles Bedard: "All day long, I went in and out of a coma... Then I saw myself from the ceiling. I was nine feet higher than my body and I was looking down at the people around me.... My vision expanded and I went into a place like a cosmos where there were twelve people standing in a half-circle. They were all pure white lights and they had no faces. I somehow knew these people although they weren't family or people I could recognize. It was as if they were waiting for me. I asked them what was happening, and they told me, 'You are not going to die. You are going back to Earth. You have something to do.' I asked them what it was, and as soon as I asked it was as if I knew the answer... What I remembered most is the music I heard when I was out of my body. It was fascinating.[83]

The following is a session between Scott De Tamble, and a successful musician and actress from Los Angeles – I call her "Sean." We met in a roundabout way; a woman who lives in Capri, Italy, was a fan of my book and we began a conversation online which eventually led to her suggesting her friend in Los

---

[81] "Homeless man turns haunting noises in his head into symphony" The Express May 2, 2013

[82] http://www.bibleprobe.com/mitchell-meadows.htm

[83] Gilles Bedard's Near-Death Experience and Music Research by Kevin Williams http://www.near-death.com/music.html

Angeles try a between-life session. I put her friend Sean in touch with Scott; I had no prior knowledge of what it was she might want to explore.

Scott and Sean

Scott De Tamble: I'm going to ask you some questions I want you to respond with the first thing that comes to mind... (etc) So talk to me is it daytime or nighttime?

Sean: Day

Inside or outside?

Outside. I'm standing on dirt. I think I'm wearing something. Sandals.

Are you a small medium or large person?

Like medium. Male. Young, about 14

Standing on the dirt there with your pouch, what's going through your mind? What are you doing here?

I'm not really sure, I feel like I'm separated from my group of people – I'm on my own. I don't feel lost though. Feels like its dusk. And I feel like I need to know where I'm going because it's getting dark.

If you haven't already done so drift outside of yourself to observe this young man; the face the hair, the eyes. What color?

Black. It's long, straight, shoulder length. Skin's kind of brownish, like tan. Olive-y.

What about the eyes? Light or dark?

Dark. Dark brown.

What about racial characteristic? Caucasian? Asian? Something else?

Maybe South American. I'm not sure. Something.... not Caucasian.

A native, Indian?

Yeah.

So notice those dark brown eyes of yours and move inside and look out through those brown eyes and connecting with the thoughts and feelings of this guy. So what are you aware of? What's going through your mind?

I have to go back and take care of my little brother.

How old is he?

6 or 7.

See him, describe him.

He looks like me, but littler. He runs around a lot, very hyper.

What does he call you?

Ferrazan.

Tell me about your home where you live.

It's like a hut, very simple, very... I see smokestacks, and it's got a chimney.... Mud or Earth or something. Baked.

How tall is it? Taller than a person?

Yeah. And there's a bunch of them around – like a community. 30 to 40 people – our group.

So let's go inside the home and I'd like you tell me about that.

Ok, there's big table, little stove, very simple; cots or something like a cot. I'm seeing one room.

Where do you sleep?

I have my cot in the corner. My brother and I sleep kind of close to the stove, so at night it's warm.

Does anyone else live here?

My mother. She's short, she's always baking, preparing something, so she's not around a lot. I'm in charge of my little brother, so I have to be the man of the house.

So let's go to a time when you're having a meal with your brother and your mother. Where do you sit?

There's a round table and we sit at that. My little brother doesn't sit very often – he's hyper.

Tell me about the food.

Bowls and plates. Food is bird meat. Like soups. Sort of a porridge.

Tell me about your mother's temperament.

Pretty serious, quiet; a good mother who looks after us. She's serious a lot because she feels she's got to raise two sons –

How do you spend your days?

I like to explore – to find new places and I like to study, I like to read about the stars, astronomy – I'm curious about traveling and the stars and things like this.

When you say you like to explore, what do you explore?

Just wander off on my own and find new places, off the beaten track and just be by myself and ponder. Find new trails, I like trails –

First impression, what country are you in?

I want to say South America, like Peru or... Uruguay.

What year are you having this meal, what number pops into your mind?

1876.

I want you to go to a time when you're bathing... One, two, three. Be there now. How do you do that?

There's a tub and I kind of just get in it by the fire so it's warm and we have like a ladle or something to pour the water over; a scoop.

Do you have any products like soap?

I scrub, a lot of scrubbing, I don't know if there's soap – there's like a spongy brush.

All right, let that fade away as I count to three I want you to go to a very proud moment in your life. So one, two three... Be there now. A proud moment. Tell me are you inside or outside?

Outside.

How old are you in this proud moment?

Like 16. I hunted something big and brought it for everybody, was able to hunt something, some sort of... And share it with everyone.

Let's go back to that moment when you were hunting – did you have a weapon? Or a trap?

I want to say... Not a bow and arrow. Not a trap, but a... projectile. I killed a boar.

All right, so you're carrying this home?

It's pretty big. I'm not sure how I got it back there (laughs) maybe I had help with that part.

What do they say upon your return?

Just it's more like you're a man and not just a boy. My mother is proud of me and that's important to me, and my little brother is looking up.

Excellent moment. Feel good, enjoy that. Let's skip forward in time, getting older, older, older, let's go to a very important... on my count one that is perhaps a turning point in the life of Ferrazan... 1, 2, 3 be there now... important moment, perhaps a turning point. What are you aware of? Are you inside or outside?

Outside again. There's like – my child is being born. Yeah. My woman's having a baby. It's a son.

That's exciting. And everybody's ok?

Yeah. People all around, it's like a joyous occasion, like a celebration.

Tell me about your wife?

She's very sweet, very a lot like my mother in some ways, less serious... she's a good mother.

So what's it feel like, to become a father for the first time?

Feels amazing, I feel proud, like I'm going to honor that in the way that I never had a father.

What happened to your father?

Killed. He died when I was really young.

So let's let that fade away... fade away. Let's skip forward in time, getting older and older, to some significant moment in this life, skipping forward... to some significant moment... where are you?

I'm inside. Inside one of the dwellings. I'm laying down. Feel like I'm... sick. I think it's something I may not survive.

Skip forward to the very last day of Ferrazan, you have not crossed over, but let's go to the last day. Be there now.[84] Are you lying? Resting?

Lying. I feel like I'm on the verge... I don't want to leave I want to make sure my family is taken care of.

How old are you on this last day?

56...?

What do you think about this life you've just lived?

I did well because I was honorable; it's a simple life, but I feel like I took care of my mother, took care of my wife, provided for them, it was ok, nothing crazy...

All right. What do you think you may have learned from this experience?

I learned how to take care of those I love; how to be a solid foundation for others... and to give; give of myself, to not put my needs first...

So without pain or discomfort it's time to move forward to the moment just after death... etc... Where are you in relation to the body above it or off to the side?

Just floating. Slight pulling.

---

[84] Ferrazan is a common Spanish name, I found it mostly in Uruguay and Central America.

Before you go is there anyone you need to say goodbye to or attend to any unfinished business?

I want to say goodbye to my family. I kiss them on their foreheads. I'll always be with them and they'll be fine. Energetically, I give them a little reassurance. I feel like I've gone already and I've come back to just give this energy to them, so they can feel I'm still with them.

By the way, what does it feel like to die and cross over?

I feel really light. Just like, sort of soft light around me. Yellow…pale yellow… Pink and yellow.

So be aware of that pink and yellow light, knowing that you're entering a soul state that's connected to the highest consciousness of your mind, like a vast computer holding all the stored knowledge of your existence. What are you thinking now?

I just want, I'm curious to meet my soul group I guess; see if I'm not alone.[85]

Let's go ahead and skip forward and do just that. One, two three… Be there now. What are you aware of now?

A Visit to a Soul Group

Being in the midst of energies…. I don't know who they are, but they're energies. A cluster. Like 12 or so. They feel like peers.

And what's being communicated to you. What are they communicating with their energy? What is that doing for you?

Like comforting… feeding me - sort of comforting, surrounding me. With comfort, friendship…. Love…. Hmm. Seem to be three or 4. In a semi-circle.

---

[85] For those with a score card, she's specifically asking to find members of her soul group. One may argue that it's wish fulfillment when she does find them. That still doesn't account for thousands of people who have never heard of this research who find soul groups without looking for them. And when people do find their soul groups, as we'll see, sometimes it's a surprise who shows up.

Let's check in with this inner circle of yours maybe there's one of them who wants to greet you and come forward first. To connect, reconnect with you. So that first to come forward is it a male or female energy?

It's a male.

So what is that energy he's communicating to you? If you could put it into words?

(Sighs) Like he's proud of me in some ways.... But I have a lot more to go.

Is it like a light or human form?

I can see a human, but it's a light that's shaped, looks like chess piece sort of – kind of human but made of light.

What color is that person?

Yellowish. Core is blue.

If that person was holding a mirror up to you – what would you appear to him? What color are you in your core?

Pink. Yellow too... And green. Yellow all round on the outside. Green around the pink.

How does it look?

Definitely flowing, it's pulsating, flowing...[86] He's smiling at me, putting his hands on my shoulders, yeah, sharing that moment, not really giving me any information but.... touching me.

What is being communicated to you?

Showing me to always be in touch with that gentleness within me, that it's always there even when I have to be brave, or a warrior. That I'm still connected very much to a divine mother spirit.

---

[86] Michael Newton began asking his clients "If I could hold a mirror up to you, what color would you appear?" And when he did that he discovered that the colors represented a number of things; how far along the path a soul is in terms of progression. He cataloged that young souls have a lighter color, and older ones have a darker color. However, these colors don't represent a hierarchy, just progression.

All right then. What about one of the other souls? Is there a 3rd person who wants to come forward? A male or female?

There's a male.

What is he communicating to you?

Humor. Heightened awareness and humor just to be flexible. And take things lightly... That I can connect with my energies and it's a gift to be able to do this, because I'm able to be flexible, I can adapt to many things, I can spread it out wherever it's needed. Different capabilities to channel different energies. [87]

What else is special about your soul?

Compassion. Speed. Swiftness. Bouncy... I get the word "bouncy" energy. Like fun, being able to do something in leaps and bounds.

Does this feel like the cluster group you grew up with, or a specialty group?

A specialty group; I get recharged from each of them. Sort of recharging and reminding. Like comrades.

What is this specialty here – do they aspire to the same specialization?

Just evolvement. Taking chances, taking risks, but for good things. In good ways. To remind us always, I forget I guess, I get focused on other things... they're like cheerleaders in a way. Not in the typical way.

(Note: Soul groups may specialize in a particular area. So everyone in your soul group might be a healer of some sort, for example, or working on a particular experience over many lifetimes.)

And so... is there anything else you'd like to do with your group? Some activity? Or are we ready to move on? Another exploration?

Yeah, I just want to find out maybe what I need to be doing better.

---

[87] When a person first enters this arena, the thoughts and images seem to come in a haze, or in bits and pieces. As the comfort zone changes, the images and answers come more quickly.

Let's thank your group for being here. Let's share some of that uplifting energy with them. Shall we talk to someone wise who knows you? Or a group of wise beings?

Sure. Some Wise beings are always good.

Are you getting an impression of a male or more of a female energy near you?

Kind of male.

All right then. So what is he communicating to you?

He's saying "go forward." Just keep going forward.

How does he feel about your performance as...

Ferrazan? It was good. I did the right things. I was honorable. And a good person.

A Visual of the Grid

What else his being communicated to you by this wise energy?

Something about.... staying connected to the grid. I'm there at all times. I know that all the time.

Show her the grid.

It's like a spider web like a light connecting all things, I think Sean has seen it before.... and it's there all the time.[88] Like energy dew drops.... but it's light instead of.... Like shooting lights connecting things like a beautiful tapestry, but it's always there.

So energy moves along those filaments... How do we stay connected?

Trusting. Just the whole moving-forward-with-trust thing.

And this male energy. Is he a spirit guide?

---

[88] This is similar to other accounts of NDE's and LBLs where people say that they can see the "interconnectedness of all things." Sometimes that's described as a giant tree, or a spider web, and they can see the filaments of light that connect all beings.

He said "yes."

I'm curious how you're in touch with Sean in her daily life?

He says "always."

How can Sean know that you are communicating with her versus her own thoughts; what's the difference?

"Steady." He says communication is steady. Just more of a knowing. Something to do with pushing forward.

Imagine in your heart center opening up, to your guide's heart center so that you meet and connect so your heart energy is melding together and you can even communicate along this beam, this connection.

I feel tingly all over right now. In my head. Tingly in my head. My palms are warm too, like there's a lot of energy.

So when she feels these sensations what is she supposed to do?

Trust in that and pay attention.

I'm curious, why were we shown this lifetime today? What's the connection between the past and current life? What's the message?

Self-reliance. Just balance. And providing for myself as well as my family being able to do that.

I'll ask the questions Sean wanted to ask and you can just answer through her or in her mind and she can translate. She asks "Why have I not been able to find a mate?"

It's not been the time for it yet, its coming. Had to find out who she is first. Had to be strong in that. To be able to know that first.[89]

---

[89] It's one of the most asked questions by people during these sessions – the ability to find a soul mate, or that person you normally incarnate with as a mate. And the answers are always a bit different, depending on the circumstances – sometimes people agree not to be together for a particular lifetime. But then, there's the possibility of not being able to discern the answer, as it might screw up the ability to connect in the way that's needed.

"Why did I set myself up not to succeed in this life? Would it be ok for me to abort this mission? If you don't get punished for suicide would it be ok for me to exit gracefully?"

No. This life is a gift, even though it's hard there are still gifts in that too. I don't think she really wants that - I think it's just that patience is needed and belief and trust, it's not what she wants to do really; she just needs to be patient and trust.

What were these strange dreams, she's had, mosaic patterns? Tapping into things?

Just downloading. Always she was always been able to connect with other portals, or other energies. **It's part of the artistic soul that also downloads and development of the soul too, and with these it's the ability to tap into other worlds for creation of art or healing.** Healing.[90]

Fractals

They have a side effect of weird patterns?

Yeah, those are all intelligence, any of those patterns are sort of intelligence in themselves, they're templates of a sort.

What was she learning (when she had these) as a child?

It was developmental. Like getting an extra jump on some things, **a lot of information encoded in small places and that's what these patterns are, they're encoded information, fractals.**[91]

She's worried she's "doomed by some agreement" not to be successful in life.

---

[90] "Downloading" has appeared in a number of sessions, where people might feel a buzzing sensation in their head, and when asked during a session, will say "I was downloading information from previous lifetimes into this body at that time." Dreams appear to be a way of downloading needed information, like the computer is on "sleep mode" but is still updating programs.

[91] There it is again; the word "fractals" to describe patterns of information that are visible – like mini hard drives in the shape of snowflakes for lack of a better metaphor.

No. No, no... **there's no agreement to fail. Its agreement to be tested, to prove to herself that she can do it to take that on, especially in the role of a woman in this time and yet have a warrior spirit and keeping the compassion.**

So there's a balance and it's sort of an example for others too, and also moving forward, and moving along and just pure love, being so in love with what you do and creating that for others. It's a gift to others, so it's not a failure by any means, it's just a step on the path.

She needs to learn her own strength - to really believe in that. To believe that she is strong and capable and can manage on her own without feeling incapable. Or like she needs someone to care for her. So the lesson is self-reliance once again – self-reliance and boundaries, setting boundaries with others. It's very important.

Open Up Your Heart

She asks "Why don't my guides listen to or care about me enough to show my path?

We are. We do. Start to believe us. She just questions a lot of what is being shown. Situations that are set up or synchronicities, or things coming together when they're meant to. **All she has to do is just tap into us -- and we're there.**

What's a good way to tap into you and become more aware of these divinely guided situations?

Meditation and the trust, and being centered, finding stillness within. Finding peace within - and that's when you hear the voices or the feelings, it's when the chatter starts, that the confusion sets in. But also at night in her dreams, she doesn't always remember them, but there is information in dreams.

She wants to know "What are my major lessons for this lifetime?"

It's the strength and belief that she's loved and that she's supported and that she's doing the right thing without doubting – to not have so much doubt – but also going past her limitations. Whether the ones put upon her by herself or by others. Just ask for it to be shown, and it will be shown. It's a phone call way (laughs). It's really true; it's just in asking, **"open up your heart."**

For an artist, it's hard not to be influenced by critics and people's opinions. Do have any guidance for us about that?

Well it's important to be aware and to be open – but the inspiration is coming from within. And that's always steady and that's what must be followed. **It's coming from a divine source and that's what's going to pull it through whether other people think it's good or bad - that won't matter, because if it's coming from a pure source, then the right people will find it.**

She wants to know "Is there free will?"

Of course there's free will. There are agreements, but we work with them for many years... And certain things are set up, but everything is negotiable.

Lotus City

Let's show her something beautiful.

I'm seeing a city sort of place, with lights. It's beautiful! A city with just pure energy, nothing solid. All lights. Different colors mostly purples pinks, looks like a lotus flower, but a futuristic too... This is just another place that exists always that you can go to, draw positive energy from.

Do that now. And when you feel like talking, tell us what you're experiencing.

Everything just seems so radiant and calm, like a combination of the two. There's movement but it's peaceful movement. Alive, like a flower, like a lotus flower.

Find a place of healing and I want you to go there and spend some time in this place. A place of healing that can wash away negativity and doubt and fear and fill you with trust and love and confidence.

Yes. There's a fountain here that washes away the bad.[92]

---

[92] In "Flipside" there was a session where a person felt his soul had been "scorched" in his lifetime during the Holocaust. (Chapter "River of Souls") He was asked if he could find a place of "healing" to go – and said that he walked down into the "River of souls" and helped heal the memories of that lifetime. Here again, a place of water with healing properties.

So be there and do that. Be in the fountain and don't come out until you feel complete.

It's pretty invigorating. Mm. Feels good.

Let me know when you're ready to go... I have another idea – I wonder if in this "Lotus City" if there's a huge concert hall a place where there can be a huge concert.

Oh yeah, there's a lot of music here.[93]

Be there now. Experience that.

Mmm. I'm in a beautiful place, looks like a seashell. Sort of like the Sydney opera house. Like an amphitheater. Just beautiful music. Great ballads, very celestial sort of, very dynamic, intense but celestial sounds; there's light that goes along with it, accompanying it.[94]

So how do the souls partake of that? Do they sit in a place?

Yeah, they drink it in. It's like nourishment. Dance too. Souls dance, they vibrate with the sound. Sort of a dance, it's like a vibration with the sound itself. It's very natural because it's part of us, just an expression of what's inside.

Is there something else you'd like to explore, to find?

I'm in the back of the amphitheater. Floating or something.... I can see the lights of the city, it's so pretty.

Is there anywhere else you need to go in this session? What else does she need or find today?

Just what was told, these big lessons of belief in the self; that's the main thing being shown here. She's starting to get it. Just needs gentle nudging.

---

[93] Scott told me he had never heard of a place quite like she was describing, but felt because of her background in music, perhaps there might be some music to listen to.

[94] One of the events they point to in NDE's is "hearing celestial music." This is an example of that kind of music, but a visual to go along with it.

I would ask why Sean was brought to this session today. What does she really need to get from this experience?

To make a decision to follow through and become the woman she's capable of being and to not let anyone else convince her otherwise. To show her she always has love and support. To really renew her, to resolve to accomplish her goals and to love herself no matter what; as much as we love her.

How do you feel about everything we've looked at so far?

I kind of feel like I knew it deep down inside, I knew the answers, but I have my moments of doubt.

Does your guide have any last words for you?

"You go girl." Just like - joking – but like "go forward." It's really what the truth of the matter is, move forward with confidence in the fact you're not alone. You're never alone. It's funny, they're all saying "Yay."

All right then, are you ready to come back to the here and now. Take a last look around.

I'm going to come back and do a show at the Lotus City amphitheater! It's a great state to be in.

Well as long as I get a ticket. All right, then as we begin to leave the soul world, I want you to remember this loving world is always with you all the insights confirmation will be retained in your mind to help you empower you as you complete your life with renewed confidence etc....

After the session, I asked Sean to go over some of the details that she learned. She revealed she's a vegan and was horrified by her experience of hunting down and killing an animal – she could smell the blood and felt the weight of the animal over her (his) shoulder as she brought it back to her family. As a musician, she was profoundly moved by the experience of performing at "the crystal palace" in this other ethereal world.

This was the first time I heard (or filmed) a person making a visit to another city in another realm. This was unusual for a number of reasons – mainly because she saw the city below her, and went to visit it, and it seemed like it was her first experience of being in this place. So if it was something she had created with her mind, you'd think there'd be more familiarity with it.

And then when Scott asked her if she could perform in the amphitheater she was visiting, it was easy for her to do so – there appears to be no rules or regulations (or auditions) for how people can or should behave in that city. She was able to see herself performing on stage, just as she had just been watching others perform.

The question becomes – who created these structures? Who's the architect, or the builder? On one hand we could suggest that the person observing these structures is the architect – so when you visit a library of souls, for example, or a temple which appears to be place for the council of elders, one might suggest that we create the columns, the floor we're walking on, the marble, the dais – or in Sean's case, a crystal city complete with an amphitheater where people could perform.

"After you climb up the ladder of time, the Lord God is here. Face to face in the vastness of space, your words disappear. You feel like swimming in an ocean of love, and the current is strong. But all that remains when you try to explain is a fragment of song... Lord is it, Be Bop A Lu La or Ooh Poppa Do Lord, Be Bop A Lu La or Ooh Poppa Do; Be Bop A Lu La." From the song "Afterlife" by Paul Simon

Chapter Eleven – "Near Death Experiencers"

Dr. Eben Alexander, Colton Burpo

"When you have eliminated the impossible, whatever remains, however improbable, must be the truth." Sir Arthur Conan Doyle, as stated by his character Sherlock Holmes

As noted, Dr. Beauregard and Dr. Greyson's research indicates that near death experiences have occurred when the brain is not functioning, such as when someone has been declared "brain dead." If near death experiences are not created by the brain (and there's plenty of evidence to show they aren't) then what is happening?

From the Wikipedia page on "near death experience:"

> The Near-death experience is an experience reported by people who have come close to dying in a medical or non-medical setting. The aspect of trauma, and physical crises, is also recognized as an indicator for the phenomenon. According to sources, it is estimated that near-death

experiences are reported by five percent of the adult American population. According to IANDS, surveys (conducted in USA, Australia and Germany) suggest that 4 to 15% of the population have had NDEs.

Some general characteristics of an NDE include subjective impressions of being outside the physical body; visions of deceased relatives and religious figures; transcendence of ego and spatiotemporal boundaries. NDE researchers have also found that the NDE may not be a uniquely western experience. The core experience seems to be similar across cultures, but the details of the experience (figures, beings, scenery), and the interpretation of the experience, varies between cultures.

Materialist science often point to studies that show brain waves that occur when people take hallucinogens, or have an epileptic seizure. Or claim there must be a part of the brain that remains functioning when people think they're dead.[95]

In the NDE we have reports of: *Positive emotions. Out of body experience. Moving through a tunnel. Communication with light. Observation of colors. Observation of a celestial landscape. Meeting with deceased persons. Life review. Presence of a border.*

Sound familiar?

As we've seen both NDEs and LBLs report similar observations, "moving through a tunnel" or some other mode of transport, flying, or "being pulled like a magnet." Communication with light, or light beings, or beings that look like light. The colors that they're seeing, the spectrum of light in a particular individual. Celestial music or landscapes. Buildings as well – as well as classrooms and other similar observances.

Both report meetings with deceased people, sometimes members of the family they didn't know existed. Both report cases of a "life review" - sometimes done with help from their "spirit guides" or "wise elders" in both.

So how are they different if they're nearly the same?

---

[95] Dr. Mario Beauregard reports there have been over 100 cases where no blood or oxygen was in the brain when people were having their NDE, and has also shown that there's no single locus for where the brain has "spiritual experiences" aka "the God spot."

A Place Called Home

I'd suggest trying to define the word "Home."

The word home means something different to all of us. One interviewee described it as a "place of safety and comfort." They have their point of view of home – however, we can all agree that "home" generally has characteristics of safety, or loving presence – or even just shelter. But when these people in the middle of their between-life sessions are asked "Where would you like to go?" Inevitably, nearly everyone I've filmed, says "I'd like to go *home*."

Where is home? Is home this between lives place?

Well, it's a bit like saying "Where is heaven?" Pretty hard to pin down. People describe traveling through deep space to get to their "home" – sometimes they see them from a distance as lights, as tree like structures with pods – but other people feel a "shift" in speed – a quickening if you will, of their energy and they kind of "appear" into this area they refer to as "home."

Is this a location in deep space? Or is it an illusion of traveling through space when the location is "outside of time?"

There's a sequence in the hit movie "Contact" where Jodie Foster makes a trip to meet with another civilization. And the travel involved takes a few seconds of Earth time, whereas in her recording of the event, it actually took over eighteen hours.

I've written how an out of body experience I had felt like I traveled through a worm hole and into another universe, and how a man honking his truck horn outside my window had brought me back. But how I had the sensation of actually making a physical return – zooming back through the worm hole, back through deep space, hurtling down into the island of Manhattan, all at lightning speed, until I was back into my body. All of that travel occurred from the moment he honked the horn, to the moment he took his hand off the horn. Less than three seconds.

The following is the case of Dr. Eben Alexander, who spent an entire week traveling into this other realm, and came back to report on it.

"Proof of Heaven" – Dr. Eben Alexander

"Extraordinary claims require extraordinary evidence." Carl Sagan

A Harvard trained neurosurgeon firmly in the materialist world, Dr. Eben Alexander hadn't considered there might be anything outside of consciousness at all until he had a near death experience.

There are some unusual aspects of his particular experience; while he was visiting this "other realm" he was aware of a feminine presence that seemed familiar to him, that guided him during the journey. It was only after the NDE that he discovered he had an older sister who had died before he was born – and when he saw a photograph of this woman, recognized her as his guide during this journey.

There was a refutation of his book written in Esquire Magazine by a scientist who blasted Dr. Alexander for including an account of a "miracle" in his book. This particular miracle happened to his living sister – she was praying for his recovery and saw a rainbow outside the hospital on a clear day. This Newsweek scientist searched the weather records to prove there were no clouds near his hospital on that day, therefore there could not have been a rainbow, "therefore" the near death experience did not happen.

Granted, there are many reasons to see a rainbow – an errant lawn jockey for one. And in the Tibetan lexicon of "auspicious events" there are many accounts of rainbows, hailstorms or lightning associated with spiritual events.[96] But because one person sees a rainbow doesn't prove or disprove anything other than that person saw something unusual that particular day.

A close friend was at the funeral of acclaimed film director John Hughes. And according to this person's account, it was a clear sunny day by the lake, and as the casket began to go into the ground, a wind storm suddenly blasted through, followed by a fog that enveloped everyone around the casket. And when the box

---

[96] A pretty amazing rainbow appeared at the funeral of HH Penor Rinpoche in March of 2013. There's a youtube link showing the "clear light rainbow" coming out of his tomb in "Rainbow Appears During Paranirvana of Tibetan Master." Of course, it's nearly impossible to prove why these events have occurred.

was finally lowered into the ground, the sun came out. A miracle? Hardly. But an unexplained weather event in concert with a life event? Most assuredly.

As Gary Schwartz put it; "Let's put it on the table."

That fact that Dr. Alexander's sister saw a rainbow is not his fault, nor should it have any bearing on whether or not his near death experience is accurate. *He* didn't call it a miracle. His sister did. The scientist went on to complain that Dr. Alexander was distorting what really happened, that he was *"nearly dead"* but not actually dead, and that all of what he saw or experienced can be explained by materialist theory.

But that wouldn't account for Dr. Alexander seeing the exact same things that other people see on similar journeys. We would have to believe that everyone who has had an NDE is somehow sharing the information. There are thousands of documented cases and thousands more yet to be examined in Dr. Greyson's office at UVA – he showed me the stacks of papers and letters he gets every day. The fact that Dr. Alexander spent his life skeptical of anything that he couldn't observe or learn through science is important groundwork for his story. He was a skeptic. He no longer is.

The materialist scientist argument goes that "people see what their cultural background wants them to see." But in the case of Dr. Alexander, he was guided by the spirit of his older sister, someone he didn't know existed until after his experience. Someone who had passed away before he was born.

He was not aware of her existence, because he had never been told of her existence. She was a relative he had never known, and yet showed up to guide him through this realm. She could not have been in his conscious mind as he wasn't aware of her existence until after the event.

So by examining the common examples of NDE hallmarks, as experienced by Dr. Alexander and others, and by finding the same reports in between-life sessions or other NDE's, we'll be closer to finding the truth, whatever it is. [97]

---

[97] Dr. Bruce Greyson's study on the hallmarks of NDEs has a list of common events that characterize a near death experience. They majority include "A feeling of unearthly realm of existence" (67%), "Feeling of Joy," "Feeling of cosmic unity," "Mythical or unearthly being," "Unnaturally brilliant light," "Sudden understanding." Others had an experience of a "life review" (35%), and less had an experience of seeing or being in a "tunnel like dark region (17%). More people saw "deceased or religious spirits, (43%)" or heard "meaningful sounds (34%)." This study was with 74 patients who had

According to Dr. Alexander, he died and went to heaven.

> **Something... appeared in the darkness... it radiated... white-God light, and as it did so the darkness around me began to splinter and break apart. Then I heard a new sound... the richest, most complex, most beautiful piece of music (I've) ever heard. Growing in volume as a pure white light descended... the light got closer and closer, spinning around and around and generating those filaments of pure white light that I now saw were tinged here and there with hints of gold.** (emphasis added)

Here are examples of seeing bright light and hearing meaningful sounds or "celestial music." As we'll see in detail in ensuing chapters, during a between-life session people have similar descriptions.

> **At the... center of the light... I was no longer looking at the spinning light but through it... I began to move up, fast a "whooshing sound," and in a flash went through the opening into a completely new world, the strangest, most beautiful world I've ever seen.[98]**

Dr. Alexander observed "you realize a part of yourself... **remembers the place** after all, and is rejoicing at **being back there** again." (Pg. 38.)

The feeling of having been there in this place in the afterlife before is also prevalent. As a point of argument, it's hard to "remember" or feel one has been somewhere before if they haven't. It's the same sensation of running into people you feel you've known forever; maybe you have.

I've been asking people to describe the moment they recognized the person they married or are partners with – the precise moment when they "knew" they were going to be with or marry that person. One friend saw her husband-to-be interviewed on a talk show. She told her roommate; "I'm going to marry him" and she did.

---

experienced a clinical and profound near death experience. See "The Near Death Experience Scale – Construction, Reliability and Validity" at www.medicine.virginia.edu

[98] In Volume Two of "It's A Wonderful Afterlife," in the Chapter NDE and LBL of Sarah "Everything is energy" she uses the same term of "whooshing" as if being sucked into another realm during her NDE.

As mentioned in "Flipside," I met an actress in college. I asked the 18 year old ingénue if she would appear in my student film, her first and my first. While we were shooting, she announced she was going to marry a famous rock star. I asked her if she'd ever met him. She said "No, but I just know I'm going to be with him." She was 18 at the time, and years later they were a couple of a number of years.

My brother-in-law said he walked into a classroom and recognized his future wife from a glimpse of the back of her head. He says he thought "Oh, there's my wife." When I asked his wife to describe the moment she knew "he was the guy," my sister-in-law said it was around the second date. "Something in his eyes and his voice seemed familiar to me." I asked what that meant. She said "He made me feel like I was *home*."[99] I've had dozens use nearly the same words to describe why they suddenly felt *comfortable* with someone they'd just met.

But what about the folks that appear in our NDE? Are they familiar to us?

In his NDE, Dr. Alexander saw a few other people as well:

> People sang and danced around in circles and sometimes I'd see a dog, running and jumping among them, as full of joy as the people were." "Someone was next to me; a beautiful girl with high cheekbones and deep blue eyes... millions of butterflies were all around us... as if they were a river of life and color moving through the air. (pg. 39)

In "Flipside" I recount the LBL of "Steven" who remembered dying in the Holocaust, being a young Danish girl who was shot in Dachau. He said his "soul had been scorched" by the experience. The therapist asked if there was any place he could go to be healed. Steven said he was led to the "river of souls" where he was able to bathe in that stream and heal the psychic wound from that lifetime. I wonder if there's any connection to this "river of life" described above.

There's also an experience of being loved completely. As Dr. Alexander recounts:

> Without using words she spoke to me. The message went through me like a wind, and I instantly understood that it was true. **"You are loved and cherished, dearly, forever. You have nothing to fear. There is**

---

[99] Once I'd heard that there are "life planning" sessions in the afterlife, I recalled how I met my wife in a Starbucks. We started speaking and within a few minutes I suggested we "skip down, get married and have a couple of kids." She now says that I say that to everyone at Starbucks.

nothing you can do wrong." Then… "We will show you many things here, but eventually you will go back." Then later: "Each time I posed… questions, the answer came instantly… thoughts entered me directly… to effortlessly understand concepts. (pg. 39)

The idea of speaking without words is often reported in both NDE's and between-life sessions. It's by and large reported that people "speak" to each other telepathically. That we are loved and cherished, is also a common message, that we have nothing to fear and that we can do no wrong is echoed in a number of the sessions I've filmed and Michael Newton's research.

These are sentiments often heard during LBL sessions; sometimes told by a spirit guide, other times during a life review at the "Council of Elders." This same idea is repeated often. "You are loved. There is nothing to fear. You can do no wrong."

The concept that there is nothing to fear is easy to say but hard to comprehend. The list of things to fear is long and comprehensive.

Dr. Alexander was being told "You have nothing to fear." That's one way to conquer it, by hearing that it only exists in your mind. "Fear is horrifying, until you conquer it."[100]

But then he was told "You can do no wrong." What does that mean?

In the thousands of cases Dr. Newton has examined, and in the 25 sessions I've filmed, the concept of wrong is turned on its head. People don't report a kind of nihilistic afterlife where pain and suffering are rampant and random. Rather, the opposite; they report that no matter what wrong you do – that when you get back to the between lives realm, you are still loved, and are forgiven for your trespasses.

However it's very hard to step into someone else's shoes to understand why someone might commit a negative action. All we can do from our perspective is to imagine there may be some future benefit behind every action, and even if we

[100] "Fear" a poem by Olivia Martini. *"Fear is the voices in your head whispering terrible things only you can hear, Fear is black butterflies swarming in your stomach, Fear is a ghost with the bright yellow teeth who enjoys putting his hand on your shoulder when you are not looking, Fear is a lightning bolt that strikes your mind with surges of panic, Fear is gigantic black spiders that crawl up your spine, Fear is a whoosh of wind up your throat forcing a shout, Fear is a mummy that entangles his bandages of terror with your eyes, covering all sanity; Fear is horrifying, until you conquer it."*

can't perceive it in our lifetime, we will eventually come to understand and embrace it. As the Dalai Lama has said "You can't control how others behave, but you can control how you react to it."

Dr. Alexander also experienced an unusual orb in the realm he had entered:

> Pitch black as it was, it was also brimming over with light; a light that seemed to come from a brilliant orb that I now sensed near me. An orb that was living and almost solid... (It) was so close that there seemed to be no distance between (it) and myself. Yet at the same time I could sense the infinite vastness of (it, and I) could see how.... miniscule I was by comparison... **The orb was a kind of "interpreter" between me and this.... presence surrounding me.** (Pg. 46)

This is also reported in between-life sessions and is identical to David Bennett's NDE mentioned earlier. In many of the cases that I've filmed, people describe seeing light coming to them, or being pulled to a bright light – sometimes describing it exactly the same, as an orb that is living.

The therapist might ask "who or what" the orb might represent. Often the answer is a form of guide, sometimes a higher guide than the guide they normally have looking over them. In this case, Dr. Alexander felt he was closer to a Divine Creator.

> (This) vast inky black core that was the home of the Divine itself; an inky darkness that was also full to brimming with light... the "Voice" of this Being ... **told me that there is not one universe but many.... more than I could conceive – but love lay at the center of them all. Evil was present in all the other universes as well, but only in the tiniest trace amounts. Evil was necessary because without it free will was impossible, and without free will there could be no growth – no forward movement. In the larger picture love was overwhelming dominant."** (Pg. 47) and later **"I saw the Earth as a pale blue dot in the immense blackness of... space... the sum total of all that evil was as a grain of sand on a vast beach compared to the goodness... unconditional love (of) the universe."** (Pg. 83)

The pale blue dot may be a reference to Carl Sagan's comment of the Earth as a "Pale blue dot" – but it's interesting to note that this "overview effect" is reported on from many astronauts who've had that same view of Earth from outer space. As noted in Dr. Beauregard's interview, the "overview effect" is a term coined by astronauts who've been outside the Earth's atmosphere who have come to regard the planet as a place that is entirely interconnected. Often, people who have a near death experience come back with this same perspective.

The concept that there is little or no evil in heaven, or in the various universes that Dr. Alexander got a glimpse of, is also repeated in the between-life research. That evil appears to be a construct may be more prevalent in a world based on polarity (as the Earth is). In the between lives realm, it "barely exists," or as he puts it "in the tiniest trace amounts." The message seems to be that "love" is the dominant characteristic of our universe.

In the NDE and LBL of Sarah (examined in Volume Two of "It's A Wonderful Afterlife") she also experienced a darkness that was brimming with light. As Dr. Alexander observed:

> **I saw the abundance of life through the countless universes, including some whose intelligence was advanced far beyond that of humanity. I saw....that there are countless higher dimensions, but the only way to know (them) is to experience them directly.** (Pg. 49)

Also reported often in LBLs is the idea that there are other realms that people can visit, other worlds, dimensions or planets that people claim to be places they we can incarnate.

Dr. Alexander mentions that his guide tells him "We will show you many beautiful things, but you will be going back." (Pg. 67-68) The idea of letting you know that you are getting a chance to visit this realm, but only as a tourist. And that you will be heading back to Earth once the tour is over.

If I was going to sum up (this trip) in one word, it would be "Love." "The unconditional love and acceptance that I experienced on my journey is the single most important discovery I have ever made, or will ever make. (Pg. 72)

I've found that it's in the afterlife research as well, every session I've filmed or examined, the thousands that Michael Newton has collected; they report the nature of existence can be distilled into this formula; the universe is composed of "unconditional love." [101]

---

[101] Dr. Alexander's book "Proof of Heaven" is available at Amazon, Barnes & Noble and other bookstores. I highly recommend reading it.

"The old paradigm of birth to death represents an outdated concept that is woefully inadequate in defining the unfolding reality of expanded awareness... Materialist science is at the end of its days as most scientists are changing their views. The old concepts are soon to be relegated to the same dust bin as 'the Earth is flat' as we develop a more mature understanding and transcend old beliefs." Eben Alexander

---

"Heaven is for Real" – Colton Burpo's NDE

"It took a lot of thought over a long period of time," (while researching his film "Defending Your Life"). *"It would be great if the movie was right. If someone said to me "You still have a lot of fears, but you figured it out, so come with me." If I'm right, I'd like to be awarded a posthumous Nobel Prize; more than that - free parking."* Albert Brooks (From "Discovering Heaven" Time Mag. by Lisa Miller)

Five year old Colton Burpo died and went to heaven as well.

It's worth noting that Dr. Alexander had an experience with an area or realm that made him feel he was in the presence of "God" or some form of a creator, or creators and Colton Burpo had an experience where he literally saw Jesus and a host of other folks.

Well, in both NDE cases, how does one know they are in the presence of "God," or even in the presence of "Jesus?" As I'm fond of saying, it's not like they're wearing name tags. There's something unique in the experience, but also familiar. Else how would they know where they were or who they were talking to? "Oh, there's a dude over here, wearing a toga, he's got a beard, and he looks like... well, Jesus." That's not how these events go – people in many near death experiences see someone whom they "know" is Jesus. And almost always, he's there to tell them "It's not your time yet, you need to go back to Earth and finish your work."

The combination of seeing the fellow, feeling some kind of spiritual event, and this concept that "it's not your time yet" are quite powerful for those who've experienced it. I would only mention that Jesus doesn't show up in every NDE, nor does he show up to Buddhists, Hindus, Jews, or other folks who aren't of "his persuasion."

One could argue that this fact alone points to *cryptomnesia* – that some vision or experience with seeing a photograph or movie of Jesus is what's influencing these reports. It's possible. But as we'll see, when examining the reports fully, a different portrait of Jesus emerges.

All we can really say is that there are a number of reports of people who have a Christian background saying they saw someone they thought was Jesus. What are the similarities between the young Colton Burpo's account and the Harvard trained scientist's account? Both saw relatives they didn't know existed, both saw a higher power with whom they felt a deep knowing and profound sense of calm, both saw and experienced things they've never experienced during their lifetimes on Earth, and both came back to tell their stories in the hopes of helping others.

So is one more credible, believable than the other? Since Harvard doesn't teach that consciousness can exist outside the brain in their medical school then why would his account be any less correct or accurate than five year old Colton's story? Is the five year old's experience any less real than the neurosurgeon's? To my mind, they're both dealing with topics that we rarely speak of on the planet, and therefore we have no common language to begin a dialog about them.

As in Dr. Alexander's case, Colton Burpo also saw someone in his near death experience that was a relative of his – a sister whom he had never met, never heard of, never knew existed because she died in childbirth. And yet he met her as his sister. She exists. Just not here.

So how does a five year old's NDE compare with that of a Harvard trained neurosurgeon?

Colton Burpo's NDE

From the Wikipedia entry on Todd Burpo's book:

> In the book, "Heaven Is For Real" (by Todd Burpo and Lynn Vincent) Christian pastor Todd Burpo writes that during the months after his emergency surgery in 2003, his son Colton began describing events and

people that seemed impossible for him to have seen or met. Examples include his miscarried sister, whom no one had told him about, and his grandfather who died 30 years before Colton was born. Colton also claimed that he personally met Jesus riding a rainbow-colored horse and sat in Jesus' lap, while the angels sang songs to him, He also says he saw Mary kneeling before the throne of God and at other times standing beside Jesus.

There's been criticism from the Christian community for this account:

> A variety of Christians have expressed criticism or concern about the book's content and message. "The Berean Call," a Christian ministry and newsletter, criticized the book for its "extra-biblical" and "problematic" claims, as well as the lack of any medical evidence that the boy was clinically dead during the surgery. Author and Pastor John MacArthur has criticized the book for presenting an un-Biblical perspective on the afterlife. Writing as the "Spirited Atheist" in the Washington Post's "On Faith" forum, Susan Jacoby said that the success of the book shows that "vast numbers of Americans" lack the reasoning ability of adults. [102]

Happy to note that if box office returns represented the amount of reasoning that American adults can make, there are quite a few other fantasy films and books, Harry Potter included, for Ms. Jacoby to make negative comments about. It's equally possible that what people experience while hearing a compelling story (and which may translate into box office success) is because they've actually experienced these events depicted in some way before, or in some way they aren't aware of.

But as Gary Schwartz Ph.D. puts it; "Let's put it on the table." What does Colton's NDE have in common with other NDEs?

First we're examining an account that is not in the near death experiencer's own words, and we will have to take the authors' word that the events reported in the book are accurate, or without undue influence. There are other cases of parents writing about a child's profound spiritual experience. In "Soul Survivor: The Reincarnation of a World War II Fighter Pilot," James Leininger's father wrote the story of how he was skeptical of his son's past life memory of being a World War II fighter pilot until the son remembered names and dates and people that the father could verify. And he did verify these people, who indeed remembered the person the son was claiming to be.

---

[102] "Heaven is for real" Wikipedia entry

Two fathers, both skeptical of their children's accounts of other worldly events, and both wind up writing books about the experience. Both experiences happened to their children; it's only because we live in a world of obtuse skepticism we find people discarding these accounts. Why not just examine them and see what details can be verified?[103]

From the book:

> It was that conversation in which Colton said that he "went up out of" his body, that he had spoken with angels, and had sat in Jesus' lap. And the way we knew he wasn't making it up was that he was able to tell us what we were doing in another part of the hospital: "You were in a little room by yourself praying, and Mommy was in a different room and she was praying and talking on the phone. (Pg. 61)

Colton reports "I saw Dad in one room, and Mom in the other" while he was supposed to be operating on in the hospital. This is common in the NDE accounts of observing what's happening in the operating room while supposedly under anesthesia; while in the operating room, NDErs often report seeing their body, hearing and observing their doctors and others (and as we'll see in a number of other accounts). There are cases of blind patients seeing colors and describing them during these events.

But it seems when Colton describes "Jesus" that many materialist minded folks tend to use the "mute" button while listening to the account.

> "What did Jesus look like?" "Jesus has markers... brown hair and he has hair on his face, and his eyes... are so pretty!" ... What about his clothes? "He had purple on... his clothes were white, but it was purple from here to here." (Todd writes "A sash.") "Jesus was the only one in heaven who had purple on."

In Michael Newton's second book "Destiny of Souls" he realized that he could ask his clients under deep hypnosis "If I held a mirror up to you, what would you look like?" And people started to describe colors. What Newton found was that depending on their "progression" as a soul, people saw themselves as different colors.

---

[103] As Dr. Jim Tucker from University of Virginia does with his account of James Leininger's past life story in Dr. Tucker's book "Return To Life."

It's become part of the Michael Newton method, during deep hypnosis, the therapist will ask "And what color do you perceive this person to be?" Often they describe them in terms of "light" – bright light, sometimes with a halo effect, sometimes glowing, sometimes tinged with gold. They describe their soul's light in terms of the spectrum of colors that travel from white to yellow, to orange, to green to blue, to purple. In Newton's thousands of cases, he found that the older the soul, the darker the color observed.

He also found that certain colors represented certain characteristics of a soul's progression – green colors seem to represent those who teach or work in the healing arts, blue seems to represent some form of wisdom, red denotes some kind of lessons in fierceness, or intensity, and purple, seems to represent those involved with teaching or wisdom. In many accounts I've read or filmed, members of a person's "Council of Elders" are described as "wearing purple robes." Perhaps this is one of the reasons why purple robes have come to symbolize judges and judgment.

According to these reports, it's not uncommon to see someone else in the afterlife, or during an NDE, "wearing" or "cloaked in" in a particular color. Seeing someone wearing "white robes" is very common. Sometimes people clarify; "They aren't robes, exactly, it's more of an energy field around them." There are accounts of white, brown, purple robes. It depends upon the energetic pattern of the person appearing to wear one.

The question might be asked "How does Colton know this fellow is Jesus?"

During his NDE Colton is only five years old. It's not like he's seen a lot of films with actors playing Jesus on film, and not every long haired guy with a beard in a blue toga might answer to the name Jesus. The argument has been made that someone "projects" what they'd like to see during an NDE, and that logic tells us that Colton, the son of a preacher, would want to see Jesus while having this profound experience.

Michael Newton has had many clients who saw religious figures in their sessions; Buddha, Mohammed, Jesus and others. What he found was that when he examined them more closely, these figures "dissolved" or "turned into" the person's spirit guide. And he cites a number of cases where a spirit guide reveals him or herself during a session – at first appearing as some kind of mythical deity – sometimes to "calm the fears of the person having the experience."

However likely the above two scenarios are, there is a third possibility; that it actually *is* Jesus. That somehow, the person or energy of the person who was Jesus still exists – outside of time – and can appear when needed to console and help those who need his counseling and help. (See Volume Two of "It's a Wonderful Afterlife" for a more in-depth discussion of this topic.)

Perhaps Colton had what is categorized on Bruce Greyson's NDE scale as "seeing a "mystical or unearthly being (55%), having a "meaningful vision (50%), and seeing "deceased or religious spirits" (43%).

> What did you do in heaven?" (His father Todd asked). "Homework... Jesus was my teacher... Jesus gave me work to do, and that was my favorite part of heaven. There were lots of kids, dad.

In "Flipside," just prior to my friend's passing, my friend Luana told me she had a recurring dream she was in a "classroom where everyone was dressed in white..." It was Michael Newton's accounts of classrooms in the afterlife that prompted me to want to make a documentary about his work.

And in my four between-life sessions I've visited a number of these "etheric" classrooms. There are numerous accounts of people being in classes in the afterlife, so when Colton says "Jesus was my teacher" – imagine for a moment that this person that looks like Jesus also functions or works as a teacher.[104] Colton is confirming at least one aspect of LBL accounts here: classrooms in the afterlife. But just what do the students look like?

> "What did the kids look like? What do people look like in heaven?"
> "Everybody's got wings," Colton said. (Pg. 70)

People who have NDEs or LBLs report a number of unusual things about what they see or perceive in the afterlife. If the therapist is willing, the client can look closer at items: "Describe the wings in detail. Are they feathery? Soft? Hard?" When examining details, the story usually expands to include how and why something is constructed.

The same goes for the word "heaven" – it's not a concept or word repeated in many accounts. As we've seen in Dr. Alexander's description, it's only after he's

---

[104] In "My Life After Life" by Galen and Ken Stoller, there are a number of accounts of classrooms.

done exploring this other realm that he decides that the word "heaven" is the only one we have to describe it.

For example, Colton's father asks him how long he was in heaven. "Three minutes" he says.[105] Is that three minutes of Earth time, or three minutes of Heaven time?

But it ultimately seemed to be the emotional revelations that Colton made that ultimately convinced his skeptical parents. Colton said he met his sister, who told him she had died in utero. "Who told you I had a baby die in my tummy?" (Colton's mom) said… "She did, Mommy."

This same kind of report is found in Carol Bowman's work "Children's Past Lives."[106] There's one account of a child who spoke of originally being in her aunt's "tummy" and then appearing later in her mother's. What the child did not know, and was revealed to Dr. Bowman, that the aunt had a miscarriage, and later the mother became pregnant and gave birth to this child who claimed to originally be in her "aunt's tummy." And it wasn't until the story was being investigated did the aunt confirm that indeed, she had lost a baby that she didn't tell anyone about.

But then Colton got to see his grandfather, Todd's father, whom he called "Pop."

> Pop came up to me and said "Is Todd your dad?" And I said yes. And Pop said; "He's my grandson."

The obvious question would be, "Why does his grandfather have to ask Colton his father's name?" How could he not know that? His gramps is proud to announce to the crowd around him "Hey, this kid is my grandson!" like one would in an old folk's home. If you're in a room of prescient beings, they might have to be snickering at this moment. "Really, Pop? Where have you been?"

But I think this example actually points to the verisimilitude of the account. "Pop" has been up there some time. He's got a few grandkids to consider and think about. He also may have reincarnated by now, as we'll see in future

---

[105] As mentioned, in the film "Contact," Jodie Foster's character travels to deep space to meet another group of beings that have reached out for contact. In Earth time the event took only three seconds, but in the tape recording of the event took 18 hours.

[106] "Children's Past Lives: How Past Life Memories Affect Your Child" by Carol Bowman. Bantam

chapters in this book. So asking Colton "Who the heck are you?" is in keeping with the other accounts people have had with members of their "soul group."

"What are you doing here?" is a question that is often asked. The souls in question know that your "due date" isn't up – and seeing a loved one appear too early in their world might be as disconcerting to them as us seeing them show up in our world. "Why are you here? You're not supposed to be dead yet."

Colton's dad showed a photograph of his father to Colton and he initially said "that's not him." Then his dad found a picture of the grandfather, younger, and Colton confirms that it's him, but that he wasn't wearing glasses. "Dad, nobody's old in heaven... and nobody wears glasses."

When I was working on the feature film "Salt," one of our technical advisors, a Detective in the NYPD, pulled me aside after hearing me talk about this research. He took me into a side room, locked the door and said "I think my house is possessed." I asked why. He said "Because my daughter is seeing ghosts and now she claims she's "reincarnated.""

I suggested he separate the two events to examine what was happening. "Who's the ghost?" I asked. He said "Well, that's the odd thing, she sees him in our kitchen. She said "He dresses like you daddy." So the detective found a picture of his deceased partner and showed it to his daughter. She said "That's him, but he's younger and thinner now." The Detective wanted to know how that could be; his partner died ten years ago, and his daughter is 8.

I said "Well, according to these accounts, between lives we appear as however we like to appear. If we see ourselves as thinner and younger, then we might appear to others that way." I asked if he liked his partner. He said "I loved him." I said, "So having this person you loved look over your daughter isn't such a bad idea, is it? He said "Not when you put it that way."

I asked the Detective about his daughter's reincarnation story. He said his daughter claimed she lived and died in Australia in a past life. I asked if they'd ever been to Australia or were watching a television show about reincarnation. He said he didn't own a television and he'd never been outside of New York State. I suggested he take home a map of the "land down under" and open it and then ask his daughter to describe what she remembered, without judging the answer.

He came in the next day, pulled me off the set, walked me into a room and locked the door. He told me how he opened up the map and his daughter had pointed to the Australian city of Perth and told a long story of being a farmer and how there had been a drought and her whole family had all died. She then burst into tears. It was as if she'd been waiting eight years to tell her father that story.

So when Colton said that "In heaven, nobody wears glasses" it bears out in the many accounts of NDEs and LBLS, and in this case, a ghost who was hanging out at a New York Detective's home. His partner not only didn't wear glasses, but he also appeared to be thinner and younger.

El Diablo

Todd asked his son about Satan. Colton said "Satan's not in hell yet. The angels carry swords so they can keep Satan out of heaven." That's interesting. Satan's not in hell yet. Nor is he in heaven. Where the heck is old Beelzebub hanging out?

Michael Newton had a client who saw "Satan" during an LBL. He was a fire and brimstone minister who came to him for a between-life session. And during his session, under hypnosis, he suddenly saw this fire breathing creature with horns coming for him.

Newton had thousands of cases by then, and he had already observed that the between-lives realms didn't contain many descriptions of hell. So Newton asked "What's he wearing?" And the minister saw instead of cloven hooves, tennis shoes.

It was then that the minister realized that this "creature" in front of him was his spirit guide putting on the "mask" of Satan. The guide said to him "I did this so you could feel what you made all of your parishioners feel for so many years; you used fear to gain power over them." And indeed, that's what this minister had done.

So – did Colton see someone identified as Satan? Not in this account. But he said "he's not in hell" and that people "carry swords in heaven" to keep the fellow out. (How would he know either of those details? Was it something someone mentioned? Was there a wanted sign posted? And why carry swords?) Colton said "There's going to be war, and it's going to destroy this world, Jesus and the angels and the good people are going to fight against Satan and the monsters and the bad people. I saw it… the women and the children got to stand back and watch… and Dad, I watched you, you have to fight too." "We're fighting monsters?" his father asked. "Yeah… like dragons and stuff."

Colton's dad equates this account with the Bible's account of the "battle of Armageddon." Aside from the idea that Colton doesn't mention Armageddon, or see anyone named Satan – it's important to examine this account with regard to what Colton actually said.

He saw his father "fighting a battle." In "Plato's Republic," Plato recounts the first case of a reported NDE 2500 years ago – there was a Greek warrior who died and returned to life ten days later, and reported visions of the afterlife which included battles from his previous lifetimes. Since we find in this research that reports of future events are based on likely scenarios, the future can't be certain because of free will. There's never a guarantee of any event, including a war, unless every soul agrees to participate.

Various possibilities come to mind. Perhaps Colton was reporting seeing his father fighting a battle during a previous lifetime, or as is reported in some LBLs, fighting a battles in another realm, or another universe altogether. The only way to pin these details down would be with the help of a hypnotherapist, or even doing a session with Colton's father.

All of Colton's experiences, including this one, are now stored in his memory banks, and a visit with a trained hypnotherapist would allow him access to his memory of these events. With the help of a "guide" – or a therapist who's been in this realm before asking questions about what he heard or saw – Colton, or his father could access them with more clarity.

The research shows that we experience the afterlife based on the journey our soul has taken over many lifetimes. The information we receive fits who we are spiritually at that moment in time. And our reporting on it is based on the language, symbols and ideas we are capable of expressing. So the NDEs of David Bennett, Dr. Alexander, or Colton are no more correct, nor less correct than others. As we've seen, each near death experience has a number of things in common, and yet relate to the spiritual progression of each individual.

We tend to get caught up in the idea that if someone reports something in the afterlife, it exists for everyone. It's a bit like swimming in the Caribbean, and then telling people that "underwater, there's coral and brightly colored fish, and that's about it." The afterlife is reportedly a vast ocean of information and places to go. Each NDE or LBL may have similar characteristics, as in the research of Bruce Greyson and Michael Newton's research - they have hallmarks that are the same, but the journeys themselves are never identical.

In like form, when people experience a "library" in these accounts – as many LBLs do, it's not to say there is a physical library that everyone perceives as the same. A library appears to the person experiencing it in a fashion that makes the most sense to them.

I've found no two accounts of libraries to be the same – each has varying accounts of books or ledgers or scrolls or even high tech video screens that contain previous lifetime information. It means that we experience things in the afterlife, for the most part, based on our consciousness. So a rose may be a rose, but it appears differently to each person holding it.

One of the wonderful hallmarks of a meeting at the various International Association of Near Death Studies (IANDS) meetings I've attended nationwide, is that they always begin with the proviso; "We are not here to judge other people's reports. We are here to share spiritual experiences with people from all backgrounds, and all perspectives." It's a great way to open oneself to other people's reports, and this research. By just observing them, and not judging them, we can hear more clearly what the reports have in common.

By comparing a Harvard trained neurosurgeon's NDE with a 5 year old's, it allows us to see what these experiences have in common and what differentiates them. It bears repeating what Dr. Alexander said was his great discovery during his near death experience; that the universe is composed of "unconditional love and acceptance." Not *conditional* love. Not loved *if* you're good. *"Unconditional love for everyone."*[107]

---

[107] "Heaven Is For Real" (by Todd Burpo and Lynn Vincent) is both a book and feature film, and I recommend both.

I recently spoke with Kimberly Clark Sharp, one of the founders of IANDS, who had a profound NDE earlier in life. Her heart suddenly stopped and as she lay on the sidewalk...

"Suddenly, an enormous explosion erupted beneath me, an explosion of light rolling out to the farthest limits of my vision. I was in the center of the Light. It blew away everything, including the fog. It reached the ends of the universe, which I could see, and doubled back on itself in endless layers. I was watching eternity unfold.

The Light was brighter than hundreds of suns, but it did not hurt my eyes. **I had never seen anything as luminous or as golden as this Light, and I immediately understood it was entirely composed of love, all directed at me. This wonderful, vibrant love was very personal, as you might describe secular love, but also sacred.**

Though I had never seen God, I recognized this light as the Light of God. But even the word God seemed too small to describe the magnificence of that presence. I was with my Creator, in holy communication with that presence. The Light was directed at me and through me; it surrounded me and pierced me. It existed just for me.

The Light gave me knowledge, though I heard no words. We did not communicate in English or in any other language. This was discourse clearer and easier than the clumsy medium of language. It was something like understanding math or music - nonverbal knowledge, but knowledge no less profound. I was learning the answers to the eternal questions of life - questions so old we laugh them off as clichés.

Why are we here? "To learn."

What's the purpose of our life? "To love."

I felt as if I was re-remembering things I had once known but somehow forgotten, and it seemed incredible that I had not figured out these things before now.[108]

---

[108] "After the Light: What I Discovered on the Other Side of Life That Can Change Your World." By Kimberly Clark Sharp. William Morrow.

Perhaps it's the same for all of us. While we are here, we can't experience what it's like to be there – but on certain occasions, we can get a glimpse of it: "I felt as if I was re-remembering things I had once known but somehow forgotten, and it seemed incredible that I had not figured out these things before now."

Why are here? To learn. What's the purpose? To love.

Profoundly simple, yet simply profound.

"I'm not the first person to have discovered evidence that consciousness exists beyond the body. Brief, wonderful glimpses of this realm are as old as human history... Our spirit is not dependent on the brain or body. It is eternal, and no one has one sentence worth of hard evidence that it isn't." Dr. Eben Alexander

Chapter Twelve – "A Wild Ride"

"But how can the characters in a play guess the plot? We are not the playwright, we are not the producer, we are not even the audience. We are on the stage. To play well the scenes in which we are "on" concerns us much more than to guess about the scenes that follow it." — C.S. Lewis (Photo: My grandparents Ed & Mimi Hayes waiting to meet the King of England in London – Ed was National Commander of the American Legion 1933-34. Center of photo)

Not long ago, I ran into a talented writer who had some major success in her career, and I noted that she seemed to be suffering from some kind of physical ailment. I asked about her condition; she told me she'd been diagnosed with Parkinson's. Something told me to suggest that hypnotherapy might be of some help. I admitted to her I felt it was something I needed to pass along.

In "Flipside" there are two people who claim symptoms disappeared after their sessions. In the chapter "Aquaphobia," a woman who claimed she'd suffered a lifetime of the fear of water had her symptoms disappear during her session, and in the chapter "Oh, There You Are" the person suffering from a lifelong kidney problem claimed 95% of his pain disappeared during his session. Dr. Brian Weiss' book "Many Lives, Many Masters" delves into this arena. Under hypnosis, one of his clients claimed her illness was cured during a past life regression; that revelation led to Dr. Weiss' lifelong work.

By the time my friend called about doing a session, her Parkinson's had progressed quite a bit; every few seconds she had an involuntary twitch, a body contortion or movement of her hands. But for a few hours during this between-life session her symptoms completely disappeared, as if she no longer had Parkinson's. Her only movement was an occasional flick of her fingers, but for all intents and purposes, her Parkinson's was not present. After looking at the tape of her session, she too thought it uncanny.

The following session with "MaryAnn" was filmed in Scott De Tamble's office in Claremont, California. I've included some of her pre-session interview, as they relate to events during her session:

Scott and MaryAnn

Scott: What are you looking for?

MaryAnn: Looking for answers because I feel like, I know the answers already but I feel like I've been ambushed off my path. I don't feel human, I had a clear path and clear vision and this Parkinson's has knocked me off my path. I was a writer, a teacher, I had a good voice, a great sort of presence in the world; now I don't feel present, like I've been scraped off into some abandoned parking lot and now I'm just riding around on a bike... (Cries) I'm sorry, I didn't mean to cry.

Like you've been sideswiped by a truck.

Right. I feel like how could this happen, is this a mistake or something intended for me to go through? What are my spirit guides thinking? There are relationships I need to know about... (She talks about her affair with a married business colleague "Michael") We've been together for 15 years; we've had a connection for a long time...

He has a hold on your heart?

My life; my whole esteem. I feel my work is wrapped up in what he thinks, it's sad because he doesn't consider me at all in his life – but I feel this connection, a strong pull... he's very famous, and he's very unavailable.

So the main thing is this condition (Parkinson's) and what it's all about.

It's giving me a sense of shame – I feel like I have earplugs and I'm missing the party – I feel like I've let a lot of people down by getting ill and dropping the ball, I feel like my life just went by.

So why did you do that?

(Laughs) I don't know. I'm feeling a great deal of shame. Even saying his name – I have this fear people will overhear me and spread rumors. It's a burden being in love with a famous man – it's hard.

Okay... (The session begins)... before birth now... in the womb, feel the dark warm environment, this floating environment. This dark warm peaceful place. Drifting, floating. How do you feel?

I feel like I'm floating in the bathtub. Nice. She's moving around a lot, a lot of rocking going on at this point... she's very careful with me, very gentle. She wants me – she's really excited about me coming into the world. I have this feeling that being in her womb is a good ride so far. These two came together and they had me – just entered the body right away, their love was so passionate, so intense, I want to be their love child, I want to be the reason for everything getting into action.

What month did you choose to come?

June. On their wedding night, I followed them from the church. They got married at the justice of the peace, they eloped.

Was she already pregnant?

No, conceived on the wedding night. I didn't make myself known to them. I was sort of hovering, she was having dreams and I was sending her dreams of this crying child...

In June when you enter this fetus, when is this?

Right at conception. I took a risk, I was just ready to come back and so this is a chance of like sparks – two rocks making a spark and I wanted to be that spark.

As the baby develops, are you there with the baby?

I move in and out. It's so cramped, stifling in here, I like sleeping here, it's warm and nice, I need to be out and about.[109]

What's the emotional system like?

Very emotional. I feel like I'm meant to come to this woman to educate her about feelings and that things matter and that things have a consequence to them. She doesn't want to be a baby again – she doesn't want to be a baby.

You don't want to go through the whole baby thing?

Yes, very tedious a lot of lying around, crying and pooping.

Something you have to go through?

Yeah, you have to. I just want to be a teenager right away, speed things up.

What are your gifts? What makes you unique?

In the lifetime before this one, I had hidden talents, no one expected me to be anything. I wanted to be born to a family that wanted me to be fruitful.

Lifetime before this one, are you inside or outside?

I'm inside, my glass studio. I shape things with stained glass.

How old are you?

42.

As you're inside your glass studio, what's your name?

Amanda.... Brooks.

What's the name of the town?

Lindhurst, Virginia.[110]

---

[109] As mentioned, MaryAnn is suffering from fairly dramatic Parkinson's and is being treated medically for it. So when she stopped moving, it was notable, and Scott looked over at me as if to say "Look. She's no longer moving." Also Scott mentioned in his talk how "on average" people don't show up to the fetus until the 4th month, and people have the ability to "go in and out" prior to birth.

[110] I found Lyndhurst, Virginia, a town that MaryAnn says she's never heard of, nor been to. I have yet to find the account of Amanda or Walter Brooks from this particular small town in Virginia.

As you're there, Amanda, what year is this?

1941.

Tell me about your life.

I like to find things, I collect things on the beach when I walk, and I got really interested in natural tinting glass, and it occurred to me I could buy the glass and mold them and make shapes and make people happy, spruce up their – it's a hard time right now. We're at war and it's very confusing time.

Do you have hardships?

I don't eat very much, I learned to control my appetite.

Because of money or lack of food?

Both. My husband died, he was in the Army during the war. No children. His name was Walter. In Germany, he fell out of a train and was killed. I live by myself, my sister worries about me; she lives in London with her children and they want me to come to England (in the countryside) where it's no longer part of the landscape of war; it's just a hard time. (She is moving and curling up).

Let's go back to a happier scene when Amanda is just a girl, happy. How old are you?

I'm 8. I have a new dress. It's blue. It's my first tea length dress. Just below the knees, sort of spins when I spin. Makes me feel, if people could see me. I had to wear the old shoes because new ones didn't fit me. There's ribbon in my hair, it's yellow.

What color is your hair?

It's red, auburn sort of. It's pulled back like this, mom brushes my hair every day and she hurts my head. She pulls my hair and pulls it really tight, sometimes I have to loosen it when she's not looking. She's very strict, she grew up with very strict rules she imposes on me and my brother. My sister will be born next month. My brother is older.

As your mom brushes your hair... where are you?

France. My mother's French. We don't know who my father is. He's missing. He left when I was a baby.

Does your mother have a new mate?

Yes, this older man who married her, saved her reputation, they're having my sister; he's the father of my sister. He's like my grandfather, he's old. He's gruff.

How do you spend your time as an 8 year old?

We have school, raids, we have to get ready for. At school we have raid drills... at school there was a bomb.[111]

Ok, let's skip forward now to some time in your 20's or 30s, curious about when you find a husband, let's go to that time... one two three, be there now. Tell me.

He sings a song that I like. And he kind of knows – he just knows we're meant for each other. Very simple, not very – it's not as dramatic as I thought it would be – I just want to put my arm around him and walk a long way. Walter is very talkative, shorter than me, he's got a short man's complex, gruff and mean to authority figures... I'm 5'8". I'm willowy. They call me a "handsome woman."

Tell me about your life with Walter.

He's quiet, very fragile and he knows me, sees me, he gets me, in front of other people he acts like he doesn't – in the world we have a strange relationship, but inside, it's close and satisfying. It's like he has to "put me in my place" because of his manhood.

But in private?

He's very tender, very sweet, like the roles reverse, I'm very sexually aggressive and he's very glad that I am. I bring him out.

Tell me how you spend your time?

Walter is an engineer. And makes things... goes to a plant, manufacturing...

What city?

---

[111] I'll assume she means during World War I

We moved around a lot. It's about an hour out of town, we live in a small town in Virginia.

Where'd you meet Walter?

In Europe. He's Cuban. Grew up in Cuba but he's not native Cuban – he's a mix of Latino and Spanish, speaks Spanish – he changed his name.

When Walter's at the plant, what do you do?

I make things. I cook, I bake, I'm a housewife, tend the fires until Walter gets home. Velvet cake with cream cheese frosting. Bread pudding and custard.

Tell me about the town.

It's in the country, makes me sad because I found out about Walter there – in the garden. These two men come up and I just knew. Soldiers, uniforms, very formal, kind of ... they don't have to say anything, they just, feel sorry for you, want to get it over with, so they told me and they left (holds her head). I just try to keep him to myself, Walter had a lot of friends, but his friends dried up, I don't know.

After he perished...

I walked on the beach more, collecting things....

Let's go to an older moment in Amanda's life... inside or outside?

I'm in my garage in my studio. And I just sold some things. Some pieces that I make, glass pieces. Makes me feel connected to the world, something I made is out there, and someone – it's a good feeling.

Just enjoy that.

I see we're meant to give ourselves to people, shape things and give them back as different shapes. We're meant to shape things in our path, and give them back to other people.

So it's time to move to the last day of your life as Amanda. Be there now.

I'm inside. I'm terrified. This is terrifying. I'm 50, 51. These kids have gotten into my house (holds her head).

Float above this scene. As if watching TV, you don't have to feel anything, but describe the scene.

I was looking at some things I've done and I was going to make a cake and go into the kitchen and I see the doors open and I feel like some people have gotten in, and I call "hello?" and then go up the stairs, call the police, hear a noise, and... Someone hits my head. (Holds her head) Bleeding everywhere.

The kids steal her keys on the counter in the kitchen, three kids, she knows them, they're kids that help her sometimes; they steal her car. She's slumped... she doesn't know what comes... She doesn't know what they did to her. There's a lot of blood. She doesn't move, she's not moving. (Lots of Parkinson's movement)

Let's move forward to the moment just after death.

Oh God, thank God (sighs).

Let your awareness expand. Remembering who you are, what this is all about. How are you feeling?

I feel so good, so relaxed, free of disease and constraints of some pathetic nobody – and I feel like I'm somebody and I'm back to myself again – and experience more of the light and (I can) get with the program.

Let's experience the light as you float up. Feeling lighter and better. Tell me about the life you just left. What did you learn?

I feel sorry for her (her incarnation just past), one point I didn't feel connected to her at all. She had these 3 teens who worked for her, jealous of her car, a Porsche. Her husband left her some money so she bought herself a car for pleasure and these kids stole it – they didn't have to kill her; ridiculous.

How do you feel about the death of Amanda?

I feel free. It's like having an orgasm for 24 hours, it starts to hurt – it's not a feeling, it's a state of being. Everything is just weightless and light (At this point her body movement slows down quite a bit).

Ok, do you want to say goodbye to anyone?

No. (Stops moving around completely) She's ready to move forward.

Into the Light

Please describe as you move up and away.

I feel a blue light, streaking through the sky – whew – into outer space, everything you've ever seen astronauts report back. I'm a comet. I'm arcing through the sky. I feel speedy, a sense of urgency to get to where I'm going, so I make this sound like "shwww!" I'm burning up, like on fire, burning and getting cooler and cooler and cooler.

It's into the voidness of space. I'm just floating. I can see the planets of the solar system, little dots that are fading away. There's this light, approaching from all corners, as if it's a tumbling tsunami of light; I can hear the thunder of it. It's white and pink, approaching and it totally envelops me with its warmth and sound; it's coming from all corners of my space.

Is this a natural force?

It feels like a catastrophic storm – a tsunami. I don't have a body so I'm just feeling very overwhelmed. It's a thrill![112]

Let's skip forward and see what happens.

It's good, an amazing light show (sighs). It's a sense of joy of fireworks, times a hundred, just light bursting like a lava lamp breaking on your head. You can touch it, it's beautiful; hot, and sparkly, and like it electrocutes you.[113]

It's like an electric shock feeling. But it doesn't hurt you, it pumps you up. Makes you rise, like yeast; it thickens you, makes you feel like you're all powerful and invincible. It's like a very mind altering spirit; it feels amazing! Amazing's not the word, I can't describe it. It's too much, too much! It's too beautiful.

---

[112] "A tumbling tsunami of light." Similar to other NDE accounts, where in the voidness or inky blackness of space a bright light appears that becomes all encompassing.

[113] Another description of fireworks during a session that is repeated in a number of others during their NDE or LBL.

(Note: There is no bodily movement at all for the next hour and twenty minutes – effectively no Parkinson's can be seen by me or my camera).

Just let that course through you.

I feel clean, rinsed like from a really good shower; I felt so dirty coming off this life. I'm refreshed, I feel beautiful, just beautiful and fit and healthy; I feel very like a presence. I don't want to go back, I like being in the spirit world.

Where do you want to go?

I want to know who I am.

An Unusual Request

Let's find a wise and loving teacher where we can sit down, to talk to you – male or female?

A male. A human dressed in an Edwardian costume. Looks 35. He seems very sad and he's leaning on one knee like he's going to propose to me or something.

What is he communicating to you?

He's warning about the garden. "You'll always receive sad news in the garden." I'm just sort of there, I can see him, he doesn't see me; he senses me. Feels like he has some sad news for me.

Are you up to hearing it? Let's ask him.

"You aren't through." He says. I'm not through.

What does he mean?

He's very confused; he's talking to me like I'm a hallucination. (A pause as she listens to what he's saying to her) This is so weird, sick and twisted; he wants me to be in his lifetime with him, that he's in now.

He's stuck, he's asking me about going into the lifetime he's in and save him – and be the one he's supposed to love.

What lifetime is he in?

He's a wealthy landowner in the South – Edwardian period. [114]

Before Amanda's life or the same time?

This about a hundred years before, but – I can't compute time, all I know is that his eyes are begging me to come and be in this lifetime with him which seems unfair and weird.

What can we call him?

It's Michael.

All right, I'm going to speak to Michael directly, and put Michael's responses in your mind directly.

He doesn't like it, but just do it.

What's your relationship to her?

He says "I saved her life."

And what was her name in that life?

Charlotte.

How did you save her?

I rescued her from a burning house.

And in that lifetime as Charlotte what was your relationship?

She was my sister.

---

[114] The Edwardian period is from 1901-1910 and sometimes extends to World War I. For those keeping a time card, this life she now describes may have been in the 1800's, as the outfit a person wears in the afterlife is usually one they're comfortable wearing. In Newton's research, he found a woman who normally appears as a Viking between lives, because that's the life she felt most comfortable in, and her soul group referred to her as such. When asking dates, the numbers don't always match up, and that could be for a variety of reasons (outside of cryptomnesia) including reports that not all of our energy comes into our lifetime; two thirds may be available to live other lifetimes. (In response to this question, one spirit guide said "Do the math.") Sometimes people say the first number that comes to their mind, and later revise it during a session. And there are reports that time outside of earth time has its own rules. If she was 38 in 1941, and 8 during the Great War (1914) she couldn't be showing up as Michael's wife in the actual "Edwardian" era. Perhaps she meant "Victorian" (1837-1901) which would match the dates. However, her description of his clothing may reflect Michael's preference in attire.

Why are you asking her to save you?

She owes me one, she has to come save me. I killed my wife and she can't be dead.

So how is this soul going to save you?

(I want her to) come into my wife's body and take over her body for the rest of its days.

Why did you kill your wife?

I didn't mean to. I didn't know my own strength.

Did you strike or push her?

No, I was helping her. I was helping her across the room; she fell from my arm and I snapped her neck.

So your wife died for a while from a snapped neck? And after your wife died you came to talk to MaryAnn and asked her to inhabit the body of your dead wife so she could be alive again?

She owed me.

So how did she respond?

She came in.

So how can she come in to a body with a snapped neck? What's the use of that?

She's a healer.[115]

Explain what happened.

---

[115] This is pretty unusual in this research. MaryAnn answers questions from the consciousness and voice of Michael, her sometime boyfriend in this life, and according to this session, his spirit came to her in the between-life realm and begged her to inhabit the dead body of his then wife, Charlotte. This account would be considered a "walk-in" – which Michael Newton's research claims is not something that occurs without specific reasons. As Newton puts it; there's one soul in one body, and that's pretty much the contract carried out in each lifetime. MaryAnn is saying Michael came to ask a favor – that his wife had died accidentally, and he needed her to come forward (from the spirit realm) and take over the life of his wife, as he was convinced he would be killed for his wife's murder if she didn't.

I called on her, she came in, put her energy in the neck and healed it. And our love is so strong that we just continued.

So after healing that neck, MaryAnn inhabited that body?

Mm-hmm.

What about your wife's soul? Was she okay with this?

(A pause)I don't know what happened to her soul.

Let's call her forward and ask her – what happened. Did you want to leave that life? I want to hear from her. What does she have to say?

"He tricked me." (Sighs). He was always tricking me – he'd kick me under the table and when I said it hurt, he'd say "Oh sorry, I didn't mean to hurt your leg."[116]

So when you fell? What happened?

I fell forward and he grabbed my head and snapped my neck.

Deliberately?

I don't know. It happened so quick.

So then as a soul spirit – you left the body?

I left the body, went back to the light.

What did they tell you about that life you just led?

That I was torn, that I'd be tempted to go back, but I decided not to.

So MaryAnn came into and lived as Charlotte, is that right?

That's right. She outlived Michael.

---

[116] In many forms of regression, when a person says "this happened to me," the therapist notes it and moves on. Scott is familiar with how things normally work in the afterlife arena; confident he can call upon this previous soul and ask her to verify this version of events. Interesting that each person in this discussion had their own point of view of how events occurred. Michael says "Our love is so strong, we just continued" but his former wife Charlotte says "He tricked me." Maryann seems to agree that Michael's a trickster, but reports "it's not how it happened." A true "Roshomon" story of three differing points of view of the same tragic event.

So MaryAnn.... can you confirm this story?

No.

How do you feel about this story?

It's too revealing.

All right then. It's time to get some higher guidance about all this. Michael we're going to leave you for now, perhaps we'll spend time with you later, let go of her, release her, she needs to go to a higher source. So let's find your true spirit guide or mentor or teacher. Can we call that person forth? Male or female?

Male. It's just my muse; the person who is my muse in life.

A human form?

Human. Male body, curly dark hair. He's the other half of me – he's someone I've yearned for my whole life.

What shall we call him?

David.

I'm going to speak to David directly. What is your relationship to this soul?

(Voice changes) Just pure love.

Are you on the same level as her?

Higher frequency.

Can you answer these questions about her life as a soul?

On this plane, she reunites with me many times. She comes back and I can sense that she's here. We find each other.

I'm trying to understand your relationship to her. Are you a friend or teacher?

I'm on her council, committee or board. I stay here in the spiritual plane, never leave.

Would you answer some questions she has?

(Nods)

What was the goal of her life as Amanda?

She wanted to experience love at its basic level: unconditional love.

She had that with Walter?

Yes, but only in private, never public.

What does Amanda have to do with MaryAnn?

MaryAnn is never to repeat that smallness again; she is about the large gesture, large and bold. Even though we've given her a difficulty to face, she has to push past it, push through past stereotypes, fears. Doctors will tell her she'll never do this, never do that – she has to fight.

MaryAnn has some questions, and a lot have to do with her affliction. Would you address these? "Am I on my (right) path?"

She's on her path in many ways; she has spiritual resources she doesn't even know she has. She has not tapped into them yet. By filling her heart with compassion for herself, by forgiving herself for doing things she's done in the past, she doesn't have to live in secret any more. That's why we presented her with this challenge. I'm reminding her of Amanda so she can break past the small. This condition. She needs to push past it. By tuning in spiritually and realizing who she is.

How can she do that?

Start to celebrate herself, start to appreciate small gestures that she makes and see that they're not small at all; she's got a relation to life now that's not centered. She's got to fight.

She told me she felt ashamed to be ill.

She's working out the shame she felt as Amanda, when Amanda and Walter moved (to Virginia) they were shunned by the community because they were childless.

How can she let go of that pain and shame and move forward??

Notice how quickly you come back here and get refreshed? Well, you can always go back (to Earth) again, but you choose lifetimes that are constricting. We've given you one that's potentially large; only you can make it small.

The Purpose of Parkinson's

What's the purpose of being afflicted by Parkinson's? Is there some higher purpose?

It's an illusion. (Her) Parkinson's is not a disease, that's why it was so hard to diagnose. It's in the mind, in the body; the mind/body gets poisoned, but it's not real, it's just conditioning. And then the nervous system starts to deteriorate, because it's expected to. Consider it "group thought" and we want her to fight against group thought.[117]

Can this be arrested or reversed?

Yes. She's got to look at this as a spiritual crisis, not as a physical crisis and not be apologetic for what she does or what she says, or how she moves in the world.

What precipitated this illness?

Secretiveness. She had an affair with someone - it was very physical and just threw away her power, gave it all away because she's so gullible. Just the fact that she came to live in a body called Charlotte and never missed a beat, she lived falsely for a half a life; hidden! Called by someone else's name.

It is possible for a soul to enter the body after a soul leaves? Isn't that body calibrated for the soul that left?

It is, but there are special circumstances; in this case we took pity on Michael in that lifetime, he was reforming, he meant well. It was an accident, and there had

---

[117] For those concerned about her saying "Parkinson's is not a disease, it's an illusion" her guide may be referring to MaryAnn's Parkinson's in particular, or may be referring to the idea that all disease is an illusion per se – that it is created in the mind, combined with external factors (environment) or internal factors (predisposition) – or the idea that all reality is a form of illusion, since it's based on energy waves that we interpret with our brains. ("Group Thought" is defined as: "A psychological phenomenon that occurs within a group of people in which the desire for harmony or conformity in the group results in an irrational or dysfunctional decision-making outcome.") (Wikipedia)

been violence in that household before, and her family would have killed him. He wasn't ready to end his life.[118]

So you deferred to her free will and their karma so to speak and let her do that?

It was a mistake.

What does she need to know about that experience?

You have to live in your own body.

What does she need to hear to live as MaryAnn as a healthy person?

Stop truncating things. Own your power, own your speed, your charm, your wit; we've given you all these things to go back with, don't disguise them with a disease; let it go.

She wonders, was this disease inflicted on her? Did she create it?

Her guilt for being so secretive and living a lie for half a life; it's so twisted. She just needs to let go.

Let go of...?

Living in secret. Living less than who she is.

She repeated living in secret in this life, an affair with the same person?

Another secret. He was giving her all the power and opened doors for her; she was also having to keep a really big secret.

What about this karma – he says "You owed me." Are they even now?

They sort of have a very meta-relationship; *meta* is a thing within a thing. They go against all the rules.

Should she contact him, stay away from him?

He's poison for her. A test. Michael is all of the world in every way. And with his success, he emotionally seduces her. She needs to break the pattern.

---

[118] I think this is called codependency in modern psychology. And the idea that her present incarnation would explain away her lover's callous behavior during a previous one, calling his breaking of his previous wife's neck "an accident" is an interesting turn of phrase.

What does she need to know or understand to be free of him?

That she can stand on her own. We had to do something. So we needed to knock her down, sort of stop her for a bit; she was identifying with the wrong things.

She wants to know if she can use Parkinson's to fulfill her purpose?

Yes, she's an artist and she'll continue to make art in spite of her affliction. She'll overcome it, heal herself from this condition and be an inspiration to others.

How can she heal and overcome?

She needs to get over self-doubt, take care of herself - stop eating sugar, junk. Eat fresh food, food that has energy, life. She needs to reconnect with everything that's light and good and strong about her. She needs to stop mourning and anticipating the loss of things; she's alive and needs to celebrate that fact.

Are you describing this condition as a spiritual crisis?

She needs to connect to the divine; to here. She loves it so much here, she comes back at the drop of a hat, she leaves at the drop of a hat, she's very tempestuous; we don't know what she's going to do next. She needs to commit to being on this side or that side and learn her lessons. (Sighs.) She's one of our harder cases up here.

What would the council say?

Stay the course. She has an impaired nervous system because she was extremely vulnerable during a high stress time in her life and developed neurological symptoms that mimicked Parkinson's.

Is that reversible?

Yes, if she commits to being there, and commits to just loving people that are in her life.

David, what would you like to share with MaryAnn in this session? Advice or guidance for her?

Just enjoy the ride MaryAnn; it's a glorious ride we have planned for you – and you make it so hard, don't make it hard. Just laugh and love and eat really good food and have a good time. Let go of everything that's not that.

I'm a little confused about your relationship with her; you said you're a council member, and you're like a soul mate. What is your connection to this soul?

We were friends when I was picked to be in a higher frequency; she wasn't picked. We were sort of young, like having a crush in high school.

Are you her primary soul mate?

On this plane, yes.

You haven't incarnated together?

No. We met up here. We had a bond early on and we were separated and we found each other again. I can increase her frequency; the longer she stays connected to me, the more she evolves.

Can she visit with her dad?

He has an apron on and he's been healing the sick. He spends time in the hospitals down on Earth in spirit. He reassures them, nurtures them, comforts them.

We invite MaryAnn's father to communicate; what is it that you wish to communicate with her?

He wants to sing. (She sings a beautiful rendition of "O Holy Night.") *O Holy Night! The stars are brightly shining, It is the night of the dear Savior's birth. Long lay the world in sin and error pining. Till He appeared and the Spirit felt its worth. A thrill of hope the weary world rejoices, For yonder breaks a new and glorious morn. Fall on your knees! Oh, hear the angel voices! O night divine, the night when Christ was born."* That's his message to me. That's always his message to me. I just want to say I'm sorry.

I'm going to stay quiet, so you can spend some time with him.

(She cries, sits up, hugs pillow) I love him.

A Surprise Party

David, MaryAnn wants to visit with her soul group, can we do that?

(Laughs.) **A surprise party! They're all around this table and this room is decorated; they knew I was coming up to see them, so this is a surprise. They're happy to see me; they're sloppy people, very touchy feely, very loving, kind of nerdy. I just love them, I feel myself with them.**

How many are there?

Fifteen; they just love me so much, I just love them.

You want a group hug?

No, too corny. We have this ritual where I stand in the middle of the room and they surround me with a circle and they close in on me – kind of a group hug.[119]

What does that feel like?

I feel I just know everything's going to be fine, it's going to work out. Some of them are down here, living – Mamie, my dad's mother wants to say something; "Everything you do is perfect, you can do no wrong, I'm so proud of you. You have a unique mind. Nothing is compromised, everything is going to be okay." Then she hugs me (cries). [120]

Any other souls wish to come forward??

(A pause, after a moment in a different voice, speaking rapidly) I don't like MaryAnn. I never liked her. She's a self-centered bitch.

Who's talking?

Diane. I think she's so full of shit. She has nothing to offer that's new or original, she slept her way to the top, she's an opportunist, she's a c*nt, I can't stand her.[121]

---

[119] If someone was following the direction of the therapist in these sessions, they would tend to obey or do what they are told or asked to do. In this case, that doesn't seem to happen.

[120] When she observes "some of them are down here living" it mirrors what the research shows. People during an NDE or sometimes during an LBL will see individuals in the afterlife who aren't dead – the reason, as described in Newton's research, is because only a percentage of our "life force" or soul comes down to earth for each incarnation – so we're always back in the between lives realm, or at least some version of our energy is there.

[121] At this moment, while filming this session, I was lost. I had never seen a member of a soul group berate someone like this. It reminded me a bit of the "Three Faces of Eve" where suddenly the lead character takes on a new persona. There was no hesitation in the delivery of these words; like she'd

What's the purpose of your sharing this with us?

Because this is a MaryAnn fest; everyone loves her, says she's so great, MaryAnn does this, MaryAnn does that.

It's MaryAnn's surprise party.

Well I'm the party pooper, I just came.

What's your purpose being here?

Cast a dark shadow, tell her the truth, truth is your life is going to suck, so get used to it MaryAnn. You're lucky you've lived a charmed life, you tricked us, you did something sneaky, just wait you'll get caught, you'll get your lesson soon enough.

(Scott laughs) I like you Diane you're an interesting soul.

I'm not this negative usually, but I hate her, she's a f*cking bitch; mealy mouthed and wishy-washy and she's so unconscious that she took all my boyfriends away from me. I can't stand her, she's such a flirt, coy, "I don't know what you mean by that" she's so fakey-fake, I can't stand it.

All right Diane... how do you really feel?

Hm! I can tell you that right now MaryAnn, everything's not going to be alright. You're going to end up on welfare and lose more teeth, people are going to think you're a meth dealer. These people are lying to you, you're not going to have a life partner.[122]

Tell us more, you're entertaining.

You are in your mind, you live in your head, you're just dreaming this whole dream thing; you do things that are stupid. You should be embarrassed the way

---

been waiting to take MaryAnn down a peg.

[122] Equally interesting was Scott's reaction. In this session, we're firmly involved in a discussion with a person in her soul group. His reaction to the negativity spewed by Diane is to find her amusing, even entertaining. As I was transcribing this passage, seemingly out of nowhere, a "Tums" commercial played on my computer, even though there were no websites open – I heard a loud version of "Tum, Tum Tum Tummm" as in the notes from a sci-fi or horror movie's impending doom; "Dum da dum dum..." No idea why or how, but wanted to note it.

you live your life, chaotic, irresponsible, your father was right; it just doesn't add up –

What doesn't add up?

Her choices. I'm bored with this already. So I'll smash some cake in her face and just leave.

So Diane, you're the happy face in this group.

They love me.

What do they love about you?

They tolerate me.

What's your goal in this soul group, Diane?

Keep MaryAnn in her place - she has a tendency to go flying off in the universe, she thinks she can fly, she thinks she can perform magic miracles, bullshit; she's a hack, she's the personification of a hack – I just resent these surprise parties, they're stupid.

Tell me about yourself – if this is what you tell me about MaryAnn, how do you analyze yourself?

I'm highly intellectual, I don't put up with bullshit. I'm a no nonsense person, I have had the same man in my life since I was ten, he's treated me, we're married happy.

How dull.

I'm not dull. I can talk anyone under the table.

You don't sound like you're having many interesting experiences.

MaryAnn instant messaged me the other day "Your students must love you." Her students love her, my students don't love me... I love my students, but my students don't love me.

Who's getting the most growth in her lifetime?

Little miss goody two shoes. Poor pathetic MaryAnn, learning all these lessons; they're lost on her (a pause, softens). I guess she's ok, she's all right.

MaryAnn, is there a guide for this group?

No, they're unsupervised. That's why it gets so rowdy and out of control.

If I was a visitor to your group what impression would I take away?

We have fun; we have outings where we do things. We have our meetings outside, on picnics; we go fishing, sit atop of Eiffel tower, sit on the waterfront in Sydney Australia – we just aren't really organized.

What's the common denominator of this group? What brings you together?

We all live by our wits. We choose lifetimes that honor that.

Do you aspire to the same specialty? Is this a group of artists, healers, explorers, or just a big mix?

It's a big mix. MaryAnn's mom tends to take it over sometimes, she's a spirit to be reckoned with – tries to create some order; she's bossy.

So is there anything else you'd like to experience in this group?

No. "Bye" everybody.

Any advice from the group for her?

"Just have fun. You need to laugh more, you're like a Debbie downer, talking about your symptoms and your illness. Plan a picnic, plan an outing. Do something that's out of your comfort zone. "

So David, are you still with us? Can we go to the library of souls?

It's closed today. No access on Wednesday.

(Laughs) How about the life selection?

That's open.

Let's be there now. Let's go back in time to this conference when MaryAnn was planning this life as MaryAnn. Who's there?

It's one of those crazy outings where we've decided to go to a singles bar in Chicago and we're all sitting around trying to decide what to do, table we should be at...

Who's there?

Everybody, Diane's not - thank God - but everybody's there. We've all been taken together, we've decided to have a reunion.

No one's incarnate?

Diane is.

So you're in this singles bar having a party?

And we're looking at partiers, admiring them. We're looking at people, very discerning look at people with their body language and expressions. I see something that's very curious to me – this one woman who is a very vivacious story teller, she's talking to a group of people and I feel like "I could do that, I could be that."

I hear about this couple (MaryAnn's parents); his family doesn't like her, her family doesn't like her, it's a classic Romeo and Juliet story. So I follow them on their honeymoon and they're so passionate with each other, and I just decide to go for it – and she's pregnant the next day.

So there was no guidance of any kind?

David advises me. He goes down to this woman's life, she overcomes adversity in unusual ways, I find that interesting.

Let me ask David. So why did you suggest this MaryAnn life to her?

In her last life she got short shrift. The last couple of lifetimes she felt very small, very tight, (they were about) secrecy and very covert and this is an opportunity to be expansive, to be born into a family that adores her, to bring peace to families that are warring; being in the South with its manners, finishing school effects.

She's made this progression very quickly, we were amazed how quickly she was progressing, and things got too big -- so we decided to bring her back, that's why she's there. We want to give her a glove big enough that she could do it – but she did it so quickly, we made the glove shrink and it reminded her of the other two lifetimes with fear, and it was supposed to give her the chance to push past it and fight.

Parkinson's that's not really Parkinson's.

But give her the symptoms to really scare her.

You gave her a big stage, what do you mean "it got too big?"

Some of us got jealous – putting Michael back in her life, sort of a problem. Created some tension, and some conflict – I'm not good at articulating why we did something, we just did it – we just act upon impulse up here.

No planning?

Not in our group. We have no systems in our group.

Is there anything else we need to learn about the selection of this MaryAnn life and why she's living it?

She lived through a lot of violent lives and she wanted (her) next lifetime to be sheltered and curious but not exposed. So she chose MaryAnn so she could experiment with living large. It's funny, she had a stalker around the time she got symptoms, and was diagnosed with Parkinson's; she became famous through her work and felt for the first time as if her life was not her own anymore. She changed her phone number, but still the guy terrorized her and that's where... (a pause). She chose MaryAnn's life because there was no violence in it – as soon as violence started that threatened it, it changed shape.

I wonder if there's a place where you could go to a chamber and be just surrounded by healing vibrations. Can we do that?

Yeah, I know where to go.

Good, go there and be there and do that. How's that make you feel?

Really good. I can come back her and rejuvenate, it's got light and sound; it's brilliant. I'll put it in my bookmark bar.

David, why was she brought to this session today?

She needs to just go forward and be brave, and if she dies in the meantime - she's coming back here, so she can't lose. We're rooting for you, but don't come back here too soon because you're not supposed to yet! She's meant to live a long happy life, full of human pleasures.

She's just recently turned human - in fact, the day she was diagnosed (with Parkinson's) was the day she became human – before that she was flighty; an actress who thought she was a big shot. So "Welcome to the human world, good luck and we're all waiting up here to rejuvenate you at the end."

Anything else?

These fish keep appearing. There's some big fish up here – they're like, emerged from space.

What's the meaning of that?

"The fish are just perfect. They're to remind you that you're in a different sort of place here."

Ok. I'm going to count to five and on number five you can open your eyes and be back in the here and now... with love and gratitude to those who've helped us today...

Afterwards:

(As her Parkinson's and the shaking returns to her body, she laughs.) That was fun. That was a wild ride, really fun."

The unusual part of this session was that for about 90 minutes, a person who walked in with severe shaking, twitching, all the classic symptoms of Parkinson's – stopped doing that entirely while experiencing the between lives realm. I wasn't aware of it until Scott leaned over and tapped me while he was doing the session.

And it was then I noticed that she had stopped moving entirely, except for her index finger, which was keeping a kind of slow rhythm while she spoke. She was herself again – eyes closed, face relaxed, occasionally smiling, nodding, expressing herself as the artist that she is. For a brief moment I wondered if it was the drugs that had caused that to happen (she had taken some of her medication prior to the session) or if it was something that happened when she was no longer letting her conscious mind drive the car, so to speak.

In the chapter with Bruce Greyson, he points out that there are many cases of people whose brains are no longer functioning who regain full consciousness prior to their passing. The autopsies show that their brain was irreparably harmed, but for a few moments or hours or even days before they die, the person regains all of their faculties and memories. He argues that perhaps this is because the filters that are in the brain are no longer functioning properly – meaning the filters or blocks that have prevented the mind from working properly, or are no longer operative. And when the filters and blocks are shut down or off – or irreparably harmed, then the person regains their faculties.

Perhaps this form of hypnotherapy is a way of removing those blocks, of thinning the veil, or removing the filters of the brain, and for the time that the person is under deep hypnosis, where they are fully in their subconscious minds and exploring the universe, they "forget' that they have an affliction. If this was the case, doesn't it make sense to examine the possibility of having a deep hypnosis session and then suggesting to the patient, or insisting to them that whatever filters are off during the session remain off during the day? It's certainly comes to mind and is worth examining further.

If people could see the film that I shot of this particular case – and I've promised the person I would not show it – they would see that her Parkinson's virtually disappears altogether during the session. This brings to mind the tragic story of Robin Williams, who according to his wife, was depressed over his recent diagnosis of Parkinson's. Science is on the cutting edge of treating this ailment of the brain – and as we've heard during this session, she was able to examine and clarify the cause of it. She has set about to do the therapy required to help alleviate those symptoms. God speed to her, and I hope her new therapy as well as these revelations, helps.

A woman asked the Dalai Lama "What's the meaning of life?" He said "That's easy; happiness. The hard question is what makes happiness? Money, a big house, accomplishments, friends? Or compassion and a good heart? This is the question all human beings must try to answer: What makes true happiness?"
The Dalai Lama

Chapter Thirteen – "Near Life Experiencers"

Rajiv Parti, Jeffry Martini, Jeremy Kagan

"Dear George, remember no man is a failure who has friends. Thanks for the wings. Love, Clarence." From the film "It's a Wonderful Life." (Photo: Author sitting with some Kashmiri rug dealers in Ladakh, India)

The actors Sharon Stone and Martin Sheen both have experienced near death experiences. On Oprah's show Sharon said after her brain aneurysm: "I had that whole "white light" thing... It's sort of like passing out but you sort of pass up." She had suffered a stroke which led to a brain hemorrhage in 2001.

"It's just a lot of white light and you see people that have passed on, and they talk to you, and then you pop right back into your body," she said. She also described an "incredible sense of well-being," and described the feeling as beautiful. "It's a very near and very safe... and loving, and gentle, and "OK there's nothing to be afraid of," she said.[123]

[123] Oprah.com May 27th, 2004. "Oprah's Master class with Sharon Stone."

Actor Martin Sheen says that he had a near death experience. "I got close once," he said. "It was an interesting experience. The whole thing – everything was familiar, and there was no fear. I only became afraid later when I realized how close I had come to dying. I decided to live; I actually decided to live."[124]

He recounted how the experience had come about while having a heart attack during the filming of Francis Coppola's epic film "Apocalypse Now."

> I was all alone in this very isolated area when I had this most terrible pain in my chest. It felt like an elephant was standing on me, and I had terrific pain in my left arm, I couldn't move, and for a time I was blind and deaf. It was strange because I knew what was happening to me and that I was on the brink of death.
>
> It was a strange experience. I didn't feel any kind of fear or anxiety or at that stage pain. **Everything seemed very familiar. I was aware of my mother, who had died young, being there. I was also aware that I hadn't been living an honest life. I was being two different people. I thought I was getting away with it, but I wasn't. I was only kidding myself. I realized I had to get right with whom I was, accept my brokenness and limitations and all the things that are wonderful about being a human being. I realized that I wasn't afraid of death but of living and being a human being.**
>
> Often people who have gone through near death experiences say the same thing, it's not death they realize they are afraid of but life. It actually felt quite easy to die, but I was aware that if I continued along this path, that there was no going back. It was time for me to decide. Did I want to live or die? I thought about the suffering my death would cause my wife Janet and the children and all the work I had to do and I made a conscious effort to live. I remember grabbing the grass and dirt and trying to get in touch with my senses and bringing myself back. I knew I was coming back because the pain returned. I remember being rushed to hospital and my wife's face looking at me, saying, "it's just a movie!" and it was funny because it did feel like that. Not real.[125]

---

[124] RTE. Ireland's National TV and Radio. Youtube account "Martin Sheen on what happens after we die."

[125] "The Redeeming Power of The Way" film review of Emilio Estevez's film "The Way" interview by

I met Dr. Rajiv Parti through my friend Robin Barr who runs the IANDS group in Tustin California. As I was setting up the "Afterlife Convention" speakers for an event in Santa Monica, I asked Robin who she might recommend to come and speak to our group about his or her NDE. She recommended Dr. Parti.

He's written a number of books including "The Soul of Wellness." He's a motivational speaker, and his bio states:

> Following a near death experience (NDE) in 2010, I was given my life back specifically so that I could help others suffering from chronic pain, addiction and depression. The insights gained from my NDE have propelled me to start writing, coaching and offering seminars on spiritual wellness.
>
> As both a pain management specialist who prescribed pain medication as a healing solution and as a patient who has seen the havoc they wreak on the mind and body, I am an advocate for a consciousness-based approach to healing, encouraging people to explore healing through non-pharmaceutical, non-invasive therapies. It is my firm conviction that one cannot achieve total wellness or sustained health without understanding that there is a dimension to wellness that comes from beyond the physical care of the body.[126]

Dr. Parti spoke at the Afterlife Convention in Santa Monica in 2013. This is an edited transcript of his talk:

Dr. Rajiv Parti

"My last name is Parti and I'm a medical doctor; Dr. Parti. I'm an Anesthesiologist; I'd tell my patients my name is "Dr. Party," they think I've taken the name because I'm giving them laughing gas or morphine.

Kristina Cooper. From the Goodnews archives, May/June 2011

[126] Dr. Rajiv Parti, founder of the Pain Management Institute of California and Chief of Anesthesiology at Bakersfield's Heart Hospital, specialized in cardiac anesthesiology. He's now healing people through his books and message; his latest tome is "The Soul of Wellness" and I recommend reading it.

Three years ago, I had a near death experience that changed my life forever. It really transformed me; where I lived, what kind of work I did, how I ate, how I drank, what car I drove, the house where I lived – everything changed. Some were conscious decisions, some just happened on their own. Let me give you a little background about me.

Born and raised in a middle class family in India. My father was a strict dad – I have had mixed feelings about him; he believed if you "spare the rod and spoil the child" and I had my share of beatings. In today's definition you'd say he was abusive; he used to say "When a nail is bent you have to hammer it until it's straightened." So if his son was bent - he had to hammer him.

I was an average student. In tenth grade I started smoking, drinking; I was going to movies instead of going to school, and one day I was caught. I got a spanking because of it – and there was a big shift in it –a transformation. I was at the bottom of the class in tenth grade and I went to the top; I decided to become a doctor. And my mother came to the school to add biology to my subjects, but the director was so rude, he asked (sarcastically); "Do you really think your son will be a doctor one day?" He made my mother cry over it; that day I made a promise to myself, to become a doctor to wipe away my mother's tears.

After finishing school, I came to the U.S. with only 500 dollars in my pocket. I was living in a one bedroom apartment with four guys; during my residency I worked as a security guard, sold papers, drove a taxi. I would tell people I was a struggling doctor and they'd give me a bigger tip, out of the sympathy factor.

I did my residency at Vanderbilt, then moved to California, got married. After my residency I moved to Bakersfield. I originally went there for two weeks for temp work – but 25 years later, I'm still there. My goal was to achieve the American dream. I did, but my dream became a runaway American dream. My religion became the almighty dollar; I got bigger and bigger homes, fancier cars, my last house was 10,000 square feet by a lake; we had to use iPhones to communicate with the kids.

My life was "extreme materialism," I worked 50-70 hours a week. You know the old saying -"Do I own the house or does the house own me?" I had a BMW, my wife had a BMW, on top of it, I had a Hummer; I felt like a king. But no matter how big my house got, something was missing. My wife and I were in the back yard having some tea one day, and the phone rang and my urologist called;

"Better sit down." He said "There's good news/bad news; you have prostate cancer – but if we do the surgery it'll be cured."

I was in shock. The surgery went fine but left me with complications; incontinence, chronic pain, which led to depression and pain killers, narcotics and I became addicted to narcotics. Here I used to write the prescriptions, but I know the prescription medications are a bigger problem than illegal drugs. So many people are addicted to OxyContin, Vicodin, Morphine, etc.

I was addicted as well, and then 2 years later, I went to UCLA to have another surgery, which turned out to be seven in total. I started having fever, swelling, doctor prescribed antibiotics but it didn't get better; I had severe pain, a fever of 105 degrees; they rushed me from Bakersfield to UCLA; it was a very painful trip. They put me on heavy antibiotics, Morphine, Demerol, but I wasn't getting better. Christmas day 2010 I had emergency surgery and after general anesthesia, I saw myself having an out of body experience, floating above.

The doctor was telling a joke, and I heard it. Not a joke I've ever heard before, and later when I asked him about it, he was startled and said I must have been under light anesthesia. The joke was "There was a lady who had some surgery done, and the doctor comes to see how she's doing. She asks the doctor, "When can I have sex?" The doctor was surprised, he said "In two or three weeks." The doctor looked perplexed, so she said "Doctor, what's wrong with my question?" And he said, "Well, because no one has ever asked me that question before." And she said "After an operation?" He said "Well seeing as the operation was a tonsillectomy… no."

"So the Doctor was embarrassed that I heard him tell that joke, and his reaction was "Well, you must have been light in anesthesia – hearing is the last sensation to go and the first to come back." But I had seen more during this operation; much more.[127]

I saw myself in India – I saw my mother and sisters sitting on a sofa, my mom was wearing a green sari and my sister was wearing blue jeans; they were sitting next to a heater and discussing what they're going to have to eat. These details I confirmed with my mother later on.

---

[127] As in Colton Burpo's NDE in "Heaven is For Real," Dr. Parti was able to see and hear those working in the hospital around him. The nurse confirmed the experience; the doctor claimed it was because the drugs weren't strong enough.

I would like to say my awareness went to a serene, happy place, but in my case, it went to a place where there was fire and thunderstorms and entities; I soon realized I was not in "heaven" for sure. They had horns; I was in a hellish realm and I asked "Why am I here?" And I saw that I had lived a very selfish materialist life; I had not been kind to my patients. I saw incidents where I had been rude, or refused to give them personal attention. And when I realized my mistakes, this vision of Hell starting fading away.[128]

And then I saw my father and he said to me "If you keep your consciousness clear the universe will take care of you," the same words he said to me 20 years ago, just prior to his heart surgery. And then I had a past life review; the good and the bad, the people whose toes I had stepped on to get ahead. I was Chief of Anesthesia, but I had been manipulating how to get things done.

I saw past lives, I also saw myself as child in Rome, and from there my consciousness crossed a tunnel. And then there was a bright light, and I was welcomed into another realm by two giant, robust, very lively, very soothing men. **They spoke telepathically, they told me they were my guardian angels. They guided me to a light being; I saw meadows of roses with different colors, there were mountains and when I was in the presence of the light being it felt like the light of a thousand suns.**[129]

And I had the understanding I would be fine, and I could go back; but I would change my life totally and live a life of spirituality. Also for some reason, the words "A Course in Miracles" flashed above me; which I had never heard at that time.

---

[128] I asked Dr. Parti why he felt seeing people with horns signified "Hell." According to a Jesuit priest at Loyola University in LA, (a retired exorcist that one of my students interviewed for my class in documentary filmmaking,) the concept of Satan as the embodiment of evil didn't appear in liturgy until the Middle Ages. Goat horns were adopted from the Greek vision of Pan during the Middle Ages, including "hoofs, horns and unremitting lust" according to B.G. Walker, "The Woman's Encyclopedia of Myths and Secrets," Harper & Row, San Francisco, CA, (1983). If everyone's vision of heaven is different, then the same would seem to apply to visions of Hell. There's one other vision of hell I've encountered, described during an LBL; after a lifetime in Egypt, "Grace" saw people thrashing about and smelled sulfur (but no horns). This place seemed to dissolve when the therapist explained she didn't have to stay there during the session. When Dr. Parti's conscious mind thought about his mistakes during this experience, this hell realm "faded away."

[129] Dr. Parti identified these guardian angels as "archangels" and named them as "Michael" and "Gabriel." Again, because they weren't wearing name tags, it's hard to account for how a person might identify them, as well as not having the benefit of a therapist asking probing questions about who they are and why they might be here at the moment. Also, the classic NDE experience of a "Light being" and "meadows of roses" like Dr. Alexander's vision once he went "through the light."

And then I woke up in the recovery room. I felt such gratitude for the place I'd been, for the joy I'd felt, and I recounted to the anesthesiologist the joke I heard. And the attending nurse said she'd heard these same kinds of descriptions before.[130]

After that, my life changed, either by my actions or on their own. I had been earning $50-60,000 dollars a month; I knew I'd have to sell my house, drive a simple car and have a simpler life and be a nicer person. I let all my cars go, sold my Hummer; my life went literally and figuratively from Hummer to Hybrid.

Because I do care for nature now – it's an extension of our bodies, I fell in love with my wife again. I became a more caring husband and then I became a better doctor; I have sympathy now, and I sit down with patients. I gave up my job as an Anesthesiologist, to become a healer of the soul, help people with addiction, chronic pain. Physically, I got better in 72 hours, my addiction to the narcotics was completely gone.

The truths I realized; there is life after death and we are all connected to each other and there is a loving entity, supreme intelligence (that is the) basis of all that exists. I started to study "The Course In Miracles" I found a mantra for myself; "forgive, love and heal." Forgiveness is the dharma from which healing takes place; first I had to forgive myself, then God, as I was mad at God and then I started loving myself and others and then the healing happened."

Dr. Parti is now helping others to heal by sharing his story and focusing on healing his patients.

My Brother Jeffry

George Bailey: *"Well, maybe I left the car up at Martini's. Well, come on, Gabriel."*
Clarence: *"My name is Clarence!"*
George Bailey: Right.... Clarence.*

---

[130] "A Course in Miracles" is a self-study curriculum which aims to assist readers in achieving spiritual transformation. While the original "A Course in Miracles" lists no author, it was psychologist Helen Schucman who wrote it with the help of psychologist William Thetford based on what Schucman called an "inner voice" which spoke to her. In the book, she says the voice said "This is a Course in Miracles, please take notes." Among its messages *"Nothing real can be threatened. Nothing unreal exists. The opposite of love is fear."* (1st edition, 1975) Interesting to note that Dr. Parti got a visualization of this title, although he wasn't consciously aware of the book itself.

A quote from the most famous of near death experiencers, George Bailey in "It's A Wonderful Life."

I have not had a near death experience (or "Near Life Experience" as I like to call them, because everyone claims it's more fun over there), but I know someone intimately who has; my brother.

I was probably nine or ten years old when "Jeff" died. It was during the Vietnam War era, and my brother had been drafted into the Army and had gone through officer training school at Ft. Benning, Georgia. As a brand new 2nd Lieutenant he was all set to join the other soldiers who'd been shipped off to Vietnam. (Years later, he told me that he was to join the infamous "Americal Division," which at that time had a reputation of being the most undisciplined Army unit in 'Nam. Several of its officers had been "fragged" - killed by their enlisted men with a grenade - so Jeffry was not happy with his impending assignment.)

But the Flipside intervened in his life's journey. Jeffry "died" while in advanced combat training, where he had a unique NDE.

He was out in a Physical Training exercise field at Fort Benning, doing pushups with several of his fellow officers, when he felt a series of pin pricks on his arm. He looked down and saw a bunch of ants crawling up and around his forearm and elbow. He brushed them off and went back to doing pushups.

Within minutes his other arm became covered with more ants and more bites. He brushed them off, moved to a different spot and then felt a burning sensation over his entire body. He had been bitten by scores of red ants, the very poisonous kind. They can kill a cow, let alone a human being. Trying to appear "macho" he continued doing the exercises until he slumped over, writhing in pain. One of his exercise pals came over, asked what was wrong and when told it was "ants", was familiar enough with the killer sting of red ants and called immediately for an Army ambulance.

By the time Jeffry got to the hospital he was literally the color blue. He was rushed to the Emergency Room and given intravenous doses of adrenalin and glucose.

And while on the operating table, he could feel the wave-like "pins and needles" effect rapidly heading from his toes to his chest. He remembers thinking.... "This is not good."

Suddenly, he felt himself floating just above the operating table. Looking down, he saw and heard the doctor shout, "We're losing him, we're losing him" while pumping on his chest.

He said that he experienced a sensation of being pulled onward and upward toward a very "bright light" that was indeed bright but didn't hurt his "eyes" while looking directly at it. Just before he reached the "light" he also had a past life review; two of the classic hallmarks of an NDE. [131]

During that life review, he said he saw his life in reverse motion – going from older to younger – and then back again. I asked him what events stood out for him. He said it was like watching a movie in reverse. (His account reminded me the way one would scan film on an old Fotokem editing machine, running the footage backwards).

He said that the "film" would slow down, and then speed up and then stop at a particular moment so that he could relive it. I asked him if he could remember where it stopped. He said the review stopped several times, but that the most memorable one was when he was a young toddler, and saw himself slipping a piece of candy into his pocket surreptitiously – "stealing candy from a candy store" - and had the feeling of remorse, and the impression "Oh, that's not a good thing to do." He said he suddenly felt guilty for that action.

Then he said, "The film sped forward to a moment when my best friend Tom Kozlowski and I were in a car together, and pulling out of an intersection and a kid speeding on a motorcycle suddenly hit the back of our car and literally flew over the car and into the street." It was not a major event in Jeffry's life, because the motorcycle rider did not die, but he remembered it as a "life changing event."

He said that he felt a "great calm" during these visuals, felt at peace. He also said that he felt the experience of being there was akin to a glass on the very edge of a table that was just inches from slipping over and breaking. He motioned to me with his hand to show a glass on the edge, about to fall off.

He said he felt like he was at the point – he could stay here in this new realm, or he could return to life; it was entirely up to him.[132] And he had the impression of

---

[131] He said he had other hallmarks; a profound sense of calm, or a "feeling of peace" (39%), "time stopped or lost meaning" (15%), that he was in an unearthly realm of existence (67%). He said his thoughts were "unusually vivid" (33%), and had a "life review" (35%). "Feelings of peace" (39%). (From the 1983 study Dr. Bruce Greyson did with 74 near death experiencers).

repeatedly saying "I'm not supposed to be here yet... I'm not supposed to be here yet!" As if there was something else for him to accomplish back in his body and back on Earth.

He also said that when this journey had started he was aware of and could also see the doctors working on him below. (Another common example of being "out of body" and seeing people in the hospital working on your body.)

He also told me that he had the impression that there was a thin thread, some kind of thin viscous material that connected him to his body – it was floating freely, like the web of a spider. [133] And then the doctors hit him with another adrenaline shot and he came "back to life."

He didn't have all the classical NDE hallmarks – he didn't hear celestial music, or go to another realm, or meet people that were his relatives. But he did have the hallmarks of the feeling of "peacefulness" of "insight" as well as a "past life review."

When an NDE happens, sometimes we are able to discern that this event has helped or even saved a life. In my brother's case, this odd instance of being bitten by poisonous ants on an exercise training field in Georgia ended up keeping him from going with his troop members to Vietnam.

He also had his doctor to thank for saving his life; the Army doctor, a Captain who had also been drafted, reviewed my brother's paperwork that already listed Vietnam as his tour of duty. The doctor smiled and said "We can't send you to Southeast Asia, there are bound to be biting insects and poisonous snakes there as well." [134] Never mind that there aren't fire ants or poisonous snakes in Vietnam, he changed the form so that my brother did not have to go. And my brother told me that when he checked up on it after the war, only three men survived from his unit.

---

[132] Brings to mind the film "If I Stay" which has a similar theme.

[133] I've heard accounts from other people that during an out of body experience they had the impression they were always "connected" to their bodies by a thread of some kind, but his is the only account of actually viewing this thread.

[134] Fire ants are not in Vietnam. So the doctor likely saved my brother's life. However *"Solenopsis invicta,* known in the United States as the red fire ant, is an invasive pest in the U.S., Australia, the Philippines, China and Taiwan. (Wikipedia)

And as a result of those words put onto his record, he was reassigned, where he spent a year working as a General's Aide and for the Ft. Benning Newspaper as Newsroom Chief. He did get overseas, where he was assigned to the Korean DMZ as a Mechanized (APC) Platoon leader, a Tactical Operations Center officer and President of the Southeast Asian Junior Officers Council. All of this Public Relations and Media work eventually led him into journalism and sales, where he was the National Director of Advertising for Rolling Stone magazine in its heyday and later Associate Publisher of the wildly popular LA Weekly.

I include this story because I just happen to know the person it happened to. I can vouch for who he is as a person, and his ability to tell a story that isn't based on trying to confabulate details; he's a very precise guy. He's listened to me talk about the Flipside for a number of years now, and when he first heard me talk about it, he shared this story with me.

An unusual aside; some years ago, I was in India at the "Digital Talkies" film festival showing my film "Camera-Dogme #15." It was shot on a small digital camera, and it had been given the designation of a "Dogme 95" film. It was 2001, and I was carrying some of Luana's ashes with me to place in a fountain at the Taj Mahal. And this one evening at the film festival, I saw a tall American walk past me. I got up from my chair and followed him, recognizing his voice. I got downstairs and stood face to face with former Defense Secretary Robert McNamara. This was three years before McNamara admitted in the film "Fog of War" that he and the entire U.S. government had misread the Vietnam War as a cold war conflict instead of a civil war between the North and the South. In the film he claimed if he had realized that at the time, he would have argued that we align ourselves with the North instead of the South.

Here I was, face to face with the man many consider the most responsible for convincing our country to fight in Vietnam. (Well, actually face to chin, he's quite tall.) He was there for the annual "Pugwash" conference, about global disarmament. And I asked "Bob, why is it that the U.S. aligned itself with Pakistan for so many years, when India is a democracy, it's a capitalist country and its citizens speak English?"[135]

He said "Three reasons. One, India is not a democracy, they have too many political factions." I said "Oh, and Pakistan, a military dictatorship in the 60's had

---

[135] After all, we fought a revolution so we don't have to bow to royalty, so why not use his first name; Bob?

less?" He ignored my retort and said, "Secondly, they're not really a capitalist country; they have too many tariffs." I said "Oh, and China has less tariffs? We've treated them as partners since the 1970's." Then he put his arm around me, smiling broadly. "The third reason is because the Indians are a pain in the ass to deal with."

There's no logical reason for me to run into Mr. McNamara in India, to ask him this question. This story doesn't really relate to my brother's NDE. But they both involved Vietnam and they're both good stories. The man many claim responsible for the Vietnam War, sending 60,000 Americans, countless Vietnamese to die in a war that he later claimed was a mistake, also happened to think we shouldn't deal with countries that are a "pain in the ass." Well, sometimes it takes a "pain in the ass" or an "adrenaline shot to the heart" to show how we all belong on the same planet, we are all connected, and deserve to share in its resources and beauty. But that's just my two cents.

The Near Death and Life of Jeremy Kagan

"As we live through thousands of dreams in our present life, so is our present life only one of many thousands of such lives which we enter from the other more real life and then return after death. Our life is but one of the dreams of that more real life, and so it is endlessly, until the very last one, the very real, the life of God." - Leo Tolstoy

Jeremy Kagan was in a sweat lodge in Malibu when he died.

Jeremy Kagan has a B.A. from Harvard, attended New York University's Graduate Institute of Film & Television and the American Film Institute. His directing credits include "The Journey of Natty Gann" with John Cusack, "The Big Fix" with Richard Dreyfus, and numerous TV shows including "The West Wing." He's won an Emmy, been nominated for a Golden Globe, and won the Humanitas Award. He teaches directing at my alma mater, the film school at the University of Southern California, served as Artistic Director at the Robert Redford's Sundance Institute and is a Board Member of the Directors Guild of America. He's also wrote "Directors Close Up." (Scarecrow, 2006).

A few years ago, Jeremy joined some friends in a traditional Native American sweat lodge in the hills above Malibu, California. He wasn't new to the sweat lodge concept, or spiritualism in general, but what happened to him while he was in the lodge was new to him; a trip to the afterlife.

At some point, while in the sweat lodge overcome with heat and exhaustion, he felt himself faint and die. (Jeremy's book, "The Near Death and Life of Jeremy Kagan" is available as an ebook.)

In the first part of his NDE, Jeremy saw himself in an unusual hell – it reminded him of the film "Seven Beauties," (or "Schindler's List") when a character dives into a latrine to hide; he found himself in a pool of excrement. It was foul, and he had the awful feeling being stuck there.[136]

But he also had an insight while in that cesspool:

> In this realm of consciousness I had the realization: There is no good or bad. There is no right or wrong. There just is." And further "I understood this like a bolt of lightning clarity. I knew that this realm after death was beyond judgments, beyond good and bad, I got that the continuing internal judging and interpreting and making arbitrary meaning drags us away from being present with what is. (Kindle Location (KL) 390 ("My Death A Personal Guidebook" Balboa Press)

Then he began to travel further away:

> I was headed somewhere and it felt like it was upwards. Diagonally... I was the motion and I was seeing... a smooth straight supernatural ride through a creamy cloudy grey white tubular tunnel. Heading up.[137]

Seeing a tunnel during an NDE is a common experience. According to Dr. Greyson's study of near death experiences published in 1983, 17% saw a "tunnel-like dark region."[138]

---

[136] Interesting to note that in Eben Alexander's journey, his first experience was in some "muck" or a mud-like area, perhaps pointing to the "loss of physical perception" akin to experiencing the various levels of awareness as described in the death process in the "Tibetan Book of the Dead."

[137] Kindle reference page (KL) 976

[138] http://www.medicine.virginia.edu/clinical/departments/psychiatry/sections/cspp/dops/greyson-publications/NDE8-1.pdf

I sensed/saw forms passing by... misty grey vertical cylinders... and then a jolt. An explosion of perception... filled with images... (that) contained everything I had ever perceived; actual or imagined... a life review... my whole life passed before me. But it wasn't as one event after another. It was all happening at the same time. [139]

Here Jeremy experiences more of the classic hallmarks of the NDE: the "life review," a profound "feeling of peace," or a "feeling of cosmic unity," or that "events seem instantaneous." It appears that the NDE is unique to each individual, and yet common in many characteristics.

And although Jeremy didn't experience running into any entities during his NDE, he told me he had an experience with the hallucinogenic drug "ayahuasca" earlier in his life, and during that encounter he distinctly heard two people speak to him; one said *"You are okay, right where you are."*

He said when he heard it, he felt an enormous lift of fear and pressure. The other messenger said *"You are always supported."* I pointed out to him in the numerous sessions that I've filmed, I've heard some variation on these themes.

He had more than a past life review during this sweat lodge event - almost a review of the entire planet;

> **The history of the planet flashed from the Big Bang until now. It was mostly concentrated on human events. All the proceedings of history... the heroes, leaders, etc..." "All the movies I had watched (were) playing simultaneously. All speeded up that each film took less than a nanosecond to play and were all playing at the same time, thousands... of them.** (KL 1032)

A classic hallmark in Dr. Greyson's study of NDE is the feeling that time has changed, or sped up. Since Jeremy Kagan has spent a lifetime making films, I can imagine there were a lot of reels unspooling for him at this moment.

> But what was by far the more shocking and yet completely clear, was that everything I had seen and heard – all the events, media... etc **– I had made them all up!** .... Was this then the Creative Force witnessing itself

---

[139] Kindle Reference page 1004

through the lens of my incarnation**? My mind was beyond answering or analyzing. Only experiencing.**[140]

His comment "I had made them all up!" is reminiscent of "life is an illusion" or "trick" or "hoax" of some sorts. Certainly it's not possible that Jeremy invented all the films he saw in this event, as we've seen a few of them as well. In other words, his consciousness could not the creator of these films, but is remembering them from the access points in his own memory banks. But when combined with all the events of his lifetime, he had the impression that everything he was experiencing had been created by his own consciousness. If if you consider for a moment that the universe might be sentient, and that he was tapping into the source, then perhaps that is the case.

Jeremy traveled further through this tunnel and found himself going through an **"aperture that was revealing the firmament of stars... surrounded by the blackness of space and the sparkles of star systems. An infinite array of lights. And it was quiet and peaceful..."**

And finally, when the event was complete, he went in reverse from the edge of the Universe back into his body, he felt

> **...absolute happiness... I felt love for everything and everyone. Complete, emanating, appreciative and overwhelming unconditional joy filled love; a full acceptance of and deep delight in everything. This feeling flowed through every fiber of me.**[141]

As mentioned, many people have this type of apotheosis during an NDE or an LBL. But there are a number of documented cases of people who've experienced this "connection to everyone and all things" during their waking moments.

I know of at least two friends who claim they had a brief glimpse of this feeling of "oneness" with the planet. Both of them had, while conscious, a feeling of "oneness" or connectedness with everyone on the planet, similar to the feeling Dr. Mario Beauregard recounts in his interview which led him into his field of science. As one friend put it: "Everything seemed in that moment like a Seurat or Monet painting - tiny little dots of energy - and I felt **one with everything**. As if

---

[140] Ibid. Kindle ref 1032

[141] Ibid. Kindle ref 1206

everything was a jostle of molecules and I could even see and feel the trees breathing."

I asked Jeremy if his NDE has altered him in any way. He said, "It has shifted my consciousness of who I am, not in a dramatic way, but more of a subtle way. It's allowed me to diminish a certain amount of fear, put in perspective certain anxieties and desires, and it's given me a broader choice of how to react. It doesn't mean I don't resort back to my regular neuroses, because I do, but it does remind me there's a choice (I can make). That's a major shift for me."[142]

"Life is a dream walking. Death is going home." - Chinese proverb

---

[142] Jeremy Kagan's book "The Near Death and Life of Jeremy Kagan" is available in Kindle and I recommend reading his account of his amazing NDE

Chapter Fourteen – "The Yellow Brick Road"

"The boundaries between-life and death are at best shadowy and vague. Who shall say where one ends and where the other begins?" - Edgar Allen Poe

Sometimes your subconscious will only take you where it needs to go.

In this case, a friend of mine, Jackson, a screenwriter who lives in Europe, contacted me about doing a session. He's a successful writer, and I ran into him during the Cannes film fest back in the 90's. He's had some amazing adventures in his life, has written films for Oscar award winning directors, and told me an amazing true story which I always thought would make a great film.

The story goes like this. He ran into a famous musician while she was on tour, snuck backstage, and whisked her away from her tour and her life. She was into drugs at the time, and moving into a garret with him overlooking Paris was the best thing that could have ever happened to her. It got her off drugs.

But at some point she couldn't handle the vagabond living anymore, having lived the high life for so long – she contacted her manager, got him to extend her credit, and she checked into a four star hotel so she could finally take a long, luxurious rock star bath. And that was the end of the relationship – she went back to her world, and he went back to his. I always thought it would be a grand love story for the big screen and have bugged him to write it all down for decades.

I also saw it as a "Flipside" kind of story – we never know who we're going to find on our path in life, or who our guardian angels turn out to be.

Jackson was at first quite skeptical of my stories, he'd read "Flipside" and did me a huge favor of helping me edit it. I would tease him about trying a session, and so perhaps to get me to stop telling "Flipside" stories, he scheduled a session with Scott "just to see what would happen."

He was coming in from Europe so we had to time it a bit in advance, and the only admonition I gave to him was to be open to whatever he felt, saw or sensed, and to say it aloud.

Scott and Jackson

Scott: Before birth and in the womb now... feel the protection of this dark warm environment where you drift and float inside your mother... safe and protected... the sound of your mother's voice is felt and heard as vibration. What is your impression of your physically comfort?

Jackson: I feel very comfortable, very happy to be there. Very much in the right place; loved...

Just be there. Relaxing, drifting. What month of gestation are you in?

Nine.

Pretty close to being born.

Yeah.

Still feeling good? Emotionally?

Yeah. Excited to be ready to get out, (be born) excited about the mission.

What can you tell me about the mission? What comes into mind?

Uh, I see a sort of golden pathway or line – that I'm going to be following... that's going to be pushing me. And that goldenness is behind me, under me - and it's exciting.

Like your guidance or path?

That's what I'm seeing absolutely yeah, it's just joyous - like here we go, great. How exciting.

As you look into the future of that path, can you discern anything?

(Sighs) It just feels benevolent and there, but I don't.... I don't see from the womb further than just being out of the womb and knowing that it's there, I'm sort of standing on it – and it's a presence, but it's not a progression forward.

More like in the moment.

Yeah but I'm like a week old, or....

So you can't see years into the future, but you can see a little ways.... enough to guide you.

I haven't tried to see, I just feel that presence... but I suppose if I do focus on where it goes, then I see it; I see this thing going off in front of me, ahead of me and it's a snaking yellow brick road... little twists and turns, but sort of gentle valleys.

Undulating...

Yeah. No obstacles, just "here we go."

First impression. What month did you join the fetus?

Three just popped into my mind.

Impression of the brain and body that you now occupy, as your soul mind comes by?

I see an image of sort of a pig fetus (chuckles) in the place of the brain (laughs).

What does that mean to you?

It means the "Trickster's" still alive... I don't know. It was just an image that came up.

What's distinctive of this brain or body? Or do you get a sense there's something distinctive about this person you're going to be?

It's exciting to be here, it's exciting to be this person. To have this adventure ahead of me, to join in this process. I'm just looking forward to it. Like "what a great ride it's going to be."

What's the emotional system like?

Very clean, no obstacles, no barriers, no doubt... it's just glowing energy.

Does your soul-mind feel this a good match?

Great; perfect.

Do you have any inklings about why you chose this body, this life and this mission, anything come to mind?

When you ask that question I feel a hint of fear.... like uh.... gates close... Woah, that's a difficult question -- not difficult but -- a question that shouldn't be looked at.[143]

We'll simply let it go for now.

I'm just saying that's my first impression – it's not that I'm scared to look at it, that's my first impression.

While you're in the womb, before you're born, I wonder if you can tune into your mother for a moment. I wonder what's going through her, what's she feeling?

I see her as a totally luminous being. Confident that she's doing the right thing. The word "mission" comes up.

So this is a very positive image?

Yeah, an ocean of love.

---

[143] Sometime an LBL therapist will ask this question after the person makes their way into the spirit realm – "why did you choose this lifetime?" But since Scott is intuitive in these sessions, the question "any inklings?" grows into a bigger issue or opens the door further.

Anything about this time before you were born you'd like to comment on?

I'd like to look at that barrier. Because it seems like a strange reflex. Doesn't feel like it belongs - "don't ask the question while you're there." It's strange, it feels like an alien element, and the rest feels pure and like it belongs, but this thing feels like a steel gate that's just "clang."

And that clanged shut when I asked about the mission of this life, about why you'd chosen this life?

Yeah. And I still feel that gate as we visit it now, again.

Almost like a metal gate shut?

Almost like "Don't look at it."

Do you feel it's a part of you or others?

It really feels alien, like someone inserted that or something.

So let's simply bring your consciousness to that gate and to that energy or being who closed that gate.

All I can see is a nose. I can see a sort of hovering, slightly menacing. posture or presence... uh... putting it down with his hands, putting it in place with his hands.

A Visit With A Spirit Guide

Let's ask that fellow for a name, something I can call him today.

(Chuckles) He says "Let's call him Thor."[144]

So I'm going to speak to Thor directly. I'm going to ask him to speak into your mind, through your voice. Thor, what is your relationship to Jackson?

"Dominating. Keeping him down."

---

[144] Names are for the most part irrelevant, and in this case, irreverent. The idea is to have a name or word that the therapist can use to discern between the individual doing the session and a higher version of the self, and others. However, the therapist usually goes with whatever name is presented, in this case, the name of a famous Viking deity.

And what is the purpose of keeping him down?

"He might go. "

He might go where?

"He might step outside. Maybe into a different realm, into.... he won't do what he has to."

And what is it that he has to do?

"He has to know."

And what is it Thor, he has to do or know?

"He has to know the whole of everything."

And once again – what is your relationship to this soul known as Jackson?

"I'm his chief."

Do you mean like a teacher or a leader or something like that?

"I decided his mission."

So I'll simply ask you point blank; "What is his mission? What have you decided for him?"

"To flow."

Tell us more.

"I can't tell you more. I'm not allowed to tell you more. He has to figure it out."

Who is not allowing you to tell more?

"It's part of the structure; he mustn't know." [145]

---

[145] I've found when examining other cases, or when a person isn't trained in the Michael Newton method, a therapist often allows the client to decide the answer, and they leave it at that. In this case, his spirit guide has said that he is not going to say any more about the path Jackson is supposed to be on, because he shouldn't be made aware of it at this time. However, that doesn't stop Scott from playing the detective, and probing to see if there's an answer.

So let me get this straight, as a child in the womb, he is not to know his mission because that will interfere with the mission itself. Is that right?

"It will distract him."

Because if he sees too far ahead it will prevent him from flowing?

"He must have obstacles. To purify his heart."

And so what else would you have us know at this time? What else would you share with us?

"**Keep going. It will be all right.** He is strong. There will be happiness soon."

He has brought questions to this session usually I would take him through a past life to get to you – to ask you these questions, what do you suggest?

"Address these questions? Yes."

His primary question has to do with this barrier or another form of barrier... but let me just get straight in my mind if you will. When these gates shut - was that for his earlier life, that you did that?

"**It's for *this* life. It's for – it's to give him hardship, so that he will be stronger.**"

What are the gates preventing him from seeing?

"His purpose."

And so here we are now, and I'm sure you had a hand in this session, it is no accident, it is time to be revealed; he wants to know "What is my mission?"

"To ascend. To lead. He has a strong powerful destiny, people will follow. They will get behind him."

Can you put this into Earthly terms? What does this mean? How can he ascend and lead?

"People will see his radiance and they will just know him – know that he is ... know that he is in the right and in the light."

So, again, how can we put this into practical terms for Jackson – what actions should he take?

"He must continue. He must keep going, he must go to the top of a mountain and discover his wholeness."

Are you speaking literally?

"Yes, I see a mountain, maybe not a mountain, but a rounded foothill and he's there at the top and there's that (snaps fingers). It clicks in."

What's the name of this place?

"Sayer. California. Southern, rounded drive, round hill."

Sayer? And what is he to do at this place? Walk up to this place and stand there, meditate, or?

"He just needs to go there and it will all click – it will be like he's stepping into where he needs to be."

Can you give us a time frame? When should he do this?

"Two weeks. A year. He doesn't need to go there physically." [146]

He can go there mentally? Like in a meditation?

"Like a state of mind, getting to that mountain and knowing it, having the confidence to be there, wholly. And smile on the future."

Let's burn an image of this place in his mind now. Etch it into his mind. Where is this location?

The fire trails above Mandeville Canyon is what I'm seeing. Brentwood.

He is to go to this place physically if possible, at least mentally. Can you be more forthcoming about what he's to do?

"It's like by going to that place a new confidence clicks in, a certainly about the path, just clicks in and there's no doubt after that, at all. And that power is just immensely seductive to people, to others, they'll see it. That certainty."

---

[146] At the end of this session there is a report from Jackson that I received after he went to this place. He specifically made a trip there, based on this admonition for him to do so.

Perhaps even now he can experience a taste of that feeling. He wants to know "am I on the right path?"

"Yes."

Any course corrections he still needs to do?

"There are certain things to clean out still."

What's the main thing that needs to be cleaned out?

"There are dark zones in the body which are like tunnels of energy that don't belong there, that are camping. Parasite energy and it's familiar, it's comfortable almost and he tends to go..."

Can you assist us in clearing out that energy?

"It can go very easily, instantly but he has to let it go."

Can you tell us something about the origin of this energy?

"The origin is pain, psychological pain."

And this pain has created dark zones in the body? Its camped out there?

"Yes."

So what does he need to do to be free of it?

"Just do it and renounce it. Renounce the comfort of this alien thing that he's so used to, that he relies on that (points to his abdomen)." [147]

In the abdomen? Is there a lesson or meaning to be gained from this?

"It's there because of weakness. It's there because he fails to take responsibility completely, so it gives him an excuse to not take responsibility because of this

---

[147] In many shamanic rituals I've examined or studied, people speak of negative energy traveling with us during our lifetimes. It's generally not found in Michael Newton's studies, in fact Newton's research debunks the idea that negativity might travel with us on its own, or of its own volition (like some kind of dark energy, or other form of negative behavior). Newton found that by probing further, concepts of evil or negativity usually transform in the probing questions about the nature of its existence. For example "Why would you choose to have a life where this negative energy would be part of it?" And in those questions, the client usually discovers that it was part of something he's working on.

problem. So as long as it's there, he doesn't have to complete his mission – it's dirty, it's black... it's..."

So, you're saying this is his choice. He can renounce it and it can be gone if he chooses, is that correct?

"Yeah, it's a security blanket for him. It's just there and it's his excuse for not becoming 'immortal,' for not becoming transcendent as long as he has that feeling, he can't "go there" because of this responsibility."

Can we look at the root of this pain, its origin?

"We can, but it's not necessary. It can just (clicks his fingers) disappear."

And so how is Jackson feeling now?

(Gasps.) Amazing.

So take a moment and breathe and feel free. Do you feel lighter?

It takes my breath away (sighs).

You've been carrying that a long time.

(Nods) Yeah.

Thor is there anything we need to replace that energy? A bit of an empty space there – is there anything we can do for him? Put some light?

"The light will flow in."

What needs to be done for him now?

"He needs 45 minutes and he'll be fine. It just has to flow into that vacuum. The energy is gone, the bad energy is gone, the light energy just has to flow in and replace it. It will happen automatically."

Thank you for that. You said dark zones.... are there any other dark zones?

"They're on other kind of bilateral zone, but it will ... on the left abdomen, but it will move off by itself."

Is there anything he needs to do to release that energy?

"Okay." Done (sighs).

Thank you. We have more questions. Are you ready?

"Yes."

"Why is there so much strife in my life?"

"Strife is to scramble your brains, to bring turmoil to you."

Would be nice to feel something like he felt in the womb. So the question is; why is there so much struggle in my life so many obstacles?

"I can't tell him."

Understanding Darkness

Well we've spoken of some of this. You say he has a radiant destiny but he needed to experience obstacles. Why so much struggle, so many obstacles?

"He needs to understand darkness. He needs to understand the lower state. To be worthy of the highest state."

So he's been experiencing these negative and dark things in order to appreciate love and light, this type of thing?

"If it were too easy, he wouldn't fulfill his potential, his power. He's lazy. If we gave it to him, he wouldn't use it. He must conquer his.... - he must be worthy of it." [148]

I have a question. What is there to understand about darkness? What do we need to all understand about darkness?

"There's like a layer of black tar at the bottom of hopelessness and it's the thing many people are mired in. And he doesn't have much sympathy for that; he needs to learn that but he refuses."

So he's been forced into the mire to gain sympathy for others?

---

[148] I found this portion of his session akin to saying "Why can't I read the end of the book first?" and hearing the reply "Because you won't learn anything."

"Right."

He wants to know "Am I doing what I'm supposed to be doing?

"Yes, doing it well."

Do you have any advice for him about his work?

"Keep on plugging."

He told me he felt he's been working with good intent, but being held down, stymied.

"We've put barriers there, it can't happen too soon. If it had already happened, he would just fall asleep. The barriers are there for him to remove and he'll figure it out."

You say "we put barriers" – is there a team you work with? Or more of you? Who is this we?

(Chuckles) – "There are several of us."

And you're role is what? What's your relationship to Jackson?

"What is Thor's relationship? He's the handyman. He's the "logistics" dept."

This leads to Jackson's next question. "Do I have guides and who are they?" Thor, do you consider yourself a spirit guide or if not what is your role?

"I'm the head of the barriers department. But I'm laughing at him. He's cute. It's funny to watch him struggle."

Well I'm glad you're entertained.

(Laughs.) "Well, I'm a minor employee. He has two or three spirit guides who are... (waves his hand) ascended, high up."

I would ask those spirit guides to make their presence known in this session now, in the mind of Jackson – these ascended guides that Thor works for ... would you come forward to greet us?

(Nods) "Ok."

What are you aware of? Are there other presences?

Three.

How are they arranged?

They're sort of above, very close together, white diaphanous cloaks and their arms are linked. They're smiling at the spectacle of Jackson, smiling kindly, but amused by this little being... (waves hands and fingers).

I would address these three directly for their appearance, I would ask them to speak directly through Jackson's voice – what does he need to know today?

"It's going to be all right. He is loved."

Would you tell us something about yourselves? Is there a spokesman, or higher ranking member?

"All equal. We're from the third level."

What level is Thor from?

"Fifth level."

Thank you. So how do you feel about Jackson's performance in this life this far?

"He's doing okay, we're proud of him."

What has he done well?

"He's brought joy to many people, he's been consistent, he's ... he's an emissary of the light."

The Radiance

What is the mission in the Jackson incarnation? What is the mission or goal of this lifetime?

"To show the possibilities for human beings. And it's going to cost – it has cost him, chunks of flesh, and he's still fighting. He's a warrior."

When you say "show the possibilities for human beings" what do you mean?

"The potential for glory. He tries to be humble. But that's what he's here for."

To show the potential for glory?

"The radiance, the light. Through his being."

Do you have any comments about the darker energy he was holding onto and he's now released?

"He doesn't need those things, but we're mischievous so we do this. We're playing with him. We're tricksters."

Is there a method behind your madness, a higher purpose?

"It's to encourage flexibility in him."

Jackson wanted to know "what am I here to learn?"

"To learn that you are that energy of "God.""

So what attitude or posture would you suggest he project?

"Project the radiance 100% and not worry about what people think. Not hide anymore."

He wants to know "Why do I attract these lunatics such as his former employers?"

(Sighs). "They're smaller souls who provoke doubt. Obstacles. They throw him for a loop and he allows that to happen and he mustn't."

So what is the way for him to stop or change that pattern?

"The radiance. When he takes responsibility for the radiance, those people will no longer exist around him."

He wants to know "Why did I choose this life?

"It's his responsibility. He has a role to fulfill. It's becoming the radiance, it's being infinite possibility.... as an example..."

It may be semantics, you say it's his responsibility, could he have chosen not to? Could he have chosen to sit on a cloud somewhere?

(Nods.) "Yes, he could have chosen not to yes. He understood that it was necessary."

What would you share with him today?

"It's going to be all right. There will be a period of darkness, maybe the last one."

You speak of emotional or mental darkness?

"Yes, a fog. Moments of uncertainty and despair. And there is a benevolent love presence in the form of somebody waiting for him."

Why was Jackson brought to this session today? What does he really need to get out of this experience?

"He needs to become his full power, absolutely. He needs to magnetize the proper allies. The heart needs to be pure. They're already there, but he has to do that thing first, he has to purify the heart."

How can he do that?

"Let the love flow."

Thor, how can Jackson connect with you in a conscious way on his own?

"He just has to smile. We're there."

Can he connect with his mother?

"Yes, she's here."

We invite her to come forward.

(Jackson begins to weep.)

I'm going to be quiet so you can spend some time together. (After a while) Is she communicating anything to you you'd like to share?

She's just there for me. She's just... she's love. She's ... proud of me. She's waiting for my dad.

Does she visit him or anything like that?

She does but he doesn't – he's not open.

He's not aware of her?

He doesn't acknowledge the possibility of her being there. He's too married to his pain of losing her.

I would ask your mother, "Is there anything Jackson can do to help his father?"

He should tell his father to be open; to see her smile and let her into his heart. That she is waiting for him.

I would ask what activities your mother is involved in with her time there?

She takes care of people. She greets them, she makes them feel at home, she tells them it's okay.

Do you refer to souls returning from Earth lives?

Yes. She's a comforting presence.

Is there anything else Jackson needs to experience in this session today?

If he trusts his intuition he will get what he needs; he must fully trust it. It will come to him.[149]

Take a moment and see if you have any questions for your guides today – anything else they would like to share with Jackson today?

"Make sure to keep laughing. It's a game." [150]

Take a last look around. Anything of significance we might have missed, insights or messages?

---

[149] In a number of sessions loved ones are performing different tasks. Later, a father is reported to be helping people cross over from a hospital. In this case, it's a mother greeting people in the afterlife.

[150] There is the concept of "It's a game" again. There are numerous accounts in this book of people saying "It's all a hoax," "It's just a game" "Don't take it too seriously" etc. As mentioned previously, there's a moment in the film "The Matrix" when the character Neo sees that even bullets are mental constructs and he holds up his hand to watch them fall harmlessly to the ground. Some sporting events require all of our faculties in order to survive a life or death event. I would venture that research shows those who are fully invested in their lives get the most out of each lifetime.

"Everything should be clear."

(After the session)

Jackson: Wow, what a voyage.

Scott: We bypassed a past life, didn't we? I was going to ask about colorful past lives; didn't seem necessary.

Go figure, I've got a Norwegian for a guide.

Well they wouldn't come if they didn't want to talk. Just playing coy. "Keep laughing -- it's a game."

Me: We associate the word "game" with children's play but when you consider it in the adult sense... we have this pejorative feeling to the word game. Consider it as the life and death of a chess player, someone caught up in the intensity of the game. As in "You've got to be in the game or you don't learn." If you're in the game, fully inhabiting the role, all kinds of magical *stuff* can happen.

Scott: I think of it as sport – watching the game from the sidelines you see patterns and things, until you're out there.

Jackson: Someone's kicking you in the shins... That represents ignorance on Earth; yellow cards till you get the red card. "I didn't see anything wrong, but I'm punishing you anyways."

Later, Jackson called to say that on a whim he returned to the mountaintop, the place he had envisioned during his sessions. He wrote

> I went up to that place above Mandeville Canyon and I reconnected to that. A definite smile came over my face and a feeling of "This is it. You can let go of the past now." I used to go up there with my dog sometimes with a camera to film stuff, up there with friends, sometimes with my mom. It was above our house and became a place of solace for me. And when I did the session with Scott, I thought of that place. And finally I was able to return there.

I asked him what percentage of his session felt like a direct and accurate connection to spirit?

> Perhaps 75%. But a smile did come over my face, and it wasn't a conscious thought to smile, but the smile just came. And also that feeling of "You've done it, this is it" came to me spontaneously. I may have been thinking about it, but I may have just been reconnecting to something higher.

Interesting to note that in this session Jackson did not go into a previous life. When Scott asked about what the meaning of the "Yellow brick road" in his vision, he replied *"This isn't information for you to know."* Scott's pretty adept at what he does, and despite finding resistance from Jackson's spirit guide, Scott was able to argue there must be a spiritual reason why Jackson came to this session, and that he needed to hear what it was. It was at this point the spirit guide appeared to open up with details.

This session did not follow the traditional pattern of going into a previous lifetime, then examining the last day of that lifetime, and using that as a gateway into the between lives realm. Scott began to ask him about the path – the journey that his life would take. And at that moment, he looked around to find a spirit guide preventing him from accessing that information. I think this is remarkable for a number of reasons; if you were going to make up the fact that you had a spirit guide, or that your spirit guide was some kind of higher power that guides your life, wouldn't you create someone who was easier to work with?

In essence the spirit guide was saying "Well too bad, he's not supposed to know what happens on his journey, so mind your own business." I've found working with Scott is that he's a bit like Colombo the detective who comes into a room and on his way out the door says "Oh, and one more thing" and then zeroes in on the revelation he wanted all along.

He asked "if Jackson is supposed to be here, and you allowed him to come here – then why not let him know what he needs to hear?" The guide (or his subconscious) relented and outlined a path for Jackson to take – or for Jackson to be aware of.

The extension of that question is "Why did you pick up this book, or open up this kindle? Is there some higher power that wants to reveal something to you and has conspired to open the gateway for you?" Let me know what the answer is.

"After your death, you will be what you were before your birth." — Arthur Schopenhauer

Chapter Fifteen – "This is All an Elaborate Hoax" –

Roger Ebert's Review of the Afterlife

"What we call the beginning is often the end. And to make an end is to make a beginning. The end is where we start from." - T.S. Eliot (Photo: Back of Roger Ebert's head as he speaks to Robert DeNiro at a Miramax Oscar event I attended)

"Two thumbs way down" (Roger Ebert, from Siskel & Ebert TV review of my theatrical film "Limit Up.")

My first feature film "You Can't Hurry Love," was hailed as the "Quintessential 80's comedy" by Entertainment Weekly.

It was based on a short film I had made just out of USC film school called "Video Valentino" about a guy who goes to a video dating service to find his soul mate. The film revolved around the idea that everyone in Los Angeles pretends to be someone other than who they are, and when this boy goes to a dating service, he pretends to be different people as well. And of course, the people he meets in L.A. are all pretending to be someone else too. He eventually rails at the camera: "Why do I have to be somebody else in order to be liked?"

My pal Luana Anders had a small role in the short film, where she played the father (yes, the father) of the boy's first date. It was unusual casting – Luana had been in 30 feature films ("Easy Rider" "Shampoo"), and over 300 TV shows. It was the first time where she'd played a man. She found a hefty moustache, popped it on, rolled up her sleeves and in the short film played a very funny version of her friend B.J. Merholz. In the feature film version, released by Vestron in 1989, she plays Macie, the mother of Eddie Hayes, the lead character. She based her character in no small part on my own Aunt Macie, a no nonsense matron from Central Illinois.

Some years after the film came and went I was at a party in the Hollywood Hills when a young woman came up to me and said "You're the guy who directed "You Can't Hurry Love." I loved that film and saw it six times." I looked around to see which of my friends had set me up with this "Candid Camera" moment – so few people saw the film, I assumed she was pulling my leg. [151]

She insisted she was speaking the truth. She said "I was 16 years old when it came out, and it changed my life." Disbelieving, I asked how. She said she got the message that "You don't have to pretend to be someone else in order to be liked. People in my life were trying to get me to pretend to be someone other than who I was, and it saved my life."

I said, to paraphrase a famous film; "Of all the gin joints on the planet, I would come to this one and find the one person who saw my film, who actually understood my film. What on Earth are you doing now?" She said she was currently a development executive at Walt Disney studios. "Well, that's a twist. You should hire me then!" Alas, I never knew her name, and that has yet to happen. But there's still hope.

It's a funny concept; make a film, get all those people to work on it, and the end result is that it changes the life of one person. Perhaps it's a stretch, but it reminds me of the quantum butterfly effect; you really never know who your work is meant to influence on the planet.

For my second feature film I decided to tackle a story about the first woman soybean trader at the Chicago Board of Trade. My brother Robbie was working in

---

[151] The film was made for a million and I was told by producer Larry Kasanoff that it made ten million, but learned later it had been deliberately "buried" by the distribution team at Vestron for bizarre political reasons.

the soybean pit downtown, and he pointed out there was only one woman trader in the room of 250 men. I was curious about how this woman had achieved the impossible, breaking the gender barrier at one of the oldest, wealthiest male dominated institutions in the world. After all, these fellows set the food prices for everyone in the world, their institution was one of the last bastions of males, and it was next to impossible for a woman to obtain a trader's badge.

So I wrote a Faustian tale; Nancy Allen plays Casey Falls, a runner in the soybean pit with a desire to become a soybean trader, who sells her soul to become a successful soybean trader. A mysterious character named Nike plays the devil's advocate ("Saturday Night Live"'s Danitra Vance) and claims she can help Casey become successful beyond her wildest dreams.

What Casey doesn't know is that Nike is actually her guardian angel, and works for Ray Charles, who is God. And the reason she's orchestrated this event is to get the price of soybeans to drop to help starving people across the planet.

Entertainment Weekly liked it, gave me a B+, but Gene Siskel and Roger Ebert gave it a hearty "thumbs way down." Their review effectively killed the theatrical run overnight and the film disappeared from sight. I had argued with the producer that he had to get Roger Ebert to review my film. I claimed that Ebert and Siskel's review was the only one that counted, and as it turned out, I was right.

"Compared to the genuine wit of such financial comedies as "Trading Places" or the know-how of movies like "Wall Street," "Limit up" is lame-brained and cornball" wrote Roger. "I wouldn't mind seeing a movie in which the devil tries to manipulate the futures markets (some say it happens every day), but why this wishy-washy, goody-goody copout comedy that doesn't even have the nerve to follow through on its own instincts? -- A promising mix, and yet the movie is witless from one end to the other." [152]

My flight of fancy turned into his flight from the theater.

At the time, Luana read the review to me over the phone. I asked her to edit out all the negative parts of the review and just to read me the parts that weren't negative. She said "Limit Up... (long pause) is a promising mix." (Still makes me laugh.)

---

[152] Roger Ebert. "Limit Up" Nov 3rd, 1989 Chicago Sun-Times

But sometimes one man's failure turns into another man's success. The company distributing the film pulled it, and I was stuck in Burbank one day, contemplating my fate, when I got a call from an old friend from Kindergarten, who wanted to know if I could help two recent film school graduates from Chicago.

Since I had nothing better to do, my career effectively on hold, I took them out to dinner and did my best my best to talk them out of pursuing a career in Hollywood. The pain and rejection Hollywood doles out is done in dramatic fashion. But their enthusiasm was infectious, and I found myself doing the opposite. They both wanted to be cameramen and I asked if they had shot any footage that might be able to demonstrate their talents; they had not. I told them they needed to create a "reel."

I had just met the new head of Roger Corman's production company and I called and told him I was sending over two filmmakers who needed to get a reel under their belts, and best of all, were willing to work for free. I told the boys they'd shoot second unit, the drive-bys and vistas for Roger's films, and that footage could help start their careers. But I also said to them; "But don't forget to thank me at Oscar time."

The first cameraman was Janusz Kaminski. Five years later he shot "Schindler's List," and most of Steven Spielberg's epic films, including "Saving Private Ryan." I called him before the nominations came out and said "Don't forget, you promised to thank me!" Sure enough, he won the Oscar, and during his speech paused to say "I'd like to thank... *all my friends* who helped me get here." I like to think that I'm in that mix.

And wouldn't you know it, the other cameraman was Mauro Fiore who won the Oscar for shooting "Avatar." He too said "I'd like to thank all my friends who helped me get here." So I like to think that I'm in there somewhere as well. I'd hate to think that Roger Ebert's review led to these fellows getting their careers going, but you never really know how one event can lead to a different outcome for someone else.

Is it coincidence or kismet? Or is there some more elaborate plan involved? Kismet means the same thing in a number of languages; Turkish, Hindu and Persian; "destiny" or "fate." As mentioned, people claim they have "life planning sessions" in the between-lives realm, where with their loved ones and spiritual elders, they work out the highlights of the next lifetime coming up. There's no script involved, that life is in no way "predetermined" – but that we do make contracts with people, agreements that we're going to see our roles through to the end. Was it predetermined that Roger would spend his life using words to express himself, then at the end of his life lose his ability to speak? Was it kismet that he met his wife Chaz and she became his voice? The only way to know the answer to that would be to ask Roger himself. Perhaps Chaz can answer that herself. Here's what she said nine months after his death:

> When you have somebody like that and they are not there, there's a lot of energy gone," says Chaz Ebert, who married the film critic in July 1992. "And yet, I still feel his energy with me most times. There was one period, about a month ago, where I felt like he was abandoning me. It's difficult to explain. And now I could tell he wasn't. The energy was just changing, and now he's around me even more. [153]

So the good news is that Roger Ebert's wife Chaz will see him again. Danitra Vance passed away a few years after we made the film "Limit Up" together. In my case, I apologized to her mother for not doing a better job with the film – if I had made a better film, her talent would have been more appreciated, and perhaps her life would have been different. I do know that when I see Danitra again, I'll make that point to her myself.

My brother Jeffry worked with Roger at the University of Illinois school paper at the Champaign-Urbana campus. When I ran into Roger at an airport after a film festival, I introduced myself and he said he remembered working with my brother. It was then he introduced me to his fiancée Chaz. I never got around to asking why he so disliked my film "Limit Up."

Years later Roger was diagnosed with cancer and had his own "Flipside" experience. And his wife Chaz saved his life. He wrote about it later – how he had "died" in the hospital after surgery, and how his wife had "heard" him saying "I'm still here, I still have things to do." He wasn't speaking, he had been pronounced dead, but Chaz still heard his voice in her head.

She argued with the doctors and convinced them to revive him – and they did. So when he wrote months later that he still didn't "believe in an afterlife" or that he could speak unconsciously to his wife – even though she clearly heard him – I was surprised. Here's the person he loves the most on the planet proving to him that

---

[153] Sundance: Chaz Ebert on the Emotional Roller Coaster Behind 'Life Itself' Variety. 1-12-14.

consciousness exists outside the brain, at least in his case, and still, he couldn't believe it.

Recently, an interview appeared in Esquire Magazine with Chaz about her recollection of Roger's final days:

> The one thing people might be surprised about—Roger said that he didn't know if he could believe in God. He had his doubts. But toward the end, something really interesting happened. That week before Roger passed away, I would see him and he would talk about having visited this other place. I thought he was hallucinating. I thought they were giving him too much medication. **But the day before he passed away, he wrote me a note: "This is all an elaborate hoax." I asked him, "What's a hoax?" And he was talking about this world, this place. He said it was all an illusion. I thought he was just confused. But he was not confused. He wasn't visiting heaven, not the way we think of heaven. He described it as a vastness that you can't even imagine. It was a place where the past, present, and future were happening all at once.** (Chaz Ebert on Roger's final moments (emphasis added)) [154]

Roger was a wordsmith. He spent his life using words to describe what he's seen up on the screen, championing independent filmmakers, or European films that people weren't aware of, rooting for the underdog. He was passionate about his craft, and he was at the top of his game for a long, long time, writing for the Chicago Sun Times. By the time Roger had this experience, the cancer in his jaw had robbed him of the ability to speak, so writing what he wanted to express was something he thought a lot about. This was how he wanted to express this profound revelation to the woman he loved most on the planet.

"It's all an elaborate hoax."

He might have said "It's all a movie" or "It's all a theatrical piece" which is echoed in this research. "Hoax" implies there's someone behind a curtain, like the Wizard in Oz, pulling something over on people. Hoax is defined as a "malicious prank." But he added that reality is an "illusion" – which is the same word heard in many NDEs and LBLs. I'd argue it's the way film is an illusion. Ironic the world's most famous film critic didn't use that metaphor.

---

[154] "as told to Chris Jones" Esquire 12-24-13 "Oral histories of 2013: Roger Ebert's wife, Chaz, on his final moments"

But it appears that each of us interprets these visuals and experiences in our own way. What appears to some during an NDE as an incredible interconnectivity of us all, was not what he observed.

When Apple founder Steve Jobs was on his deathbed, he also experienced a strange phenomenon just prior to his passing. He reportedly stared at his wife, children and sister "for a long time" and then looked right past them, as if seeing something or someone else. According to his wife, his last words were, "Oh wow. Oh wow. Oh wow." Sometimes people's last words seem to be the first words they say upon entering the next realm. [155] Was what Steve Jobs observed similar to what Roger Ebert observed?

The question is, who's behind this "malicious prank" called reality? And is that what Ebert meant? Or is it more of a construct that reality doesn't have inherent meaning, but is acted out, the way performances and stories are acted out on stage. "It's all an act" might be more appropriate (and less harsh than "hoax.") Still... It could all be a trick, or "just a game" perpetrated by someone with a great sense of humor. (Rod Serling perhaps? Cue the "Twilight Zone" music)

During a session in "Flipside" one person claimed that there are other places to incarnate, but this is the ballpark everyone wants to come to; ballpark meaning a game. And when someone enters the game, like a gladiator in the Coliseum, it's a life and death event. If you aren't fully invested in the play, then there's no point to it. Or if you already know how it ends, it lacks any power to teach.

When we examine these reports from the "Flipside" we find that no one but you is pulling the strings - albeit with help from spirit guides and other resources - but we experience events and problems in our paths because we put them there, to examine them, to learn from them - to learn compassion for others. We are instrumental in constructing the game, whatever it is.

Perhaps "game" is too light of a word, or "theatrical event" seems too whimsical to describe the vastness of human experience. University might be a more apt description, being on Earth is like being in an intense class where we all participate on the level of understanding and learning that we're accustomed to. Some of us are more invested in the day to day experience in that classroom environment than others, and as some excel at their lessons, mastering them fully, others have a more difficult time of it, not really comprehending why or how they've signed up for what appears to be an insurmountable assignment.

[155] "Steve Jobs's last words: 'Oh wow. Oh wow. Oh wow." The Guardian, 10-31-11

But at the end of the semester, we're all get off the bus so to speak – we gather up our schoolbooks and paper, our toys and our pencils, and we celebrate the ride we've just taken.

It's odd – I gave the following speech at my high school graduation 40 years ago, and it's just sprung back into my mind and seems an apt metaphor for the journey we all take during a lifetime. It seems like I've always had the "Flipside" in the back of my mind. Let's dissolve back to 1973. I was 18 years old.

After taking the stage I paused and screamed at the top of my lungs for 10 seconds. Then I apologized and said "I'll bet everyone here has wanted to do that at least once in the past four years, and now seems like as good a time as any." I looked down at my family, grandmother and friends in their seats and said:

> I could stand here and say what everyone knows – it's the end of four long years... four tedious years, filled with complacency and excitement all on the same ride. But what intrigues me about these four years - which may be seen as one long bus ride - are not the places we have been nor the places and plans we are heading towards in the future.
>
> A bus ride is not a bus ride without people; screaming kids, screaming teachers, even reckless bus drivers. Each year of school is like a bus ride with its huge chuck-holes and its small bumps that keep us on the edge of our seats in anticipation of the next jolt.
>
> Freshman year has to be the most hectic of all, getting on a new bus, seeing new riders, sort of flitting around in a state of bliss, thinking about days to come and people to meet. Pretty soon one gets to know the ins and outs of the bus, grabbing a favorite seat, the best place to sit, finding who to sit with, what part of the bus to sit in, whatever. Sophomore and junior years, the traumas slip by quickly, making them seem to be just another railroad crossing ... or just another rest-room stop. In retrospect, some fell off the bus, while others were pushed.
>
> The rest of us hold on for dear life. We learn how some riders shelter themselves from us... and how to shelter ourselves from other riders.
>
> But this year is the end of the line. Already there are new faces on the bus; the Class of <u>1976?</u> Of course, during the ride we even find the bus drivers are as much rookies as we are. And riders get bored going over

the same bumps and they get tired of themselves and each other. They say, "Man, I can't wait to get off this bus... I'm tired of these drivers and rules and NO SMOKING, the dirty seats and lousy rest-rooms – I just can't wait to get off this bus!"

A handful of people and I have lived in this small town, Northbrook, for 18 years. And getting off at the end of the line seems pretty scary – even terrifying. But here it is – tonight the doors burst open and the drivers yell "everybody out!" whether you want to leave or not. And while most of us will scramble off the bus, climbing out the windows, others will mill around patting each other goodbye, sitting one last time in their favorite seat, getting once last glance at the graffiti on the back of the seat in front of them which will forever be there.

And here we stand, on a street corner of time, looking down streets that lead us forward ... or backward – streets that lead us to any way we want to go. Five hundred people scratching their heads, wondering what can have brought it on, and wondering why it was so long coming. A humorous sight, bewildering to say the least.

But in light of this metaphor there's a point I'd like to make from my heart; wherever you go and wherever you find yourself, there's one thing to remember – these years have been an experience – whatever you make of the ride, at least you've gone somewhere and met and shared with others on the way. Many you'll never see again – ever ... many you'll never want to see again – ever. But each person has left their footprints on you – they've left an indelible mark that won't disappear with age. Thank you for sharing the ride with me. [156]

This speech reminds me of a sentence that popped into my head the other day. "Who are we but the echoes of each other's footsteps?" We are the carriers of each other's memories, and those memories will never go away. It appears I've been thinking about the journey of souls for quite some time.

Recently, Roger's wife Chaz was interviewed about her ongoing connection to her husband Roger. She prefers the term "wife" to "widow" as she's still married to him.

---

[156] 1973 Graduation speech Glenbrook North High School, Northbrook, IL.

Anna Sale: What changed between you two when he was no longer able to talk to you with his voice?

Chaz Ebert: Almost nothing, because Roger and I developed almost a mental telepathy. We were so in tune with each other that we actually could speak to each other without words or without even being in the same room.

Like a deep ability to understand what he was prompting, like what he wanted to communicate?

I don't know. To me, I actually heard his voice in my head.

Really?

Yeah... Sometimes when he was in the hospital, I would wake up in the middle of the night and I would call the hospital and... say, "Oh my God, he is so cold, would you please go in and put the warming blanket on him?" And the nurse would come back and go, "Well how do you know? Did he call you?" And they would say, "Well he couldn't call you, he can't speak." And I said, "I don't know, but he just told me it was cold."...

When was the last time you heard his voice in your head?

Hmm. Very recently. He still talks to me.

You feel his presence? And you hear it, I mean you hear it?

Yeah, I do... I don't know why Roger and I were brought together, I do feel that there's — it almost feels like a destiny to it, because there are some parts of our getting together that didn't make sense. And our bond was so strong that I wondered about it. I mean, and now the fact that he still is in touch with me and communicates with me, that's also — I mean it's a wondrous thing.

Does that make you feel less sad?

It does. It's very comforting, because he lets me know that he's okay. He's more than okay. He is blissful.

Because when he was nearing death, in the documentary, it shows that he died when he was ready to go, and you weren't quite ready for him to go.

That's correct.

And do you feel like it's been reassuring to know that he was ready?

It is so reassuring. It just makes me smile to know that he is this, I don't know what he is. I don't know what form we're in. But I know that it's something that's comforting. And it feels so natural and so normal and I know that there are a lot of things that we shut down talking about in our society, because, (there are) things that we can't prove. But now I firmly, firmly believe in an afterlife.

Did you believe in an afterlife before he passed?

I don't know. I don't know what I thought happened after death. I haven't had this experience — I've lost several family members, my mother, my father, two brothers, and two sisters, and the rest. I haven't had an experience like this that I'm having with Roger, where he kind of reports back... I have zero fear of death. Zero. What I do talk about with my children and grandchildren is living... And telling them to find their passion in life and live it. Because we don't know how much time is promised to us.[157]

I'm glad Chaz still has Roger with her. They're obviously deeply connected, and it's rare to hear about it in a public forum. And what she's saying about their connection, is repeated over and over again in the research.

And despite the perceived negativity of his review of the meaning of life - "It's all an elaborate hoax" – we don't know if he considered that to be a "thumbs up" or "thumbs down" revelation.

But I'm sure Gene Siskel will set him straight.

They both get two "big thumbs up" from yours truly.

---

[157] "Chaz Ebert on Life Without Roger" August 27, 2014. WNYC interview by Anna Sale

"O my love is like a red, red rose, that's newly sprung in June, O my love's like the melody that's sweetly played in tune. So deep in love am I, and I will love thee still, until all the seas run dry." A card from my dad to my mom on their 49th wedding anniversary.

Chapter Sixteen - "Swing for the Fences"

"Being a Humanist means trying to behave decently without expectation of rewards or punishment after you are dead." — Kurt Vonnegut (Photo of Marcus Aurelius from Capitoline Hill in Rome pointing to the next home run)

When I was a Humanities student at Boston University, I attended a Kurt Vonnegut lecture where he challenged students to rhyme the word "orange." Some twenty years later I saw him on the street in Manhattan, went up to him and reminded him of the challenge. "What rhymes with orange? Door-hinge." He smiled, nodded, and without missing a beat said "Now try purple."

In "Flipside" I reported my two between-life sessions, each one two years apart. My first session was at the suggestion of Michael Newton and was conducted on the spur of the moment by hypnotherapist Jimmy Quast. At the time, I felt it was the perfect opportunity to prove or disprove this method, as I was determined to not be "led" into seeing something I did not see. However, that didn't turn out to be the case.

And then two years later, after finishing my documentary, I was offered the chance to do another session. I felt it was an opportunity to examine what I'd seen before, and to see if any details might be different in this second experience. It turned out, the second session was more powerful than my first, and lasted six hours.

I had the feeling as if a gate had been left open for me, as if my "higher self" had been waiting for two years for my return to this realm, so we could pick up the conversation where we had left off two years earlier.

As recounted in "Flipside," I was able to learn a number of details about the between lives realm; I learned there are classrooms where teachers taught the manipulation of energy in various forms. I visited these classrooms where students appeared to learn how to manipulate, or clean up geometric shapes, or fractals of energetic memory that we carry during our lives. I visited a classroom where my friend Luana was learning details of how to help transfer healing energy into doctors, healers and others in health professions here on Earth.

I learned a number of profound insights about my own life, and ultimately is what's kept me doing this research. Scott De Tamble did the second session, and asked if we were going to do a third session for "It's A Wonderful Afterlife."

We wound up doing two. [158] The following is the first session, conducted in Scott's office in Claremont, California (lightbetweenlives.com).

Scott and Richard

Scott: *One month, two weeks, before birth and in the womb now... feel the protection of this dark warm environment... what do you perceive?*

Richard: Laughter and music. My mom is a concert pianist, already I'm hearing the sounds of someone playing the piano. I guess it's her.

How do you feel physically?

It feels like there's plenty of room; I'm comfortable, up for the adventure. Ready to rock and roll (chuckles).

---

[158] The second part of the session is in Volume Two of "It's A Wonderful Afterlife"

How about the music and laughter?

It's pleasant, like "what a great place to be!" Mom's got a great sense of humor, great outlook, upbeat personality, pretty happy. Yeah. Good choice all around.

Why is that?

I get the sense that I'm coming along for a ride with my dad whom I've known before, and it's all part of our journey together. My dad has found this magical, musical, funny ball of light for a wife, my mom.

What month is this?

I'd say around the 8th month at this particular moment – 7 or 8.

The Ferrari

What month did you join?

The fourth (I said the same in my first session of "Flipside" – so I can't be sure if I was influenced by that memory or if this was a confirmation).

What was your first impression of the situation? The baby?

The metaphor that comes to mind is dropping into the seat of a Ferrari. It's already traveling at a great speed, (and) you're adjusting to the speed, (you quickly) adjust the dials - you're in one realm and then boom, you're in the seat of this car that is going really fast! But it's fun, a great ride to join.

It's like as if you're shifting your energy from one realm to the next - in this case, going from another realm to this realm - you have to adjust all of the circuits simultaneously. (It's) almost like being in a jet/rocket ship kind of vehicle, but traveling on Earth, let's say, and suddenly you're going to shift down to... You're going a thousand miles an hour to (down) shift to 200 miles an hour, and so there's the jerk your body feels – all - your - *everything* feels.

All (of) your energetic ethereal body has to downshift and then match things up, simultaneously, super quickly. Connecting all of the energetic pieces and shifting so that you can get used to this realm and this ride.[159]

So it's not like you dip your toe into the pool?

Not in my case, it may be for others. What came to mind was just falling into a Ferrari seat, of a car that was already traveling quite fast. But I feel (it's) like I'm downshifting to a slower speed, but still going pretty fast, you're trying to – only (I can) see it as a pilot in a jet plane (suddenly) trying to get all the switches connected (while the car is racing). (It) makes me think that some people don't get a proper connection in order to make it work right, but that could be just me.

How does the soul downshift? What do you need to do?

The metaphor I'm sensing is mixing oil and water – they don't really mix - but in this case they have to – so you're making all the oil molecules that are viscous and thick and slippery sort of shift into the water molecules. They all have to blend and move simultaneously together.

And if you can think of water molecules as energetic systems, like electricity – you're blending these two – here you are blending the faster energy into the slower energy and there're spaces between the atoms. You have to fill each space simultaneously; the best picture I can think of is taking another substance and blending it in at the same time. And as it sort of blends into the body, you're connecting with the electrical pattern of the human; for lack of a better term.

Do you will this to happen, or do you do this at the molecular level? Are you like an artist doing this?

The decision's already been made all along the way, everyone's in agreement where you're going and you're showing up into this little tiny Ferrari that's growing. You know; it's from fish to the fish tail and all that stuff, and the central nervous system is starting to construct itself, and cells are multiplying all the time. And so the trick is to find the right entry point- time wise and energetically.

I mean some people don't show up till later, but when you decide to actually shift your gears - shift your energy into this Ferrari, that's when you make that move.

---

[159] This car metaphor hasn't appeared in sessions I've filmed or am aware of. During this experience, I have the unusual feeling I'm connected both consciously and subconsciously to the questions – as if I'm never "under" in the classic sense – but not stressed or worried that I'm not. I try to allow whatever pops into my head to be said, to come onto the page so to speak, and I do my best not to edit whatever is being said.

And of course, when you're suddenly inside the cockpit, you're now aware - because (up until this point) it's theoretical. Prior to being inside - you're thinking "What it's going to be like?"

You're thinking "I've done this before, how hard can this be?" But then (when) you actually make the shift, you now have to adjust everything. "This (switch) is working, but this (panel) is not working," "Ok, where are all these things eventually going to go in terms of your switches?"[160]

And that's why you can have problems. You can think you're going to have a smooth or blended induction, (and) there can always be bumps along the way – but in this case (of my own induction), it worked out just fine.

How do you determine the right entry point time wise?

We flip a coin. (Chuckles)

It's hard to say, it's like saying "at what point does the sun rise?" and you're sort of waiting and waiting, and then finally here it comes, this is the right moment as this ray of light blasts across the Earth's surface, that's the moment I'm going to do it...

Does somebody tell you it's the right moment?

I imagine somebody could tell you (when to make the transition) but in my case it wasn't (done) - it was "Now's the time, here we go." Certainly you can show up earlier (to the fetus), from inception or prior to inception. You can show up and hang out, check out what the energetic patterns are of the parents, sort of gauge when would be the good time. And then there's the (question) "Do I really want to jump into this Ferrari at this moment?"

Because once you're in, you're in. You can float around (the body) and check around other stuff (prior to that), but by and large, you've made that commitment to that entity, to that (car) race. You're going to jump in the car and (are) not going to get out for a long time, so you want to get in at (precisely) the right time – you know, it's just "everything is timing."

---

[160] In my mind's eye, I'm seeing a pilot who has suddenly appeared in this cockpit of a speeding bumpy red Ferrari and he is trying to adjust or flip the appropriate switches, reaching above and over his shoulder to turn them on or off, but finding that some do not work as planned, or when flipped the instrument panel doesn't work as planned, so he must make immediate adjustments.

In your case as Richard, when you jump into the cockpit, is it like what you expected, are there any surprises? Dials going into the red, or you go "Oh, woops!"

In my case, I don't see that - as a construct it's a possibility. You could say "Oh my gosh. The emotional triggers in this entity are much greater (than I thought they were)" but at this (fetal) stage, they're very rudimentary. Plus you're adjusting (yourself to enter) as an artist, as an artist pilot, (so) you make the adjustment.

As you discover broken switches, you're thinking "Okay, this is going to be a problem." And some people think "I can handle this," but they can't. It's too much, it's too fast, you're trying to turn around and adjust the levers or switches as you're making the transition and the car is suddenly out of control. But in my case, it feels like I've chosen somebody ... Not "connected" - it's the wrong word – more like "aligned" with kind of what or who I am, in-between lives.[161]

So this body or person you're going to be is as a vehicle, is a good match for you?

Yeah absolutely. Yeah, I get that.

Any contrasts between this soul and your current vehicle or personality?

Sometimes you really want to put your (gas pedal) foot to the floor and really take off - and there's regulators – you know, the thing you put on an engine that dictates how much fuel goes in? And you have these regulators, one of those things you can tighten or loosen up (to adjust the performance of the engine); it's a delicate balance.

Meaning if you choose somebody (without consideration) and you think "Well, I'm (just) going to jump off the cliff, I don't care what happens to other people or what happens to this person" – it can be disastrous, like driving without really looking in your rear view mirror or (knowing) where you're going.

In this case, it's like there are filters in everybody, every brain -- that you have to adjust to. But ultimately it's like, "Ok, we're in a Ferrari, we're going for a ride, what's the big deal?" Some filters work and some don't.

---

[161] I was speaking quite rapidly at this point, and I've added parentheses to explain the concepts, as they are now available in my conscious memory to remember what I was trying to say. Odd, but true.

It's like your soul is saying it's going to have so much energy... It's got some Chutzpah.

(Laughs) It has a lot to do with chutzpah, when you're going to jump into this car... I mean I feel like it's always the case, everyone's different, everyone has a different experience. Some jump in and (immediately) say "Whoa, where's the brake? How do I slow down? I don't like this!" or "I've really got to floor it, this car needs a tune up."

Part of it is (understanding) what you are here to do. Where are you going with the car, where are you taking the car, (where are the) pits stops along the way, who is your crew? Is your crew going to be talented and helpful? But it is interesting as a metaphor, it popped into my head, it kind of fits.

Because the car is already going when you climb in; and some people don't show up until the ninth month. Talk about having courage! "Just jump in man, here you go!" Whew!

Or another metaphor would be bull riding. If you think of a lifetime as that eight second bull ride – not a lot of guys can climb onto a bull that's ready to buck you off. And (really) ride that thing, it's anticipating what's going to happen next, and being part of the bull, going with the flow and all that stuff maybe it's an extreme metaphor – but it's like eight seconds of riding the bull it's equivalent to an entire lifetime.

If you slowed the ride down and watched every decision in slow motion; everything's a choice, turn right, turn left, put your weight this way, the same goes with joining the fetus and hanging on for dear life.[162]

In For A Penny, in for a Pound

When you entered the fetus do you stay put? Or do you still move in and out from time to time during the next five months before you're born?

---

[162] I directed second unit for the film "Cowboy Up" – Kiefer Sutherland and Daryl Hannah, about the sport of bull riding - which meant six months of shooting bull rides from inside the chute. A successful ride is counted by eight seconds; if the rider can stay on that long he's "ridden the bull." Many don't make it that long, but I'm pretty familiar here with this cowboy metaphor.

In my case, I feel like I just stuck around. I was "in for a penny, in for a pound" as they say; it's an immersive experience and you signed up for it -- so why not just experience it? I know some people feel like they want to hang out or go and visit their friends; they're always connected, never separate, but in my case I really felt like we're in the car, so let's go. I'll have plenty of time to be outside the car - that will happen soon enough, but until then, let's see how this goes, experience it.

At this point, do you have any inkling about why you chose this body? This family?

I feel that I'm following my dad, Charlie; we've done this before, and it just went without saying we would have another adventure.

And this particular individual that I've chosen, I had a sense he was going to be involved in filmmaking, and I thought it was an outside the box kind of way to use what I consider to be healing energy, helping people, something I've always been interested in.

And as a filmmaker the idea was for Richard to become somebody who through the use words, music, creative energies, could heal people through film. I kind of was aiming in that direction, but not all of the dials, not all the switches lined up exactly as they should have. But that's okay.

(Note: I explored this concept in my first session as to why I chose Richard, as discussed in "Flipside." When I said it for the first time, it was a revelation, it felt like this time I was repeating what I'd already learned on the process. "Not all the switches lined up" is a reference to not being as "successful," let's say, as I imagined I would be.)

Well you're still in the game.

Exactly. We haven't run out of gas yet.

Anything else you notice in this time before you're born?

Just that it's also akin to jumping onstage. Not to keep mixing metaphors, but there's a moment before the curtain goes up and you stand backstage with your friends. You know your script, you're in your costume, and you're ready to go onstage. You can't see the audience, but you know they're there, you can hear them rustling out there, there's a moment before, when the butterflies kick in.

Some say if you don't have butterflies you don't care; there is that moment before incarnation, before joining the fetus, where you're literally offstage, and you're anticipating the adventure of the curtain going up.

Literally it comes up as you're coming out of the womb; there are the bright lights, sometimes there's applause, sometimes there's a spank - as happened to me - so you can catch your oxygen. That's a wonderful feeling that I'm aware of, just prior to the curtain going up. The excitement of the adventure; lights, music, and... action.

I get the sense there's some folks here (in Scott's office). I close my eyes and I can see lights moving. I can tell you the experience I'm having, is almost like I'm allowing my conscious mind and my subconscious mind to have this conversation. The image of dropping into the Ferrari – something I've never thought or considered ever - my conscious mind allowed me to examine it. The images that come forward are allowing me to explain it – it feels like I'm split, but it feels right.

Friends Waiting to Speak

When we've studied this as much as you have, it's not the same as the first time.

I'm not judging myself as I'm talking. There's usually the yin yang of the feeling of "I'm making this up." But I'm fine with it.

It's okay to have your conscious mind participate?

When I first heard your voice I went into this vision of a closet; I saw this party going on, including people we might talk to that might be accessible to us.

Now if I ask your soul mind, who is here with us?

Luana.

(Note: Luana Anders is my oft-mentioned friend who died and came to visit me, and then seemed to escort me to a place in another galaxy where she resides. Luana's passing was the catalyst for this adventure into the afterlife.)

What is her message for you?

"Wake up." She's responding to my request be here. My mom comes to mind, my dad, and my spirit guide Ray – Rayma. I'm being told "Everybody you asked for is here." I guess that's a matter of putting the call out and saying "who wants to talk or speak up?" Who has something to say?

(Note: When I met my spirit guide Rayma during the first session, I saw him clearly as a friend and mentor. In my second session two years later, I was able to achieve a moment where it felt like I had transported my consciousness into Rayma's point of view for lack of a better term. I was able to see myself through Rayma's eyes as Richard – but as "the higher-self Richard." That was a humbling experience, because for all the exuberance I have, seeing it from another's point of view can seem, well, a bit over the top. But in this case, when seeing Rayma, I feel now like he's always around, just around the bend, on call if need be.)

We're going to take Rich into a past life now. If there's guidance as to which past life he needs to look at today, we welcome that. (Takes me deeper into the subconscious) Three two one, be there now. Day or night?

Daytime. Outdoors. I'm standing in a pool of clear blue water up to my ankles. It's comfortable, feels like it's the Mediterranean. Weather is warm, sunny, clouds, blue sky. Clear water. Sand, but not too far from a city of some kind.

Is it still water?

It's like a sea. Like the Mediterranean Sea. Smooth, maybe an inlet of some sort, but very clear blue. It feels like maybe Greece...

The name of this city?

Piraeus. Port of Athens.

(Note: When I went to school in Rome we spent our spring break in Greece. I traveled to Athens, Piraeus, then some of the smaller islands like Hydra and Poros. I had no special feeling of a connection with Greece, except perhaps a dramatic afternoon on the island of Corfu.[163] But when I say "Piraeus" – I know where that is, and have been there.)

---

[163] Easter in Corfu is quite dramatic. Thousands of unlit candles are handed out and one flame from the church is passed until only candlelight from thousands of candles lights the Greek night. There's an outdoor midnight mass, which ends in soldiers firing machine guns with tracers into the sky and a massive fireworks display. Easily the most dramatic, noisiest Easter I've ever witnessed (in this life).

What's the environment like?

Behind me is the port where the ships and trade (occurs) and (there are) people and the general nonsense of the city.

Are you male or female?

Male. I'm 23. Medium sized. Wearing cotton tunic - people wore of that era. Goes to my thigh, so I can be in the water up to my knees and not get wet. There's like a rope that ties around the middle. The tunic is sandy colored, color of sand.

Notice the appearance, the face, the hair, the eyes.[164]

The hair is dark, not black, brown with a lot of tight curls. A little shaggy. Skin is bronze color – like olive color but in the sun a lot. Olive and tan, but a bronze color. Clean shaven. Grey-blue eyes. Thin and handsome, and sort of an athlete. Not muscular, just healthy, athletic.

Move behind the grey blue eyes and look out through, connect with the thoughts and feelings of this young man. What's going through your mind?

He's thinking about his girlfriend, she's not available, she's been married off to somebody else. Sort of that poetic angst of looking out at the ocean and trying to figure out what it's all about – that heartache of loss, feeling like there's something more eternal by just connecting to the ocean, a bigger message, it's part of nature or something.

(Note: Since I was young, I found sitting by the ocean and staring at the waves a profoundly calming other worldly experience. It wasn't until I wrote this sentence that this memory returned to me.)

Scan back and forth through time, how do you spend your days?

I'm an apprentice, working for an artist in casting of statuary, bronze, learning the skills of putting casts together and how you melt – you put wax between the clay between the outer thing, then you put in the bronze, then you polish it, that's how you create statues.

---

[164] For the sake of editing, each answer came with the question. I've edited the questions out so that it's easier to read.

How did you do that?

You melt the bronze in a huge kiln until it becomes liquid, so the artist, the maestro, the master creates the statue, and then wax is put around the clay statue, and then another level of clay is put around that, you leave holes in it, and you melt the wax out of the statue and you replace it with bronze.

(Note: When I was in college, I studied sculpture with Peter Rockwell, son of the famous painter, and at some point learned of this "lost wax" process which I'm describing. As I recount the process here however, I am seeing the elements of how it occurs in my mind's eye with the tools used centuries ago.)

How is that done?

The wax is heated, so it's pliable and you can pack it, slap on clay onto something, you're plastering it on, then you do this outer layer, which is another shell – not quite clay, some other substance, it's colored like clay. It's like a mold, an outer mold. You heat up the statue and the wax runs out like a candle – you replace that with (molten) bronze – it's a timing thing because the bronze has to be at a certain temperature, it's dangerous.

What does the bronze look like before it's solid?

Rocks that you have to melt down and you sift out the impurities, until it's this copper colored goop, liquid, very hot, and you have to be super careful to pour it into the mold – there's all kinds of huge calipers to lift the stuff up, move it over, and I'm doing this because I'm hoping to be an artist one day. [165]

Do you make your own statues?

I do on my own, not the way this guy.... I'm just one of the apprentices, he's got a whole bunch. You know, (ones) who showed a little aptitude and you were brought into his school.

What's the master's name?

I don't have a fix, just a face of a bearded guy with a yellow blondy beard, flowing robes – Patros, something like that – Petrosian – Petros.

---

[165] Bronze is a combination of copper and tin – I've subsequently looked up how the process is done, which is reportedly correctly here; "rocks" in my minds-eye refer to what tin and copper look like in their raw, clumped form.

(Note: "The House of Petros" is a common term in ancient Greece to refer to a master's home. Petros means Peter. The term appears in the "Hellenic fragments" of the Bible, but I would assume there were many patrons with the name in this period.)

How old is he?

In his 50's. But he's like ancient, overweight, feels like an old dude, old school.

What's his persona?

Gruff, very class conscious guy, aware of the fact that he's from an upper class background. You know, (it's a) very patrician society where you don't exist unless you're part of an upper class group. He treats his plebes, workmen, as slaves really, just not focused on him.

What's your status? A slave?

No, I'm freeborn. My parents might have been captured slaves, it's possible.

Let's go back in time to a scene from your boyhood between 5 and 15. Where did you grow up?

Dad's a fisherman, owns fishing nets, catches fish, I've got a few brothers and sisters. From an early age I liked to make little creatures, dolls, figurines, out of mud and clay and sticks and whatever was available, eventually it's what caught the attention of a teacher who brought me into his school which brought me to the attention of this Sculptor. There's a transaction, the sculptor pays my dad a certain amount of money for my servitude – you're not free to run away, but you're just an apprentice, you're learning a trade and part of this guy's group – from the House of Petros, that allows you a certain amount of credibility and ego.

You liked to make clay figures?

Yeah. A little figurine I make for my mom, made of sticks and strings, little pieces of jewelry, it's a bird that I've crafted. Jewels for eyes, a little playful thing. I can make the wings move when I pull on the stick – I'm like six or seven – she seems to appreciate it. "Mom, check it out."

When did you give this to her?

The number 87 comes to mind.

Before the 87?

I just... 8... or it's 78 or it's 87. It may be BC, before numbers started changing, right around the time when it was zero – I want to say beforehand. 87 BC feels like it's right – before those events.[166]

Demetrious

When you give this to your mother, what does she call you?

Dimi. Demetrious.

Tell me about her.

She's not from the region, outside the region – darker hair, hazel eyes and she's short and fun. She's had a few kids, different than most moms, as she has a sense of humor and playfulness. Father works his ass off fishing and my brothers are doing that as well. It seems nobody's bothering me and making me do work; this idea of going to an artisan school is great as I'm not a fan of the fisherman stuff.

Let's move forward to your days as an apprentice. Tell me about this girlfriend.

She's the daughter of one of the patrons who pays my boss. And I meet her when she's about 17 maybe. It's even late for her to be promised, but she's startlingly pretty. Her hair's not like everybody else's, kind of light brown, more blondish and her eyes are hazely green and she's got long hair and she's – people have painted her, so she's an object of beauty, a lot of people talk about her.

What's her name?

Ariadne. [167] I think that's it.

Do you feel she's attracted to you?

I think there's a bit of the element of that she's unattainable, I've talked to her, stared at her and.... there was a connection there that gave me hope that it was

---

[166] The Roman general Sulla sacks Athens and the port of Piraeus in 86 BCE.

[167] Ariadne is a common Greek name, in Greek mythology she was the daughter of Minos, King of Crete. I'm not familiar with anyone, nor have met anyone in this life with this name (or Demetrious.)

going to go my way – her parents shifted things, she was like 16 when I met her, I was like 21. I'm just an apprentice; I knew it was doomed. She's from the upper class, her father's one of the patrons, they have a lot of money and they're going to marry her off to some old man with a lot of money. It's heart breaking to realize you're not going to have kids with someone and they'll live their life with someone else.

What's the place where you sleep?

Like a barracks, all the apprentices are on slabs of wood. Not very comfortable being stuck in a room with guys, but it's ok. Our patron is fairly wealthy so we have everything we need. You're not starving and you're not unclothed, there are nice clothes. The food is good; *Retsina*, a Greek wine, there's cheese, lamb – lots of lamb – seafood, squid, or calamari, lot of salt and olive oil. The food's very clean and healthy. The old man overindulges; he's put on the pounds.

A Big Turn of Events

Let's skip forward a few years, several years, find you in some different phase. One two three, older now.

Just an old man, never married. Living in some kind of hovel, close to the ocean, making art or jewelry for tourists.[168] The people who come from other ports or other countries to Piraeus wander around and stop by my place to pick up trinkets, little medallions, jewelry, necklaces. Harder to get real or good fine silver, create the good things because it costs money. You wind up using cheaper alloys, but the artistry is still pretty good, I make earrings and necklaces, things that women like to purchase.

Do you enjoy this?

It's like my form of meditation, always looking at your work, mold it, shape it. I have someone who runs the shop, an older woman. (She's) my age; she's a cook, maid, takes care of stuff and pays the bills.

Let's go to an important moment in this life, a major turning point. Be there now.

---

[168] "Tourists" for lack of a better term. People from other cities that come to visit Piraeus and want to bring home a souvenir of their trip.

The master accused me of stealing something. I was 31, pretty old for an apprentice. I hadn't stolen anything, I'd used some of his metals to create my own things. He accused me of robbing him, was just trying to get rid of me; time for new apprentices, this was his way of letting me go. Somebody else accused me of theft, he picked up on it, turned me out. That was a big turn of events.

A disgrace?

You're no longer considered at "The House of Petros;" you're on your own. I stayed with friends in Piraeus and eventually started making this jewelry and trinkets for tourists[169] – it's a hard scrabble existence. I'm happy with the work, the artistry, the creativity; you get caught up in creating something and you don't know what day it is, what time it is. When you're done, you're on to the next one; it's very meditative. You're not thinking about what your life could be or should have been; you're really just putting one foot in front of the other.

Any sight of Ariadne?

She married some rich guy and went to Italy; a distant shore and never heard of her again. Just unrequited love, didn't happen.

Did you have any relationships?

I don't see any connection to anyone – I'm sure there was sexuality – normal and average and whatever it was, but no love relationship I can see.

Let's move to the last day of Demetrius.

In my hovel, and I have some kind of stomach illness, like cancer. I've been drinking heavily for a long time now, maybe an ulcer, and ultimately that stomach illness does me in.

How old?

56. Old man. For that era.

What do you think about this life?

I look back and I see the positive things were the artistry and focused on that, it's what the journey seemed to be about. Not connecting to anyone doesn't seem to make any sense.

What about the artistry that's so interesting?

Creation of things requires a lot of focus and energy, and you get better at something. You're more of an artisan than an artist, and you get better at your craft – it's a metaphor for getting wiser, as you get wiser as you keep creating, keep forging ahead.

There are a lot of adventures I could have had, but avoided. I wasn't involved with soldiers or wars, and there wasn't any violence other than self-violence, drinking too much, but no major trauma. It was like the art was always something I could fall back to and it gave me a lot of pleasure, as long as I kept working.

Okay to the moment of death. One two three. Where are you now?

Above it looking down. Amused by the sight of this old beardy fellow, now with beard and white hair, feeling a little compassion and sorrow for him; what might have been, what he should have done. He certainly had skills, and things just didn't turn his way.

He might have had more courage to strike out on his own, find another patron. He had talent and skills and stayed protected until he got kicked out and it was too late to find a new artist to work for. He was happier with security and camaraderie of his fellow workers and he just didn't show a lot of courage, or spunk.

You're looking down? Thinking about that life?

Not so much, just eager to go home. There's no one to notify but the matron to connect with – I can't wake her up, she's sound asleep (laughs). There's no one to mourn me, or mourn this passing.

As you move away, please describe.

I'm feeling the opposite of what we talked about earlier, shifting gears, I'm accelerating, quickly, through the clouds into deep space, moving rapidly, eager to get back to my friends and companions. I'm shooting through, I feel I'm directing it, I'm not being drawn - even though it's the equivalent of magnets being pulled across the table – or it's like gravity, falling back to your home base.

What do you perceive around you?

Feels like I quickly return to this energetic field. **To look at it from the outside, like a beehive of various lights; think of it as dim lights in the distance. Like a tree perhaps and each hive area is like a leaf in this glowing lit tree, I'm passing millions or billions of leaves, all of these are different almost like stars.**

But they're all connected, and as you're passing them you get closer to your group and when you finally get there it's a little bit like a transporter in Star Trek where your energy arrives and you're aware of other entities around you.

And inside, some entities are busy and some are there to greet you and some are focused on other things. I'm aware of about 20-25 entities but it's not like they're waiting to greet me – it's almost like – there's like four or five waiting and the rest are kind of like -- it's like I went off to do an errand an now I'm returning back.

Into a Classroom

Not enthusiastic?

A bit like "Oh, you're back, cool." There's Rayma, he appears in his 60's, hazel eyes, a few wrinkles, kind face. One of those faces that always makes you feel comfortable or welcome, he's happy to see me. Well, happy is a relative term, he's there. I'm getting a woman, maybe two. Kajeera, we've met her before, here. She's quite welcoming.

What's she communicating?

Always very generous and effusive, very complimentary; she's showing me all the wonderful things in that lifetime that I wasn't focused on – the beauty, the things of beauty. **She's pointing out there was something of beauty to experience; sunsets, sunrises, the ocean, the artistic things I made, the people I connected with; all the things that have the energy of beauty.**

She's reminding me, like a teacher would, "Look how good this was." Like a recap. **"You're too hard on yourself, complaining you didn't really accomplish much, it's so much work to be there."** Nobody's judgmental here; everyone's **positive.**

What's her name again?

Kajeera. It's more of a sound than a word. She is somebody that is a teacher; she has a classroom of students.[170]

Is she on the same peer level as you?

I think these four or five people, this is my core group of people; they're teachers. Each one has their own classroom – and the other 15 or 16 are affiliated with us, but just not part of our core group. They're still associated; when we make decisions they're all part of that. I'm kind of expanding on the (concept of) "affiliated groups;" in this case we're all in the same pod when we're at rest, or greeting someone coming back from their incarnation. I'm sensing this four or 5 are the most connected to me.

(Note: Affiliated groups is a term that Michael Newton uses to describe other groups that work with or are connected to a primary soul group. I'm noting that these other groups seem in closer proximity at all times.)

Was Kajeera in Rich's current life?

I don't recognize her other than here; she's a crystal colored light blue. She has a lot of radiance about her; the blue core means she's very wise, got a lot of wisdom and that quality of radiant compassion. The blue is wisdom or oldness, that's not the right word – a level of development of wisdom. This color blue is rich, but it's got streaks of other colors, dark blues and a really crystalline quality that has its own radiance to it.

<u>*Looking through Kajeera's eyes, what color are you?*</u>

[170] In my first LBL I went to Kajeera's classroom. In 2008 I did my first session with Jimmy Quast, I asked my guide Rayma to take me to a classroom and he deposited me at her door. As I entered her class (literally, students in desks, she was at the front of the room), I saw this bright light presence, warm and welcoming, very beautiful. She introduced me to the class as if we were the best of friends, and the class seemed happy to have one of "teacher's friends" appear. When I visited Luana's class later in that session, I had a different experience, which is described elsewhere. But I feel a strong affinity towards Kajeera, and have no other memory of her, other than a member of my soul group here.

A variation of a dark blue, little bit darker than hers – teal blue? My shade signifies qualities of artistry, but also like "You've been around for a while and you've gathered experience," and there's maybe a little compassion. **To examine that for a second; when people examine their color – for example a doctor - all the healing arts here in this realm are associated with the color green.**

A lot of doctor's teachers have a variation of green color, but when you blend these various experiences they become these other colors. As you go through these experiences, your colors add amounts of blue, or red depending on the adventure.

So if you add blue and red you get this purple color; depending on your experiences, this color I'm composed of -- I see there's a penchant for trying to heal – hence the green, which is a green-blue – which is teal.[171]

You're saying it's not just a purple or blue color, but an accumulation of layers?

Like when you take a book and take those plastic sheets and lay one on top of the other? Or like paint; if you examine a painting closely, really examine the molecules, or photons for lack of a better word, **they shimmer with a particular kind of energetic wave with what they like to do and what they've learned to do; their expertise.**

Tell me about these others in your group. Kajeera, Rayma.

My dad, Charlie – can't really focus on a name other than Charlie's.

Anything to communicate?

Always positive, reinforcement of "You did a great job." I admire his talents; he's quite a talented artist, so when he compliments me, it feels like a big deal. I feel like he's wiser and older and more adept than I am at a lot of things, but he's very, very positive.

Kajeera and Charlie – who else?

---

[171] In "Flipside" I said that I saw my own color as a blue color – but as I examine these closely, I see that colors are more like an Impressionist – many bits of color and energy and depending where you look, you can see various color combinations.

They're all within swinging distance, but for reasons of storytelling they aren't making their appearances clear to me; meaning if I figured out who they were, it would hinder my path. Does that make sense?

Nevertheless I will ask for a message from them without revealing identities. The female?

"Keep up the good work" is the message she's got for me; the male says "Don't get so full of yourself."

Conversation with my Spirit Guide

Can Rayma speak with us?

Sure (voice changes). Hello Scott.[172]

Can I speak with you directly?

Love to.

How did Rich perform in that life as Demetrius?

You don't always knock it out of the park when you step up to the plate. But it's worth it to be in the game because there are always lessons to be learned.

What was the main goal or mission of that life?

It had to do with the energy of art, the energy of creation and seeing how that is something he wanted to delve into the energy of; he was able to do that extensively throughout his life. When he began selling, he lost passion for the work and started drinking.

By and large when you sign up for a lifetime to examine the energy of something, that's included; the energy of not being focused. All are variations and aspects of what it means to be creative or what it means to live a life of creating.

---

[172] Scott pointed out to me that Rayma is an actual word; "Rhema" means an "utterance" or "thing said" in Greek. In philosophy, it was used by both Plato and Aristotle. When I note that my voice changes, it didn't appear to be a conscious decision, "Oh I think I'll change my voice here." However, there's always the possibility that's the case.

How was the past lifetime as Demetrius related to the present time as Richard?

Not to be afraid of trying things you haven't tried before, and also to allow yourself to not take outside circumstances as personal setbacks. To swing for the fences. He has a tendency to feel when things don't work or don't go his way he should start a new project, a new piece of work. He doesn't follow through on the original piece. There's something to be said for following through.

Part of the reason he came today was to remind him you can fall down and scrape your knees; it's okay, there's no pejorative there, it's just a learning exercise. If you try to create something, see it through to the end, see what it turns out to be.

Part of the reason was to persevere, what else in this life?

You can allow yourself to wallow in despair or what appears to be failure and you wind up taking drugs or alcohol or altering your reality to dull the pain. **It's important to remember pain is part of the human experience; by not dulling the pain you can experience something that will teach you.**

It's hard for people to grasp that, but by showing him a failure of a life, for lack of a better term, we can show him there's value in failure as well.

He has a question: "What about Paul Tracey visiting Carin and the dream she had?"

Paul showed Carin a transformative experience they had in college, and Paul called Rich the night he died, he was drunk and he regretted making that call – it was his way of apologizing. But he's fine now, no need to worry, and he finds it amusing he could communicate so clearly to Carin who could then call Rich and give him the message directly. [173]

Any message around Rich's parents or to his parents?

---

[173] As mentioned, our mutual friend Paul appeared to Carin in a dream, in what she said was more of a "vision" where he reminded her of a weekend they spent together in college, and that she should call me and tell me that he was "sorry for the phone call." Paul called me on the last night of his life; he normally called after a number of cocktails, and when he called that Sunday night, instead of my usual chipper "Hello Paul" I answered the phone with a cursory "What?" and he hung up the phone. Later, when I realized it was his last phone call, I felt terrible I hadn't called him back I didn't share that guilt with anyone, so when she mentioned it, I knew Paul was specifically telling me something that Carin did not know. "Tell Richard I'm sorry about that phone call." Only I would understand it.

His mom has now returned to her loved ones and is comfortable there and keeps an eye on him; appreciates his conversations with her in the kitchen and sends waves of love and gratefulness.

Would she like to come forward now to say hello?

My mom is saying "I'm always with you." She says "Play more piano. It takes you out of yourself and connects you with the energy of the universe."

And how is she adjusting to the afterlife?

It took her awhile. **It took a while to adjust to the tone - the vibrational energy of where she was – to where she is now. It's a bit like a piano in a way; she was a concert pianist and eventually she came to understand the notes of the other realm are different and she adjusted to it.**

How is she spending her time?

My mom is playing a lot of piano (laughs) and entertaining and connecting to people. She's (says she's) really enjoying seeing old friends and loved ones. "My mother and father, and Louise and my childhood friends, and the nuns I knew, from grade school; all those people are just so much fun to be around and it's wonderful to connect with them all, spend time sharing all the information we had in each lifetime; because when you connect this way, you can really share all the emotions and feelings; it's powerful to experience."

"Once Richard asked me what I thought heaven was like and I said to him that I had pictured it as a place you create in your own mind a place where you're in a comfy home with friends and sharing with them and it's absolutely that, and it is that for me. You could say that I designed it that way and that's what it's become; I'm very comfortably situated in a home of my design with my friends. I'm able to communicate with them and I can really enjoy what I'm doing and who I'm with."[174]

So you created this space for yourself by yourself?

---

[174] Mom was a concert pianist, played most every day of her life, and even played for an hour the day before she passed. Her hands were strong, her mind was amazing. She could sight read the way an actor can translate the meaning of a script at first glance. I had asked her what her opinion of the afterlife was, fully expecting a religious answer. I was surprised when she told me that she thought heaven was a place where you were surrounded by your loved ones, and you created your own environment of peace and happiness. This description fits this answer.

"Yeah, it's what everyone can do, what everyone does – **everyone has their own sense of reality of who and what they are so when they come back here, they use their faculties and their memories to create an energetic place that makes them feel comfortable.**

So if you're a person who lived in fear, for example, you may find yourself in a place of fear, but usually your loved ones and soul mates will come and try to pull you out of that to remind you that you don't have to exist in that environment. In my case I'm surrounded by the things and people I love, they're interacting with me in that way; of course they see me from their perspective and I see them from my perspective."

What about Rich's father how is he doing?

"He's having the time of his life, (laughs) – wonderful for him to connect to all of his friends from college, from high school from Niagara Falls, his parents and his brother, they're all so close and they're all really entertaining and fun people. He's drawing a lot; he was an architect, and he gets to draw here and create buildings and doesn't need a whole construction company to create them. Those designs he always wanted to do he can do here; he can create those homes and places. He designed the place I'm in, he helped me design it, let's put it that way."[175]

Any message from Rich's wife Sherry's mom?

She says that she's "keeping an eye on her," loves seeing her as a mother; it's amusing and at the same time wonderful.

Any messages from Rich's friend Jan who recently passed away?

(Chuckles.) Jan says she's experiencing "amazing adventures in amazing realms," – (I can hear her Aussie accent) and her life on Earth seems very far away from her at the moment, very distant, but of course she's always connected to her daughters.

(Note: After this, I had a dream where I was in some amazing mountainous region with these beautiful wooden homes, three and four stories, and all not far from each other in these woods. I was aware there was a crowd of people, all friends,

---

[175] My dad was an architect, designed and built many homes in Chicago, worked on the Bahai Temple in Evanston, and La Fonda Hotel interiors in Santa Fe. He worked for the famed architectural firm Holabird & Root in Chicago.

all having a great time. One of them was named Mike, and he brought me over to introduce me to his friend Jan. It was at that moment I recognized my friend Jan who passed some years ago, and she was radiant and as clever and funny as always. And she showed me around this area of beautiful homes which were open air – some of them didn't have any walls to keep out the elements. When I woke up, I remembered how Jan and I had once visited a friend of hers on a small island outside of Sydney, Australia, so remote that the mail boat only went there twice a week. But the homes on the island were open air – they didn't need to close them or have walls, akin to what friends of mine in Hawaii have. I realized that if Jan were going to create a place to reside, it might look something like this dream that I had.)

Open Your Heart

So Rayma… can we ask you some questions? What or who is God?

Examine it in your heart, and you'll get the answer. The concept of God or the creator - that which permeates the universe is beyond the ability of the brain to understand - is beyond the capacity or the random access memory of the human brain; there's just too much information to comprehend.

However, you can experience God – the way a human might describe water to someone who's never seen it. You can describe snow in a variety of ways but to someone in the desert, they're just words. But you can experience snow by falling into it, putting it into your hands and squeezing it, letting it melt in your face. It's the same with God, there's no amount of words, no syntax or correct words to use to get everyone to comprehend "God." **But you can experience "God" by opening your heart to everyone and to all things.**

It's key to examine what it means to open your heart to everyone; it means no judgment of anyone, it means only love for everyone. Very difficult to open your heart to everyone, including the person pointing a gun at you, the person who cuts you off in traffic, the person who steals from you, the person who punishes you, hurts you, molests you, kills you; very difficult to have your heart open to everyone, but if you want to experience God, that's one way to do it.

It's hard to put your mind around being open to a desk, a tree, a car, a computer. But if you can accept that it all exists simultaneously as it should be, that it all has a right to exist and that it's all part of the universe around you, it's a way of opening your heart to all things.

So to open your heart to everyone and to all things is a way to feel and experience… snow – the snow of what God is. Rich has put it succinctly **"Not that God is love, but that love – or what we can agree the concept of love is - is what God is."** Not so hard to experience.

So you're saying, to attempt to define God is difficult but you can experience God?

That's the conundrum. Imagine a computer with too much information to handle it; freezes up, doesn't move forward. The same is true for, not just God, but the idea of other realms, other multi-verses, these things are very difficult to wrap someone's mind around. But when it's as simple as "You can experience it," like jumping into a pool of water or jumping in a snow bank, it makes it easier for people to imagine.

Rayma, though a human definition of God might be difficult, if you're talking to a spirit guide friend, do you comprehend what God is? Are you able to talk about that with a friend who's not in a human body? And if so, what words or concepts do you use?

(Chuckles**.) Communication over here is a little bit different in the sense of knowing and understanding when you're communicating something to someone else.** When you're speaking to a group of students, let's say, you tailor your words and your thoughts and your explanations to the students you're talking to -- when you're talking to a friend or colleague or someone on the same level – it's not really a topic that I've ever come across where you would refer to "God" by that particular word "God."

It's just not referred to that way over here – the word God is a human construct to try to get a glimpse of something that's happening on the other side of the veil, let's say. So the word itself is just a concept we wouldn't use because it doesn't exist per se, there's not a single entity or individual that is ruling the roost. That was a human construct.

So when a human asks us or talks to us about what God is, instead of saying something like "Well that doesn't exist," or "God doesn't exist," or "It's beyond your capacity to understand," which wouldn't have any value, we tend to say, "Well, let's examine it from another angle. What could that mean?"

But if we're talking about concepts of how the universe works, not the nature of the universe, but beyond that, how energy works on all levels; unfortunately I don't have access to any particular terminology or words I could say to you, other than to observe that when I'm talking to a colleague about these concepts, they understand what I'm saying.

Rayma, I understand God may not be a single entity that rules the roost, but what humans refer to as God, when you talk about that, or something similar, with colleagues how do you speak about that?

The overwhelming energy – overwhelming is not the right word, but the "complete and utter energy," -- and energy is not exactly the right word either - again when we're trying to speak in human terms, we have to narrow the words down. Probably what comes closer to it is a like a poet's definition because poets are not trying to be specific in each word, they're trying to get at something of a larger, and richer nature.

So if I might have a conversation with a colleague where I'm discussing something about the nature of existence; we might just speak in terms of visual patterns, it's like another language completely and it's not a language that's confined by words.

I might touch you, for example, take you by the hand and you'll feel like a wave of energy that goes through you, and that might be my way of communicating to you a particular experience – now you haven't heard it as a word but I've given it to you as an energetic field. **Words are little, miniature energetic fields, that we use to communicate something, let's say to other people, but over here, words aren't really necessary. We have a tendency to use energetic fields to communicate issues or problems.**

If we're talking to humans, certainly we have to find a way to communicate with them, if they're suffering or having a problem or having some issue. I'm sure you've heard of people who've had dreams of someone who appears and shows and explains something. Even that construct is an energetic field that's been planted - like a visual, it comes off as a visual to a human, but the actual creation of it for us, was an energetic field, if that makes any sense.

It does. What projects should Rich focus on?

It's a funny question because part of the answer is, and what we learned today, is he needs to "swing for the fences.**" It doesn't matter which one he focuses on, every work project has a life of its own, but you do have to swing for the fence if you want to make it happen. The answer is always to follow the one connected closest to your heart and not your mind.** We're all waiting for this next book. "It's a Wonderful Afterlife." Clever title. We're all amused.

Anything very important that needs to stay in the book?

Focus on the heart, that's the most important part of the book. What more can I say? "Just let go." "Swing for the fences."

It's an odd sensation I've had while transcribing this session – knowing that I've filmed it, recorded it, but not aware of what the answers to the questions are going to be. I could argue that everything said in this session is in my head already, and it refers to other bits and pieces of information that is in "Flipside" and available online.

But perhaps that is part of the value of hypnotherapy – by relaxing the mind, you can access all different parts of it. I can't vouch for all of the details in this session – but I know how I felt when I said them, and how I felt when I transcribed them. I see the power they have when they're on the page. All I can hope is that whoever is meant to hear them, will hear them, and they will pass the same information on to others.

I once asked Robert Thurman if he thought enlightenment might be your brain suddenly being able to access all different portions of it simultaneously. He nodded, thoughtfully. "Perhaps." So hypnotherapy can help people do that – or if you can't find a good hypnotherapist near you, meditation can help you in the same way to access many of the files you thought had disappeared or been deleted or damaged.

You might say that death is just a phase. You might say that life is just a phase. As I'm fond of saying "The good news is; we don't die. The bad news is… we don't die. We have a mountain of work ahead of us, learning in new lifetimes, teaching and having compassion for everyone. No time like the present to "just let go" or "swing for the fences."

"I am certain that I have been here as I am now a thousand times before, and I hope to return a thousand times." – Goethe

Chapter Seventeen – "Why Kids Choose Us"

"You think just because I'm little and young, nothing great and old can reside within me, but you shall see very soon." Mozart at age 6, in a letter to his father, Leopold (Photo of the Dalai Lama's room as he left it. I snapped this illegal pic inside the Potala Palace in Lhasa, Tibet)

The curtains opened and Merv Griffin said, "Ladies and gentlemen, Richard Martini."

Charles Grodin had been invited on The Merv Griffin Show and decided he wanted to take me with him on the show for a laugh. Before I came on he told Merv I was "The most charismatic person in the United States." Charles' comic idea was to take me, someone who'd never been on television before, along with him to show Merv that *anyone* could sit in the chair and tell an interesting story. It was an improvisational idea, we both had no idea where it would wind up.

Merv wasn't crazy about the idea of my even being on the show. As I emerged from the curtains, he walked over and shook my hand, and I stared at him and said "So you're Merv?" as if I'd never heard of him. When I sat down on the couch, next to Charles, who was in the main chair, Merv said "I could have had Orson Welles in this spot. What's this guy doing here?" Charles asked the camera man to come in for a close up. "Richard has a great aura. Look at him. Don't you just feel more comfortable now?" I smiled. Merv rolled his eyes.

Charles had earlier been on Merv's show talking about a concept he and Carole Burnett had been discussing on other talk shows; "the idea of people "being more friendly" with each other." Merv dismissively called it "the Friendly Movement." Merv asked me, "So what do you think of your friend's idiotic concept?"

I said I'd been in a restaurant recently and had witnessed a celebrity of great renown practicing what he'd learned from the Friendly Movement. (At this point, Charles said, "I think Richard's ready for the main chair," and I switched chairs so I was elbow to elbow with Merv, who promptly moved his chair away from me.) Undaunted, I continued my story. "I saw this megastar at a local restaurant in Hollywood, Musso & Franks, and this woman came over and asked him to come over to her table and sign autographs for all of her daughters. And this star went over and greeted them, signed the autographs, and I know it was because he'd gotten caught up in the Friendly Movement."

"Oh really," Merv asked, dripping with sarcasm. "And who was this megastar?"

I said "It was you, Merv."

Charles added "And we all know what you were like before you heard about being friendly." Merv's face lit up. "Really? That was me? At Musso's?" Now Merv moved his chair closer to me, and started to talk about how he hadn't really believed Charles' story about the importance of being friendlier with people. And at that point, Charles said "Wait a second, why is your chair so close to Richard's now?" And Merv said "Well, now that you mention it, Richard does have a wonderful aura." The audience laughed.

Walking onto Merv's show, I had no idea where our comic bit was going to lead us, but trusted Chuck's comic genius to find us a way through. And somehow I was able to turn Merv's feigned hostility into something *friendlier*.

I learned reverse psychology from a master. My mom.

As a kid, I used to often threaten to run away from home. When I was four or five, I'd whine, "You don't love me anymore. I'm running away!" Inevitably Mom would say, "Yes, dear, we love you, please don't run away." But one day she said "You know what? You're right. We don't love you anymore. Let me help you pack."

And I packed up my Dondi-like knapsack on a stick, she put a sandwich in for me, wrapped it up, and handed it to me. I must have a pretty shocked look on my face, as she opened the screen door and said "Bye, nice to know ya!" I made it about fifty yards when a slight drizzle started to come out of the grey Chicago sky. I thought to myself, "Hmm... Maybe I can postpone this trip till tomorrow."

When my mother used reverse psychology, it startled me into a realization. What's the point if she already knew the outcome of my threat? Why threaten if she already knows I'll come back for another sandwich?

It was in my college years I started to observe that my life seemed to resemble a book or a novel. Something someone said to me when I was a teen would echo or have some effect on me later. People who appeared in "Chapter Two," would show up again in "Chapter Six." Recently a young tough kid from Detroit I met in college won the Pulitzer for his writing, and rode to my rescue at a moment when I lease expected it. Who would know that this leather jacketed cigarette puffing kid would turn into my knight in shining armor?[176] But then, the question I had was, who's writing these unusual twists to my plot?

I subscribed to the commonly held belief that chance or chaos has everything to do with how our lives played out. If you didn't make the right choice, you might spend years ruing that you'd made the wrong choice. Depending how the coin flip came down.

When I was 23, I found myself standing in the massive Roma Termini train station with my brother Robbie. I had found a place to live in Rome and was told by the famed Italian film director Lina Wertmuller there was a chance for a production assistant job on her next film. (I found her listed in the phone book and had called her out of the blue.) So I was waiting for that possible future gig when my

---

[176] None more so when a pal from college, Sheryl, whom I'd met in school in Rome. She became my mother's caregiver and best friend for my mother's last days on the planet. Who could have foreseen that our friendship in the "Rome Chapter" would become so important in the "Mom Passing" one?

brother asked "Why are you staying in Rome? Why don't you come back to the States with me?"

So when Rob went off to buy his train ticket, I took out a 100 lira coin. Cento lira as it was called, with the head of a man on one side, and his naked rear end on the other - literally heads and tails. I thought "I'm going to flip this coin, and whatever the outcome – heads or tails - is going to be my life. Heads, I'll stay in Rome and become a writer, or tails, I'll get on that train with Rob and go back to the States." I can still see it now, catching the light in that massive train terminal as it flipped through the air and landed into my hand. "Heads." *Stay in Rome.*

"Oh shit. Two out of three" I said.

But I realized I must really not want to stay in Rome, so I got on the train. When I arrived back at my apartment in Boston, I found an acceptance letter to University of Southern California graduate Masters of Writing program, which I'd forgotten I'd applied to months before. I flew to Los Angeles, entered the program, switched over to film production, and have been at it ever since, leading up to the sentence I'm writing at this very moment.

It all came from that coin flip. I used to joke that there was a *doppelganger* living in Rome, enjoying the life I was supposed to have - success, fame and fortune, all three of which have so far eluded me quite successfully!

But then, when my daughter was born, I remembered that coin flip. We were in the hospital, I was asleep on a chair and had a vision of that coin flipping – I could see it in slow motion going through the air. And it was like a lightning bolt of understanding; I knew that every event in my life had led up to our daughter's birth. Every choice suddenly made sense.

Certainly, I could have made the wrong choices along the way, and I would argue that many appeared to be so. But since they all led to the birth of my daughter, how could they be characterized as wrong? But was their some giant story generator behind these twists and turns in my life? Had I chosen them?

And what about our children? Do we choose them or do they choose us?

When I was visiting my mother in Chicago one weekend, my wife Sherry was having dinner with our daughter Olivia and our son RJ. He was 3 and she was 5. Sherry says Olivia suddenly became very thoughtful. She said quietly, "I knew your mother before she died. That's how I came to life." Sherry, not skipping a beat and knowing the moment would pass quickly, asked Olivia to describe her mother. She did, accurately, including mentioning Sherry's mother's frequent trips to lounge by the pool of their home in St. George, Utah. (Sherry notes that it was interesting that Olivia focused on that, because sunbathing was like a religion to Sherry's mom.)

Sherry's mother, Sidney, passed away five years before Olivia was born, so it wasn't clear what Olivia was saying about Sidney's death being her entry point into this life. Olivia said "That's how it works. Someone in your family dies so someone new can come into your family." Sherry then asked, "Did Mommy and Daddy choose you, or did you choose Mommy and Daddy?" Olivia said happily, "Oh, I've known Daddy for a long, long, long time. I really liked him. I watched him when he was in London." Sherry asked "Was that before you were born?" Olivia said "Yes." Sherry asked "What did you like about him?"" Olivia said "He had a happy smile."

She asked Olivia about choosing her as a mom and Olivia said she knew Sherry was in an apartment in Venice, and the reason she chose her was "You were just... Love." We'd never told Olivia about Sherry living in an apartment in Venice, California, or my trips to Europe, where I'd stop in London on my way to or from the Cannes Film Festival (the last trip being in 1997, which was about the time of Sidney's passing).

Did you pick mommy and daddy or did we pick you?

This is a question I tell all of my skeptical friends to ask their young children; it's not a tough question – it's not irreligious, or concept bending. Those who've reported back to me the results say that about half of the children claim "I chose you." (Some kids have reportedly stared at their parents and said "Is this a trick question?") So the next question is "Why?"

As to Olivia, it's easy for me to confirm both of her details were true. And I can guarantee that I wasn't in London and Sherry wasn't in her small apartment in Venice, California when Olivia was conceived, but I can also point out that Sidney, Olivia's grandmother, whose death "paved the way" for her to come into our lives, according to Olivia, died 5 years before she was born.

And perhaps it's a bit too much information, but I have the distinct memory that when Olivia *was conceived*, I heard a voice in my head say aloud "Well, it's about time." I was not at all surprised when a few months later, my lovely wife Sherry approached me on the balcony to tell me the news; I turned down the Sunday paper and said "That's great!" But to be honest, I already knew it.

Her birth itself had a number of unusual aspects to it. Just prior to her birth, I looked out on our balcony and found a swarm of dragon flies pointed at our window. I don't mean a few dragon flies, when I saw swarm it took up the entire ceiling to floor window. They weren't flitting about, but kind of bobbing in place. I looked down the balcony at the other apartments to see if they were anywhere else. They were not.

What were a thousand dragon flies doing outside our window? I haven't the faintest idea. But I am aware of "auspicious occasions" in Tibetan lore, and I noted it as an odd occurrence I could not explain. I opened the sliding door and looked at them, but they were not intimidated by my presence. They just hovered a few feet outside our window, eight stories up, as if waiting for something.

Then when we were in the hospital for Olivia's birth, I was handed a pair of scissors to cut the umbilical cord, and given a chair at the end of Sherry's bed. The Doctor was to my left, as I recall as Sherry began to give birth. Olivia's tiny little face emerged from Sherry, and she opened her eyes, looked directly at me and said "Heggadaba!"

I was aware that normally babies can't see for a few days, everything is fuzzy and dim. But I kid you not. She looked at me as if recognizing me and said "Heggadaba!" I started to recount this story to strangers on planes, asking people from different countries if they'd ever heard the word before. I couldn't find it on any database – I remember asking a Hassidic rabbi if it was a word from the Torah and he said "It sounds Italian. Ecco papa!"

A couple of years later, I was recounting the story of her birth at her Godmother Edna Gundersen's home. The revered former music critic of USA Today, I can state for a fact that there never has been a more devoted and generous Godmother on the planet. She was throwing a second birthday party for Olivia and I was telling our friends the story, and as I got to the punchline, Olivia suddenly said the word with the same tone and intonation. "Heggadaba!"

I looked over at her blue eyes and smiling face. I said, "Olivia, what does it mean?" She said "It means "I'm coming back." We all looked at each other. A few seconds later she said "No, it means "I'm coming out." I said "In what language?" She said "In the angel realm." She was two. The word angel and realm had never been used around our home.

Then, sometime later, she told me she'd thought about it, and realized it was more of a phrase that one would use upon seeing an old friend. "Oh, there you are." Perhaps because she'd heard my voice the past nine months. But I wasn't speaking aloud when she emerged.

She opened her eyes, looked straight at me and said "Oh, there you are" in a language I've never heard before. The doctor was startled, and he looked at me as if to say "Did you hear that?" Being the first birth I've ever seen, I wondered if it was something he'd seen before, but never got around to ask.

Moments after her birth, Olivia went back to being a normal baby. The nurses cleaned her up, did all the things one does with a baby, and she cried until she was put into her mother's arms.

I spoke of our son's past life memories in "Flipside" in the chapter "My Son the Monk." At the time of that writing, he was only four years old, so the details were pretty fresh. And I was in the midst of my research, and when suddenly someone so near and dear to me, so close to me happens to mention that he (or she) remembers a previous lifetime, you can bet I took out my pen and tried my best not to interfere with whatever memory that might be.

To recount the story as told in "Flipside:" I was in Chicago visiting my mother when my wife put my two year old son on the phone. We'd said a few words together in his wee vocabulary - mostly, "I love you," or "I miss you." So fully expecting him to say something of the sort, I was shocked when he said "Dad, I was a monk in Nepal!" I paused for a few seconds. Did he just say what I thought he said? "Put your mom on the phone, honey." Sherry confirmed that she'd heard him say it, but had no idea why he said it. They hadn't been talking about Nepal, they hadn't been talking about monks. It was said to me as if he'd been waiting for two years to say that sentence, and could finally formulate it.

We'd had a few interesting moments with regard to Nepal. Before Sherry knew she was pregnant with Olivia, a close friend of Sherry's told her she had a dream the night before where Sherry was standing at a bus stop in what looked like India and she was pregnant. Sherry didn't know she was pregnant at the time, so to have this friend inform her she was pregnant, was a bit startling. And no,

Sherry's never been to India or Nepal, and rarely outside California and her native Utah.

RJ was born three weeks early and had a hard time of it in his first few months on the planet. Sherry says he seemed to want to be elsewhere, almost as if he hadn't committed to *this* place. One night, while RJ was rest on Sherry's chest while sleeping, Sherry had a profound vision of white mountaintops and what looked like a monastery. Then she saw a woman in a traditional Tibetan dress, with the multi-colored apron they wear that signifies a married woman. She saw two boys next to her, both of them were young monks.

The woman was by a beautiful, clear stream of water running down the mountain. Sherry said got a powerful feeling of sadness from RJ, as if he had been "missing the solace" of that mountain retreat, wherever it was. But she'd never spoken to him of this vision.

When I came home, I asked him about what he remembered of Nepal. He said he lived "near water." I asked Olivia if she remembered RJ "from before." She said "Oh, yes, he was a monk." "Really?" I said. She said "Yes, he was an old, old monk and everyone came to see him." I asked how she knew him. "I was his doctor," she said. Then she said "and then, when he died, his robes just fell away." She said that gesturing with her arms open, as if it was a magical experience.

I looked that up on line, because I've heard of monks who in their final days are locked into a room or a cave and left alone for seven days. And when the attendants return, they find the monk has "disappeared" and only hair and fingernails are left. It's called a "Rainbow death" and there are a number of accounts of them in Tibetan literature. I have not been able to find any specific accounts of the same in Nepal.

Once we went for a drive down to nearby Long Beach to visit the Tibetan monastery there. Olivia, who was about four at the time, asked where we were going. I said "We're going to visit the *gompa* in Long Beach where the Tibetan monks live." And she said "No! We are not! I don't want to go there, I don't want to wear robes anymore! And I don't want to go without shoes anymore!" We had been there once before for a visit, and indeed we had taken off our shoes, but I guess I forgot to add that we were just going for a visit and not to leave her behind.

Granted, most parents would nod and assume their child was talking about an episode of "Scooby Doo." But in light of the fact that our son already told me he was a monk in Nepal, I tend to pay more attention to what our kids say in this arena.

One day, I had a picture book on the floor with photos from Tibet. Olivia was flipping the pages, and RJ was looking over her shoulder. She came upon a photograph of the Potala Palace, one of the most famous buildings in the world, where the Dalai Lamas lived in Tibet. It's a massive structure with multiple levels, towers that are painted white, some that are painted red. Olivia pointed to the white towers and said "I used to live there."

RJ wanted in on the story. He said "I used to live there too." She said "No, you didn't, you used to live over here..." she pointed to the front of the Potala, across the street, where common people lived in years past. "You lived here because you were from the land of no people, and I was from the land of people." Something about the way she said it rang a bell with me, and I went to the computer to search for the phrase "land of people" and "Tibet."[177]

Turns out that's how Tibetans refer to themselves, or at least those folks who hail from Kham, which is known as "The Land of People." Those who aren't from Tibet would be known as being from the "Land of No People," the same way people in Maine consider everyone who wasn't born in Maine to be "from away," whether they're from Vermont, or Sri Lanka.

A few days later, I opened up the book of photos of the Potala Palace and asked RJ if he knew who lived in one of the bedrooms. He shrugged. I showed him the picture that is at the front of this chapter. He said "Boba." I looked that up later as well - it's how Tibetans refer to themselves, as in the famous character in Star Wars known as "Boba Phett "- most people don't know that George Lucas had learned enough about Tibet to use some of their names and characters to inhabit his world beyond our world; Boba speaks Tibetan on screen. "Boba" means "Tibetan" to a Tibetan.

When Olivia was quite young I asked if she knew me from before. She nodded her head. I said "when?" She said "When I was a doctor in Big China." Big China

---

[177] "Tibetan Modernities – notes from the field of cultural and social change." Edited by Robert Barnett and Ronald Schwartz. 2003. "U-Tsang; Land of Dharma. Amdo; Land of Horses. Gyalrong: Land of Fire. Kham; Land of People." Pg. 37.

is how some people in Asia refer to Mongolia and the Tibetan region. I asked her who I was. She said "Tulken Khan."

I looked that name up and found it to be a common name in Mongolia. Later she said that she had been a doctor, a male, who lived in Lhasa, and that she took care of people with medicine which she made from herbs and rolled into balls.

She said Sherry lived in that lifetime as her servant at the foot of her bed and would help her gather herbs for medicine. (When Sherry heard this, she said, "Well, nothing's changed in this life!") Olivia told me that I was there too, and I protected her.

Whatever slim research I've done on the subject tells me that the Mongolians protected the Tibetans for a period of time, lived in Lhasa, and their warriors served at the Dalai Lama's request. The name "Dalai Lama" itself is Mongolian for "Ocean of Wisdom." I have no recollection of these details of Tulken Khan, either from dreams or doing past life regressions. (And our daughter has no recollection of these events today, and would likely deny she'd ever said anything of the sort. She just happened to choose parents who would write down what their kids say.)

I was driving around Santa Monica with RJ one day when he was three. I looked at him in the rear view mirror, sitting in his car seat. I said "RJ, do you remember Daddy from before?" He nodded. I said "Where did you meet daddy?" He said simply, "Tibet." My jaw dropped. I said "Where in Tibet?" He said "On the path."

That took my breath away. Did he mean "on the spiritual path?" or did he mean literally on a path? And when did he ever hear the word path? He wasn't in pre-school, and I'd never heard it in any of the myriad "Scooby Doos" and "Sesame Streets" he'd seen - and we had no paths near our house. But he clearly said "on the path." I hesitated. I had been on many paths in Tibet while shooting "Journey Into Tibet" for Tibet House in New York. Then I remembered something that had happened to me on one particular path in Tibet.

While I was on Mt. Kailash with Robert Thurman in Western Tibet, we had come to a point on the path around Kailash that is considered particularly sacred; the north face of Mt. Kailash, according to Professor Thurman, is the spot where an individual can make a wish, and it will come true. When he said that, I'm sure I chuckled to myself, thinking about other places on the planet that are supposed to be sources of good luck.

Here I was, having left the set of a Bollywood film I'd written and was producing called "My Bollywood Bride," starring Jason Lewis and Sanjay Suri, and an email had arrived from Robert inviting me on this amazing trip around Mt. Kailash. If I could get to Katmandu the following week from Bombay, I was going to be allowed to join a tour group from Geographic Expeditions out of San Francisco on this sacred trek.

Mt. Kailash is considered to be the "center of the Universe" for four major religions; the Buddhists, the Hindus, the Jain and the Bon all consider Kailash an amazingly sacred spot. It's said that if one makes a trip around Kailash, all the sins of a lifetime are wiped away. It's said that if a pilgrim makes 101 trips around Kailash, the sins of all lifetimes are wiped clean. It's a sacred mountain also because the Tibetan Saint Milarepa lived in a cave on the far side at one time, and every sacred pilgrim that has come to Tibet has at one time or other, made his or her way around this sacred mountain. Robert and Tad Wise wrote a book about their trip around it in the 90's. There was a passage in the book that caught my attention.

As I mentioned earlier, just prior to my friend Luana's passing, I had a powerful vision that I awoke inside of a volcano - there was a tremendous roar around me, and I could see the walls of this volcano were molten, but I couldn't feel any heat. The roar and sound was so intense that at some point I passed out.

And later, when I came to, I realized I'd only moved closer to the entrance, or exit - and that I was part of a platform of rock that was moving towards the upper regions. There was a crackling around me, like fireflies of light, sparkling and snapping as I got closer to the entrance above me, all the while accompanied by an incredible roar that seemed part freight train, part earthquake and part birth of the planet.

After I had met Robert Thurman, Sherry purchased a copy of his book for me "Circling the Sacred Mountain." In it I discovered the following passage:

> Suddenly, I felt surrounded by a buzzing, sizzling, roaring sounds, as if a gigantic rush of molten energy like a volcano was erupting within and all around. There was searing heat and yet I seemed to be in the perspective of the sacred mountain itself... A giant living crystal rock, aware of all of this within, yet completely free and still and cool. I felt an overwhelming surge of joyful giving toward all beings...Honey of life and happiness was flowing out of my crystal mountain's flaming void.

Thunderbolt energy was crackling in all directions. A roaring, seething, hissing sound exploded all around.[178]

So what's the connection? Robert and I had similar dreams. Did we both dream about the creation of the universe? Or Earth? I know when I read it in his book about circling the sacred Mt. Kailash, I knew instinctively it was something I'd like to do … Some day. Then oddly enough, the day came.

While we were camped in front of the North Face of Mt. Kailash, Bob reiterated the sacredness of the sight, and how people could wish for something on this spot and it would inevitably come true. So I thought long and hard about two possible choices; one was money, and the other was a film deal. After all, struggling as I have my entire career and now having a family to take care of, it was a conundrum; which is more important? The work, or the money? I couldn't make up my mind between "a million dollars" or "a three picture deal," and debated which one to say aloud. So I did the next best thing, I said to myself, when I count down from ten, when I get to one, whatever I'm supposed to say will pop out of my mouth.

"Three, two, one…" and out of my mouth came the words "I want a son."

I was stunned to hear it, and actually looked around as if to say "who said that?" It wasn't part of my conscious mind at all, our beautiful six month old daughter was waiting for me back in Los Angeles, and I had never considered we'd have another child, let alone to try and give it a gender.

I thought that it must have come from my Freudian subconscious, or that there's some masculine primal code. Again, it was not part of my world view, but I had to allow that it might be something that resided within my subconscious because I said it. Which leads us back to the car in Santa Monica, and RJ having just said that he found me in Tibet "on the path."

I couldn't help myself. "Was it on Mt. Kailash?" I asked him, and looked into the rear view mirror. He shook his head, no. I thought about all the paths I had been on in Tibet, and then remembered that he's quite literal.

---

[178] "Circling the Sacred Mountain" by Thurman and Tad Wise. Bantam Books. Pg. 338

"Was it on Kangra?" I asked. He nodded his head. "Yes, it was Kangra." Kangra is the name of the path that goes around Kailash, but in Tibetan. Even though I'd supplied the word, it seemed like he was agreeing, indeed, that was the place.

Some months later, I was in New York City working on the feature film "Salt" for my friend and mentor, film director Phillip Noyce. At some point, I was able to bring my family out to stay in my sublet in the West Village.

Our son went to a bookshelf and pulled two books from it. He took one and threw it into the trash. Sherry said "What are you doing?" She said he scoffed at the book; "That book is worthless." He held up the second book. "This is the important one." It was the apartment owner's copy of Robert Thurman's "Circling the Sacred Mountain" about his journey around Mt. Kailash. Sherry said he opened the book, found pictures of Mt. Kailash and said "That where I found Daddy."

She called me on the set to ask me if I'd ever shown him the book, or talked about Kailash to him. I told her that the only time I could remember ever saying the word Kailash was that one time in the car over a year earlier. Sherry noted that before he fell asleep he would do elaborate "mudras" with his hands, thumbs and fingers doing a dance in a way that I've seen Buddhist monks do, but have no idea how to perform myself.

Then when RJ was 5, we were in a Bhutan bookstore in the Santa Monica Mountains. And at some point I was speaking to the owner, and Sherry came over and said "Have you seen RJ?" It's a small shop so I said "He can't have gone far, just look around for him." He's normally running around, hiding under racks and knocking things over – your typical five year old boy.

She came back about five minutes later with a stunned look on her face. She had gone into the back storeroom and saw our son doing full prostrations in front of a mirror as a tape of prayers for the long life of the Dalai Lama played over the sound system. These are the kinds of prostrations only devout Buddhists or monks do – hands over the head, then a touch to the forehead, to the lips and heart, then kneeling down on the ground, touch the forehead to the ground, and then do it all over again.

I've seen Buddhists do these prostrations, but never with my family. And here was Sherry watching RJ do them for what she said was about three minutes.

Then he caught sight of her in the mirror. "Oh," he said, as if being caught doing something – "Mom, you need to meditate more and this is how you do it." Then he pulled her down to the ground with him and said "You hear those bells in the music?" He picked up a bell and showed it to her. Sherry said that the music seemed to be key to what he was doing because he was moving with the flow of the music and when it stopped it was like he was in a trance. [179] "Whenever you hear a bell," he said "It means peace comes into the world."

I asked a Tibetan friend what it meant when Tibetan bells were rung during a prayer service or puja. I thought bells symbolized wisdom. He said "It means peace comes into the world."

Finally, a year later, I heard from my friend Sheryl who had been taking care of my ailing mother that she didn't think she would last the weekend. So as I prepared to go home to prepare by with my mom, I thought about the first time I had been to a funeral. I sat our children down and said "Listen, the next time you see grandma, she will be different. They put make up on her, and she'll no longer be grandma."

And RJ, seeing my distress over telling this story said "It's okay dad. Spirit is like water." He looked around and picked up a half empty plastic bottle of water. "Watch," he said, and then threw it down onto the floor and stomped on the bottle rather violently. He then started to jump on it with glee. My wife and I looked at each other, trying to figure out what he was doing. Then he then picked up the bottle; the cap was still on. He held it up and said "See? The water is okay."

Easily the most profound teaching I've ever heard about the nature of life and death. Water evaporates and goes up to the clouds, or heaven, and then comes back down, goes into rivers, mountains, and becomes a bottle of water again. The bottle becomes crushed and brittle and broken and old – but the water, like spirit, is always okay. *The water is okay.* Wow.

And I'm glad our kids chose us. I tell these stories about our children, because it's been confirmed over and over again in the research. And with friends of mine who have young children, I suggest they ask their kids that simple question;

"Did mommy and daddy choose you, or did you choose us?"

---

[179] The CD was "Traditional Chants of Tibet" by the Nechung Monks, available on itunes.

You might be surprised by the answer.

"For those who seek to understand it, death is a highly creative force. The highest spiritual values of life can originate from the thought and study of death." - Elisabeth Kubler-Ross

Chapter Eighteen – "Get in the Game"

"After you die, you wear what you are." - St. Teresa of Avila

I became friends with a successful film producer who's also worked in television. I was telling her about my research into the "Flipside" and she basically said, "Richard, you're nuts!" Sometime later she told me that although she didn't believe what I was saying about the afterlife, or about between lives, she did want to arrange for a hypnotherapy session. Scott De Tamble arranged for her to come out to his office in Claremont and I offered to drive her and record the session on film.

In the car, she said the real reason she agreed to do a session was because her doctors found a cyst on her ovary, and she was having an operation the following week. She'd heard hypnosis might help in the healing process, and felt if there was a way for her to speak to her subconscious, she was "all for it."

She was concerned she couldn't be hypnotized, and let me know she was skeptical about the rest of the process; she didn't believe in organized religion and was doubtful there was any "higher power." I offered that Scott is particularly successful working with people who believe they can't be hypnotized.

During her session, when it came time for her to remember "a previous lifetime that has some effect on this lifetime" – she spent about a half hour saying variations of "nope, I got nothing." And then the energy in the room seemed to shift, a door opened, and the following was recorded on film.

Scott and Kelly

Scott: All right then, time to go back to the stairway, going to move down... I'm going to ask you some questions, and I want you to respond with the first thing that comes into your mind. First impressions. Daytime or night time?

Kelly: Day.

Indoors?

Outdoors. It's mixed up. It's like I'm a big ant. It's in the desert or something. Like I'm an insect, or I'm looking at an insect. I feel like a grizzled old man insect. Grizzled old man... but one that stands.

Imagine you can float outside yourself. Tell me about where you are.

Sort of like a pretty deserted country, desolate western. It's dirty, sandy, (there's) a cactus.

What goes through your mind?

Grumpy. And old. I'm uncomfortable. Very uncomfortable... like an insect or a person that's very uncomfortable. It's warm. It's hot.

What's your gender? Male or female?

Male.

Let's focus on the grizzled old man. Cranky. Grumpy. How old is he?

70.

Is he wearing anything on his feet?

Uncomfortable boots. Sand colored. Jeans. Shirt. Black. Worn. Greyish white hair.

How about his face?

Fair. Light blue eyes.

Move into those eyes and look out. What's he thinking?

He's frustrated. He's like "Goddammit!" – It's because he's stuck somewhere. Somehow he got left there - like his horse ran off or something. He's in the middle of nowhere. He's stuck.

Let's freeze the frame. Let's mine his brain. His memories. Even as a boy. Where did he grow up?

He's very independent. And he takes care of someone older. It's a female adult.

A mom or relative?

He looks after the house, looks after the business, he tells everyone what to do. A little tyrant... he's 10 but he's like 40. House is very simple, very clean, just clean, fresh living quarters.

What part of the world is this home?

West. America.

What does the older female call him?

Tommy.

What year is this?

1806.

Tell me about Tommy.

He doesn't go to school.

Family?

Older woman, I don't know if it's his mother or grandmother. She's thin. She's sort of see through.

Let's skip forward to when something interesting happens.

I see red. I don't know if it's a fire or an activity.

How old is he in this red scene?

In his 30's. There's another female around. Around the same age.

Tell me about the place where Tommy and this woman live.

Two story house. And the image I get is that he's always busy running around and she's very still. I get the impression it's in Arizona, near Tucson.[180]

What's the wife's name?

Agathany or something weird – not Agatha, not Betheny, but a-gathany. Last name is something with a B. ends in R. three syllables. Sounds like Bourger or Bourget.[181]

What does he do?

I see him bossing people around. "Go do this" and "go do that." He's always telling someone what to do in the town.

Does he have a position of responsibility?

Yes, he runs the town but he's not a politician. He just sort of runs the town.

Like getting water there and food? How many people in the town?

All told, a couple hundred maybe.

Let's skip forward to another interesting situation.

He's a grumpy old man. I'm going back to the place where I first started (in describing him), he's trying to think about where the woman went, and his attitude is "she never did anything anyway." It's not like she died, it's like she's not there anymore. He's stranded. He's like "what have I done?"

Let's skip forward and see what happens. Let's see how this is resolved.

[180] In this point in Arizona history, Tucson was part of the Mexican state of Occidente (Sonora after 1824). It didn't become part of the US until 1853. (Wikipedia)

[181] Thomas Bourgery is a common name in the 1800's throughout America. Also Boerger, Bourgier and Borger and Boerger in Arizona. Agatha Ney is a name in the Texas historical records. (Ancestry.com)

It's just like he's... pretty old, the idea of walking all the way is too much, his attitude is like "This is as good as place as any to give up the ghost."

Let's skip to his last hour on Earth. Be there now.

He's under a tree... A few days since saying he was stranded. He was walking, he really did just sit down and decide to call it a day. His attitude has changed. He's sad, like he's dropped his façade of being tough. He was just who he was his whole life, and now it's over. He doesn't keep it up anymore. He's lonely. He's 79 years old.[182]

What does he think about the life he just led?

It was interesting. It's sort of like he had fun being bossy and not having anyone control him for a life.

Feeling a Bit Bored

Let's move to the point where you've just died, rise from the body feeling free... feel your mind expanding.

You know it was, it was fun being a girl pretending to be a man and not having to be a female.

You choose females lives?

I feel like I am female and I got to pretend to be a macho man for a while. And when I came out I was like "Oh! That was fuuun!"

Just to see how the other side lives?

Yeah.

What other insights coming to mind now?

I was feeling a bit bored. I'm just sitting around.

Where is Tommy's body?

---

[182] According to this time line, it would have been roughly 1875.

It's under the tree. I'm just sitting there next to it. I'm bored but I'm not ready to go anywhere. Just feel like sitting there, no obligations. I'm avoiding obligations (laughs).

Interesting life you just led. When you're ready, we'll be going to a place of expanded awareness and talk to those who can help teach and explain things. How are you feeling now?

I'm kind of a like a petulant ten year old. I'm like this person saying "What? What am I going to do now? Fine... I'll just go and do that..." Constantly running around... mostly I don't like to do what I'm told... to do...

So being Tommy was...

Telling everybody else what to do. I feel like back there (between lives) I'm always in trouble for not doing what I'm supposed to do or what I'm told to do.

What do you really want to see or do? What calls to you?

The universe. I don't want to be stuck anymore. I like flying around.

Let's go fly around. Let's allow you to fly around and explore the universe. What's that feel like?

It's great. I'm very interested in the mechanics of how the Universe works, that's really what I like doing, going and figuring it out.

How will you do this?

I just go and observe things. It's a very big complex machine with a lot of cogs and things all fit together.

Like a mechanism?

Yes.[183]

So you notice how these different things fit together, how it all works?

---

[183] That was one of her questions that we discussed in the car. She wrote them off the top of her head; "Does the Universe work like a machine?" (The idea of working parts functioning like a machine) "What's the meaning of the shift?" (I suggested that one). "What or who is God?" Since she doesn't believe in a higher power, I thought this was an interesting one to ask.)

Yes. I don't really understand it - but I know.... **that it's a big machine that has A plus B equals C – one plus two equals three. There is a reason for it. There's a blueprint.** I just don't know how it works.

A coherence in it?

Yes.

A Visit to the Library

What about going to a place that holds the blueprint of the Universe, like a temple or room or space of some kind where we can ask questions and receive answers. Just be there now.

What a fantastic idea. That there can be this entire library with everything you ever wanted to know. There's no limit to it. I think this is where I'd like to be. If I could choose an incarnation I'd like to be there.

Is it a library, is that what you would call it?

Yes. It's fantastic. And **it's huge and there all kinds of books and you can pull down a book and see something or pull down a screen and look at something.**

Let's pull down a book or screen.

It's so big. I'm going to have to figure out one question that's manageable.

What's the question that comes to mind?

"Is it intentional?"

Like "Was I created? Or a crazy accident?"

Evolution, yeah.

Let's go to a book or a screen that shows the reality. Let that knowingness flow into you.

It's both. You can't separate the two. I think it's... one thing builds on another so it is evolution, and it is perchance, but it is.... intelligence can grow and evolve as well. **It's like it can build itself – doesn't have to be - some outside intelligence created it, the intelligence is creating itself.**[184]

What set the Universe into motion?

All I'm hearing is some laughter. (Laughs.) "Wouldn't it be fun?" It's like um... Just like an explosion – there's not an intention, there was not an intention... (to create the Universe).

Everything was not set out to a T?

Yeah.

"Let's create something" - then "boom?"

Yeah. **"Let's see what happens."** And (there's) a feeling of awe and amazement and it's all encompassing. That's very awe inspiring.

What else do you want to know?

I would like to know what's real and what isn't. Or does it not matter...

What do you mean?

Well, is it all imagination? And if it is, great, then it shouldn't matter.

Everyone Creates their Own Universe

So let's find a source of knowledge in the library that addresses this question.

(Pause, as if listening) Not a satisfactory answer.

Make a verbal report. What's going on?

(I'm hearing) **"Everybody creates their own world and their own universe."** That's just stupid, it sounds like stuff I've learned in books and in school – (laughs) I mean it's all up to the individual, there's not an answer in the bigger picture.[185]

---

[184] She's describing a universe that functions like a mechanism, but is "sentient."

[185] But it does seem to be accurate when a person describes the afterlife via an LBL or an NDE. Each description is unique, although it's possible to categorize the events that occur. But if you take apart

There's no one truth?

Yeah. I would like one truth.

Let's go to a source what can explain why there can be "no one truth."

(Pause) "It's too small thinking. You're thinking too small" is what the book said. The reason it doesn't sit well with me, is because I'm thinking from a very limited perspective and I want security, but that's not how it works. Until I can change my way of thinking, it's not going to be convincing... which still doesn't sit well with me.[186]

Would you go into the library to the place that has records of all of your incarnations?

All right.

Tell me about this weird ant-life thing – what was that about? Another incarnation?

I think it's me, I don't know, I don't like it – but it was kind of fun to do it.

Let's go into the record of your incarnations and see if it pops up like a search. Was this an incarnation?

I think it's where I came from. I think I am... **I think that's why this place (on Earth) I don't really hook on, is because I'm just travelling there.**

This is where you originally came from?

I think I come from a place... -- or **imagine a planet where people are individuals and not linked to other people, like to other families.** And... then they just sort of do their own thing and travel around and **I think I'm from that planet,** (where I was) looking like an insect thing.

the sentence in light of this research, it may be more akin to "Everyone's experience is unique unto themselves, how they perceive energetic fields and how those fields affect their journey or path." So my journey or path is not your journey and path, and when I experience the afterlife, it won't be exactly the same as your experiences. However, we may be able to connect, as we do here on the planet, moments where we can share our experience with each other.

[186] She's getting this information from a book that's she's been able to pull down from the stacks in the library. And the answer as she's describing reading a truth from a book – which says in essence, "When you ask why there's no one truth, it's because you're thinking too small."

Is this in our universe?

Seems to be.

It's time to get some guidance. It's time to get some higher guidance. Is that ok?

Yes.

We can call a teacher in to meet you. Let's go and find someone who knows you, loves you and someone who can answer some of our questions about your present life. Call out in your mind and your heart for your teacher, your guide.

I'm going there. Walking. It's still in the library, it's massive, can't seem to get out of it.

Let's skip forward. One two three be there now. Male or female?

Male. Tall, older, staring at me.

What is he communicating to you?

"Stop bouncing around. I really wish you would calm down."

Ask him to help you center yourself because we want to talk with him, it's very important. Perhaps he can enfold you in his energy or do something to help you.

Ok. That's better.

How do you feel?

Like I'm carved out of wood.

A Visit From a Spirit Guide

Imagine being on the same wavelength as him, opening your heart chakra sending a beam out to him, making a connection. I have some questions to ask him – and he can answer through your voice or mind. What shall we call him?

Sounds like Shhh. Something like a k (laughs). You can call him Shaka Khan.

"Shaka" ok?

It's not it, but it's okay.[187]

How do you feel about her performance in her lifetime as Tommy, the grumpy old man, how did she perform?

Admirably.

Was their goal to just experience life as a manly energy?

Yes.

What does her soul gain from that?

To grow, you need pieces. And you need to absorb things. So to evolve or to grow, she needed a different piece. It's a food.

Why were we shown the Tommy life today? What's the connection to Kelly's present lifetime?

She's doing the same thing. I supposed she's repeating everything she did before without growing.

Tell us more about the not growing part. What can Kelly add to that or bring to it that would display growth?

The good news is I've gotten myself to a place where I can now relax and observe. I don't have to fight anymore to get there, but I can observe instead of being so...[188]

Fighty?

Yeah. Had to be *fighty* to get there, now it's time to stop. Stop and watch. It's not all about me.

---

[187] In these sessions, it's common to ask for the name of the spirit guide to differentiate with experiences the person is going through. I've heard often that whatever name is spoken is "not their actual name" but a sound that is similar, "like the sound a musical instrument makes." Sometimes the names are characters from the person's life or work – either way, the names serve as placeholders to refer to other people and events during the session.

[188] The tense shifts here from third person to first person. This happens often, if Scott asks a spirit guide a question directly, the person will answer in the third person, but if the question doesn't contain a point of view, it often moves back to first person. I know in my own sessions, I've shifted between the two in mid-sentence.

To watch what?

How the Universe works - is played out and how the people interact. **If you really want to know how the Universe works; watch the people.** It's all the same. To understand it; watch it.

How can she do this in her daily life?

Good question. Yeah, we'll just drop my defenses. When you put up defenses or force fields, you just isolate yourself and when you're secure enough to drop them you can see what's really going on – **defenses stop you from really interacting.**

Does Kelly have force fields up?

Many. She always has them.

Can you show her in her mind how to drop some of these defenses?

(Her voice changes) I really don't like this conversation with my guide, he's very bossy. He's just tells me that I "need to know better," again, "do as I'm told." It's not an emotional problem other than to just stop thinking I know better.

Kelly has a series of questions... Would you honor us with addressing these questions? She wants to know "What is the purpose, why did I choose to be Kelly? What's the purpose of this lifetime?"

To unsettle people. I... have a knack for drawing people out and I make them look at things slightly differently. Unsettle them. I make them look at things differently.

"Why have I always felt out of place? On the outside looking in?"

It's because I don't fit in. I'm drawn to situations where I don't fit in. She'll do it until she doesn't want to do it anymore; she'll do it until she's had enough.

She wants to know "If I will find my soul mate."

(Sighs) I can't get out of my way on that one.

Let's come back to that. Maybe visit your soul group later. Please describe what "the shift" is all about – is it real, is there a shift of energy a shift of consciousness?

It (a shift in consciousness) is like a massive vast ocean and if a little crab at the bottom decides to open his eyes -- and see that he's in an ocean. That's what a shift in consciousness is. However, the shift is just... it's not as important as people are saying.

Why not?

We are putting way too much emphasis on things that are not important, like names, giving things a name; in terms of the consciousness of the Earth in the big picture; it's not important.

Is there something a little more positive about a consciousness shift? Is there a higher purpose? Was it seeded to us by someone in the spirit realm to think about consciousness?

Yes. That's why it's not important. Any more important than (it is) to think about why a flower seed is planted. It's just evolution.

Is there a new energy available to people?

It's the same energy, it's always been there.

So we need to be like that little crab, opening its eyes to the big ocean. She wants to know – something that might be related to a greater spiritual event...

My fibroid tumor.[189]

"What's this all about?"

(Pause) What a relief. He's saying "It's just physical." I've been telling myself it's my fault like I did something bad.

Question; "Did she create it with her thoughts or feelings?"

No. It's just physical.

---

[189] As mentioned, on the way to the session, Kelly revealed her primary reason for agreeing to do a session was to examine this upcoming operation.

The cells have a problem? Something wrong with the body? So there's no greater meaning to it all?

Surprisingly, no.

What can she do to get a healthy outcome?

Have the surgery.

And to what extent should it go?

Just remove them and get on with everything.

Is it necessary?

What I'm hearing is "Just do it and get on with it." And "there's too much time spent on things that are not important." There are things that are important but just don't focus on things that aren't important.

What is important for her to focus on?

Going back to what he said earlier. Get out of my own way and just watch what's happening. I'm just supposed to categorize and watch what's happening. Don't over analyze it, just observe it and like record it. Observe what's happening and just record it.

What's the purpose of this observation? Some project she's contributing to?

Yes, but I don't know how to describe it.... I'll be very rudimentary. **It's like the universe is this big massive you-can't-even-comprehend-it place, and everything moves around it. Like energy moves around it and by observing it in this tiny spot, I'm drawing the energy up to somewhere else.** But the energy keeps moving and growing and when I'm too busy analyzing things, like my fibroids, or "Why am I lonely," or what's going on, I'm stopping the energy that's supposed to go back from watching what's going on. I've just got to stop and get out of my own way. But that's like turning a cube into a speck; it's not really explaining.

By obsessing or worrying, it's stopping the flow of energy, when you could watch how the world works. Is there anything Scott can do about the fibroids?

Why? Are you a surgeon? (Laughs.) He's joking...

(Scott Laughs)

He's saying 'it's not a psychic thing" – it's physical, like getting your tire changed?

Yeah.

*"What about her search for God?" She wants to know; what you can tell her about the idea of God? **"What or who is God?"***

Searching for a human concept of God is like looking for somewhere to stop along an infinite wall; it's too vast. It's "security." But I have a need for a bigger understanding… and a very human need for a human God…

A need for a "big daddy God" that makes you feel protected?

Belonging to something or a safety wall, like a place that just stops, yeah. But I can't reconcile that part of me which knows God is so much bigger, with this desire to understand a human God; so it's a constant conflict - an on-off switch.

Beyond the Capacity of the Brain to Comprehend

From Shaka's point of view? Talk to us about God as you understand it.

"Just let go of the intellect and feel it. Your feeling will tell you."

You can't understand it with your head?

Right. **It's beyond the capacity of the brain to comprehend. However, you can feel it, you can experience God.**

What's it feel like?

Feels like perfection. Like it all makes sense. That all "clicks into place," but not in a mechanical way.

So when you feel God what does that feel like?

It's not "endless love" the way people describe love; that's just something we can relate to. It's a concept that is much bigger than that. Imagine an energy that connects everyone and everything in the universe. You can call that energy "love." But there is a wisdom to it and that wisdom is what people call God.

What's something we can share with Kelly?

That I'm not going to find the answers, so search only what is fun and not obsess. And I can feel this energy anytime I want.

What does that feel like?

I'm just trying to put a name to what I feel when I meditate. A sense of peace? But you can achieve it through meditation and prayer.[190]

Tell us about the gifts of this soul here – what does she have that's unique?

I'm intuitive. (Laughs). I don't like his answers. He talks about how annoying I am, how I pester people. I thought it was just the way I am (back) here, but it's refreshing to know that I can get away with saying and doing things without causing hurt.[191]

Start Having Fun

Why has she been brought to this session today? What does she need to get out of this experience?

(Laughs). I was about to say "because it's time I'm going through a change in my life and it's time to grow up" – and he said "Actually, it's the opposite; you should start having fun." **Relax a bit, have more fun, let the barriers down.** It's not that difficult. It's not so difficult. **Life is not meant to be so difficult.**

Take a deep breath to signal this change in you. You okay with that? What else does Shaka have to advise you today?

To not put too much emphasis on the words, the things I read and everything that's happening in this session as hard core reality; it's just methods of communication. Don't take everything as gospel, just take everything as a

---

[190] As noted, Kelly told me she's an atheist, but from what she's saying here, it may be more along the lines of an agnostic; someone who doesn't believe in a religious concept of God, but allows that there may be a form of higher power.

[191] She's listening to her spirit guide talk about who she is as a person – and why she says "I don't like his answers." He seems to be explaining how she can get away with sarcasm because she's not causing harm in others.

method of communication. **Whether it's a religion or talking to a guide, he's saying whether or not it's a past life; don't give it too much weight but take it with a grain of salt. It's just communication, just trying to get something through.**[192]

Is there anything else to show her?

Yes. Let's go back to my soul mates.

As you become aware of these people; how many are there?

Five, six. Tangled together.

What are they communicating to you?

Well here's what I asked them when I was untangling them; "Who the hell are you people?" And they laughed because they get my sense of humor, and they said "Just the same as you; who the hell are you?" And I saw they have the same sense of humor, excellent.

What are they communicating to you now?

Like "leave that guy (Scott) in the room - let's go! Let's go do something else!"

You can go and do something else. Take off. What do they want to do?

Oh my God! My soul group are like children. They want to play.

A Game of Cosmic Tag

So go play.

Oh God, they're kids. They want to go play a game.

What sort of game do they play?

---

[192] It's worth repeating this idea. Even when discussing past lives, future lives, or lives between lives – to not take them so seriously that they can't be examined for what they really are; explanations that are in the form of communication.

(A pause) It's like it has a lot of rules. "*You* can stay *here*, but *you* can only move." It's a big, incredibly elaborate game of hide and seek. Incredibly elaborate; too many rules (listens). What?

Hide and seek? Is that fun? How do you hide?

You disappear and you can only give certain clues and coordinates. And then you can only reappear in certain places that would give a hint of where you are. Then they have to find you. We're all looking for each other; it's incredibly complicated! You have to herd them all, pinpoint them all and then you herd them.

Are you good at this?

Apparently not, it's very complicated.

How do you disappear?

You just will it.

When you're disappeared, do they still feel your presence?

Yes. That's why there are so many rules, because if you cheated it would be too easy.

So rules to pretend not to see each other. Sounds pretty fun.

You don't get... you don't get a... but you get a lot of wisdom. When I said "they're children" I think I'm not kidding.

Are you on the same level as them? Or different?

I'm on the same level, but I'm there with my hands on my hips, tapping my foot.

Bored?

A little impatient.

Tell me about his group. What is their focus? Do they have a job to do?

We are a family. We're all like the same age.

That's What She Does

Let's see if any individuals will come forward and talk to you. Is there anyone you feel really close to?

My friend Sarah.[193]

How is she appearing?

She looks like Sarah. She said "Ha! You didn't know I was here" because I didn't know she was part of my soul group.

What else is she communicating with you?

I ask her to get serious for a second, and she says the only thing she has to communicate to me is, if I'm looking for something serious - which she's not in the mood for - is that... Oh. She's saying something like my guide said; that **when I'm (on Earth) I act like I'm alone in the world, but I've always got all of them with me at all times...** and to... you know... I should stop that.

Can I ask Sarah why Kelly decided to act like this?

She just shrugged her shoulders and said "That's (just) what she does."

Sarah do you have any advice for Kelly from the soul place as Sarah?

She said - very interesting -"Because we're together a lot here (on Earth) and we complain that we're very similar and that we haven't found the right man." But she says "that's because we're too young. We're not meant to settle down yet." She says, "So stop worrying about it on Earth, stop worrying about it here!"

Other Than Human

Anyone else?

I do not know them.

But we can meet them here. It's not like they're strangers.

---

[193] Sarah is a friend who is in her current life.

(I see a) Male, tallish, boyish. He's staring at me and I'm staring at him. He's as curious about me as I am about him.

Do you need to communicate with him?

No. I'll stare at the other two.

Tell me about them.

Seems to be a couple of boys and the rest are women. Second boy is smaller. Feels like a little brother. A lot more excited to see me; he's trying to communicate, but I can't understand a word he's saying. He's jumping up and down, happy and joyous.

What about the other one?

Not getting much, I'm feeling like they are older – the rest are kids.

So where are you in this range?

When you put me in it I'm about 12 years old. The group is in their early 20's down to about 8 years old, or how they appear.

By older do you mean more life experience?

Yeah. I'm seeing them all as other than human.

How do other groups see your group? How do they see you?

I don't get a sense that there are labels here; the impression as from the very beginning, it's a kid group.

Let's find your guide and see if there's anything else he wants to show you today.

He's just driving home what he said earlier. That what I'm seeing here - don't take it to heart, it isn't that serious. **Forms are not important, names are not important, don't get hung up on things like that.**

So what is important?

Only what you decide is important, because at the end of the day - predestined is too strong of a word, but (our path is) already created, already laid out. I

don't know, I don't have the right word, but... predetermined? It's all there, so I can decide what is important; but it's only important to me.

Get Your Head In the Game

Put another way, Shaka, you're telling her forms and names are not important. What would you suggest she focus on?

He's being very stern, telling me to get my head out of the clouds, he's pointing me back. Imagine you're in space and he's turning me around from heaven and pointing me back, his hand turning the back of my head. **"Get your head out of the clouds, get back down to Earth and stop worrying about all these other mental intellectual, spiritual pursuits."**

Then what shall she invest her energy in?

"Get your head in the game."

What part of the game should she focus on?

Participating... (he's) saying I don't participate, I need to participate.

Like the game with her friends? Get in the game?

Yeah.

It seems like Shaka is saying "lighten up and have fun and not obsess so much," on the other hand he seems to be saying "focus on the game."

Oh no, like, get in the game of being here – not – he just keeps physically turning my head around, from staring up into space, pushing me back down, and saying "Get in the game." I think it's all the same; **"Remove the barriers, stop standing on the side, stop staring up in the sky, get in the game and stop worrying about it so much."**

Is there anything else you want to explore? A place of healing perhaps?

Well, I want to go back to the library, I chose door number two and **I stepped through it and it exploded into a million lights and it felt good. I stepped through the door and it felt like fireworks. I don't know how to describe it, it's**

like losing your form, like fireworks going in all directions at once; it's fantastic, exhilarating! And fast. And you can do it a million times; it's fun. I'm doing it over and over again; it's really fun! (Laughs.) Yeah it's giddy. Like a ride. You're everywhere at once. [194]

Let's go to the exploring dome one more time.

You'd love it, you should do it.

Let's hang out with your guide for a moment and thank him for his help today and if there's a final insight for today, let's have him put that inside you right now.

He's just saying "Goodbye, come back and see me."

I would ask Shaka to do something – put a sensation in her body or mind, in the future it will serve as her calling card, when you want to get her attention – like your ring tone.

Okay. Yeah, a tug on my hair.

What should she do when she feels that?

This is the listening time.

Etch that in your mind. You need to listen. I'll count to five and you can open your eyes......"

––––––––––

I'm happy to report that Kelly had her operation and, as predicted, everything turned out fine. After her session on the drive back, we talked about some of the more interesting things she'd come across in her session. To understand a shift in consciousness, imagine being a crab walking on the ocean floor and you open your eyes and realize you're in an ocean.

That's pretty profound in itself. To imagine for a moment that everything we know about the outside world is not what we thought it was – or perhaps to realize that we live in an ocean like environment, where what we think to be

––––––––––

[194] In a few of the near death experiences, we have the same reports of experiencing "Fireworks." Also interesting to note that she "chose door number two." Where's Monty Hall when we need him?

oxygen functions like water. Or to think for a moment that one bit of pollution, effects the ocean entirely.

The idea that the universe functions like a mechanism, but that it's sentient. Hard to get my mind around, but perhaps it means that everything is in its place, and everything has a purpose, however it has the ability to change its mind, or that free will directs how we behave.

The question about "what or who is God?" also had an unusual answer.

> It's not "endless love" the way people describe love; that's just something we can relate to. It's a concept that is much bigger than that. Imagine an energy that connects everyone and everything in the universe. You can call that energy "love." But there is a wisdom to it and that wisdom is what people call God.

Eben Alexander mentions something similar in "Proof of Heaven" when he arrived at point in his NDE where he felt he was in the presence of God – describing the luminosity of a place where everything was connected.

Frequently people claim during these experiences to see the connectivity of all things. They describe them in varying degrees of light, or describe a web llke interconnectivity of all people and things. So if we consider for a moment that we're all in this ocean together, why would we allow people to pollute it? Wouldn't it make sense to keep the Earth healthy, the water and air pristine, if only for our own return to the place?

Kelly's session sums up this research; to see the world from a different perspective. To see our journey from a different perspective. Some have said life is like a game or some kind of cosmic illusion, and Kelly's spirit guide wants her to stop observing from the bench, but to get into the game. He also advised against taking things "too seriously." Including this research.

Wise words indeed.

"We are all visitors to this time, this place, we are just passing through. Our purpose here is to observe, to learn, to grow, to love... And then we return home."
Australian Aboriginal Proverb

Epilogue – "Home"

"Jeff Bridges had more to say in memory of actor and comedian Robin Williams, all triggered by an unlikely source: an appearance by New York City legend "Radioman," who ran into Williams during the filming of "The Fisher King" and reportedly coached him on his performance as a homeless person. Shortly after hearing of Robin's death while attending "The Giver" premiere, Bridges spotted Radioman outside the after-party for this film at the Central Park Boathouse:

> *'Is that Robin? Is that his ghost? No! It's Radioman.' And it brought back all of these wonderful feelings of what an amazing time we had together here in New York shooting "The Fisher King." And so we embraced, Radioman and I, and I felt Robin's spirit as I'm feeling it here now in this room with us... What a gift he was to all of us."*[195]

"Did you hear? Mrs. Doubtfire has died."

The news that Robin Williams, the actor and comedian, had taken his own life at the age of 63 came via the above sentence while I was attending a film premiere of "The Giver" in New York City. As the word spread throughout the theater like wildfire, a number of people on the red carpet paused to reflect on his influence

---

[195] "Jeff Bridges and Harvey Weinstein Remember Robin Williams at The Giver Premiere." Bennet Marcus Vanity Fair, August 12th, 2014. (Photo above: At a flea market outside Moscow with some new best friends.)

in their lives. Jeff Bridges wept openly and recalled how much he loved Robin, how much he'd influenced and enlivened his life.

I first met Robin Williams' *doppelganger* on the set of the film "Salt," which I worked on at the behest of my friend, the Australian director Phillip Noyce. As Jeff Bridges mentioned above, "Radioman" would appear wherever a set is in New York City as if by magic. He rides a bike with a radio strapped to the handlebars, and it is uncanny; he really does look like Robin - his voice, his smile... At first I thought it was actually Robin pretending to be a homeless fellow. But then I remembered the "Fisher King" and realized here was the living embodiment of a role that Robin had played on screen. As if the creation of Robin's role had jumped off the screen and sprung to life.

There are a number of things about Robin's passing that remind me of this research, the quote from his film "August Rush" being one of them: "You know what music is? God's little reminder that there's something else besides us in this universe; harmonic connection between all living beings, everywhere, even the stars."[196]

As accolades poured in around the planet, I reflected on my own brief exposure to Robin. It was over dinner at a friend's house, and I was at a table with him and Charles Grodin. Robin was both gracious and friendly, and for some reason took the opportunity for polite chatting, rather than flights of fancy.

I didn't get a chance to tell him that I had also been in the Harvey Lembeck comedy workshop for a number of years, and had heard of his legendary performances in the class. That I too was a huge fan of Jonathan Winters, and that I'd had the good fortune to attend a number of lunches with him at his favorite table at Musso & Frank's restaurant in Hollywood.

That I had once asked Jonathan a question about his father, and how that had sent him into a flight of fancy that took us to the revolutionary war, and fighting with Indians, but then realizing we were on the wrong side... but being aware of his difficulties with his Marine Corps dad, I knew that the reason we'd gone down this path was because his father was a trigger for him in some ways - that to avoid discussing something of great pain for him, he went into a place of great comedy. So at the end of this 45 minutes of amazing improvisation, I was able to

---

[196] "August Rush" written by Nick and Paul Castle, James V Rush.

pick up the thread of the question: "So I take it you don't want to discuss your dad?" To which Jonathan roared with laughter.

Robin Williams knew how to roar with laughter. David Letterman ran a tribute to him the other day, where Robin was frequently throwing his head back, roaring like a lion with laughter - David had said something that allowed Robin to release that laugh - a kick back of the head, chin pointed skyward, his legs stretched out. He was literally roaring.

Just a quick note about depression. If you know someone who is suffering from it, I encourage them to look into the scientific research on meditation. Prof. Richard Davidson of the University of Wisconsin has proven that meditation can "alleviate or cure depression" in his monumental study. [197] Meditation can actually change the shape of the amygdala where depression exists in the brain. So depression is not an ailment without cure - it's a clarion call that something is wrong. It's worth checking into these alternative methods as a combination of modalities may be what is required. (And is what helped David Bennett recover from cancer in the chapter "Voyage of Purpose.")

But the good news is; Robin Williams is not dead. Like Elvis; he's just left the building.

Suicide is a tricky subject. I can only weigh in on the "Flipside" research. We all choose to come to the planet to learn and teach lessons; we are not here by mistake or happenstance. Each person has their own path and journey, each has a myriad of reasons how they choose to experience the journey here or for exiting the stage when they do.

Once we wrap our minds around the fact that we don't die, or in this case *can't* die, then the matter of our leaving the stage is one of logistics. Do we judge an entire life or performance on how an actor leaves the stage? "Yes, I loved the play, the first and second act were great, but you tripped as you came off stage and that I cannot forgive. Two thumbs way down." We tend to write reviews on how an actor exits: "A belt, a plastic bag, a box of pills" and ignore those who are checking themselves out with each cigarette, each shot of whisky, each time they drink and drive and/or text. Are they any less "guilty" of choosing the manner of their death than others just because it happens to be a slow lingering exit?

---

[197] Davidson's meditation studies can be found at RichardJDavidson.com

We applaud those who managed to stay on stage until their last breath, surrounded by loved ones, whether its Betty Bacall or the world's oldest man, and wag our fingers at deaths we don't applaud, whether Robin or a child in a wedding party taken out by a drone. We've all got a myriad of exits and entrances behind us, and ahead of us - suffice to say it's up to us how we manage them.

Again, the research shows that we don't die. That each life is a sacred, precious choice, that we come here to learn and teach and love for many reasons, and the manner of our passing has roots in our own path and journey. Robin is ok, he's fine, he hasn't gone anywhere - he's just not here or visible to us. And that's a damned shame because he lit up the stage, made the entire planet laugh, and there's nothing more healing than laughter.

I was in a post office in Manhattan the day after he died, waiting in a long line. And when I got to the front, the tired postal employee said with exasperation "Finally. The last customer; I'm going to lunch!" I smiled and asked "What's for lunch?" She looked at me to see if I was trying to bait her, and then softened when she saw my face on the book I was mailing. Someone had come to hear me speak at Tibet House in Manhattan about "Flipside" and asked me to send a copy of the book, which has my mug on the back cover.

"What's it about?" she asked. I said "It's about what thousands have said under deep hypnosis about the afterlife." She looked at me. "I've been crying all morning since I heard the news that Robin Williams had died." I said, "Well, these people say that he hasn't died. He's just not here. It's like he got off stage too early. But he still exists, just as our love for him will always exist." She reached over with her rubber gloved hand and held mine. Tears welled in her eyes. "You have no idea how much I needed to hear that. Thank you. You've made my day."

Later, I was at a bodega helping an owner speak to a family from Spain in broken Spanish. Afterwards I asked the owner where he was from. He said Nepal. Joking, I said "My son's from Nepal." I told him the quick story of our son RJ remembering a life as a monk in Nepal (as recounted earlier) and shared a few of the stories which seem to verify RJ's proclamation. The owner asked if he could see a picture of him. I showed him a pic of our nine year old smiling son. The shopkeeper closed his eyes and said a prayer, moving his hand from his heart to his lips to his forehead. He then looked at the photo and said "You can see it in his face; serenity."

I then realized the man was weeping, tears rolling down his cheeks. He wiped his tears and said "Thank you. That was very powerful."

So then I told him the story the same story RJ had told us - how when I sat him down to tell him his grandmother was going to pass away, that the next time he saw her she'd look different. How he had picked up a bottle of water and said "Spirit is like water. Watch." And how he had stomped on it until the bottle was crushed and broken, then picked it up and showed it to us - the bottle demolished but the cap still on. "You see dad? The water is ok."

It bears repeating: our bodies may get crushed and old and broken, we may do things to them and check out early - but the spirit, like water, will always be ok. Like Robin Williams, our loved ones, no matter how or when they leave the planet, will always be okay. After all, they've just gone "home."

In most of the between-life sessions I've filmed, people report at the end of their previous lifetime, they want to go "home." I said it during my own first between-life experience when I saw myself as an American Indian, standing on the edge of a river, about to end my life. (Not entirely unlike Jimmy Stewart on the bridge in "It's a Wonderful Life.") I said "My life is a shell. I just want to go home." But I didn't have an angel Clarence who could jump into the river and save me. No one to show me all the people that I had affected or influenced in that lifetime. And after I jumped in, it seemed like I flew back *home*.

If there's a common theme in this research, it's that when we're here on the planet, we're not "home." We're someplace else. According to these many accounts we've chosen to be here – and it takes courage to be here. We signed up to be here. We've earned the right to be here. We signed up for lifetimes that may seem difficult while we're living them, but back "home," we knew it was the right thing to do.

I've had four between-life sessions now, during which it always felt like I had returned "home." I saw my spirit guide, saw my friends and spoke to and laughed with my old friend Luana as well. I got to see and hear my father's voice again, and heard direct messages from my soul group. They were all *home*.

Some find it useful to consider our journey away from home as a theatrical piece – actors going on stage, choosing their roles, costumes, props, performing night after night, improvising, jumping off stage too early at times, but basically investing their hearts and souls into their story for the benefit of others.

Here's how Will Shakespeare put his version of the journey of souls:

> All the world's a stage, and all the men and women merely players. They have their exits and their entrances, and one man in his time plays many parts, his acts being in seven ages. At first, he's the infant, mewling and puking in the nurse's arms. Then the whining schoolboy, with his satchel and shining morning face, creeping like a snail unwillingly to school. And then the lover, sighing like furnace, with a woeful ballad made to his mistress' eyebrow.
>
> Then a soldier, full of strange oaths and bearded like the leopard. Jealous in honor, sudden and quick in quarrel, seeking the bubble of reputation even in the cannon's mouth. And then the justice, in fair round belly with good capon lined, with eyes severe and beard of formal cut, full of wise saws and modern instances; and so he plays his part.
>
> The sixth age shifts into the lean with slippered pantaloons, spectacles on his nose and pouch on his side; his hosery, well saved, too wide for his shrunken torso, and his big manly voice has turned again into a childish treble, with pipes and whistles for its sound. The last scene that ends this strange eventful history Is a second childishness and then mere oblivion; sans teeth, sans eyes, sans taste - sans everything.[198]

Each one of these metaphors, from crying infant, to whining schoolboy, to ardent lover, loyal soldier, wise sage, then older shrunken man, and finally back to childish elder aptly captures the various roles we play on Earth as well. Each stage of life comes with its own dialog, props and storyline, we do our best to fulfill our sacred promises to the stage manager.

Some feel this metaphor is incomplete – because the idea of being part of a play or a "staged event" makes it seem a life is less important than it is. Perhaps "Life University" is a more apt metaphor – we all sign up for classes, we all learn at our own pace, and our own ability during each life. And if we fail a particular class, we get to try it again. We're all in the same university – a word derived from universe – so perhaps it resonates more to realize we're all in this school together, we all chose to be here, and we are all here for a reason.

But beyond that, what have we learned in "It's a Wonderful Afterlife?"

---

[198] "As You Like It." Act II, Scene 7. By William Shakespeare. Amended.

That consciousness is not necessarily created by the brain, because there's sufficient scientific evidence that shows people can have conscious memories, thoughts, ideas, when there's no blood in their brains.

While the brain does record (that's not the right word – probably more like "filters") human experiences, it appears to not be the source of consciousness. (As scientist Nikola Tesla said: "My brain is only a receiver, in the Universe there is a core from which we obtain knowledge, strength and inspiration. I have not penetrated into the secrets of this core, but I know that it exists.")

We also heard from people who have near death experiences are having similar journeys to those described in the between-life therapy sessions. Dr. Helen Wambach did her own form of research about hypnosis as Michael Newton and got the same results. People claimed to exist prior to coming here.

Experience is how we learn everything, according to this research. Whether as a healer, a teacher, an artist, a mathematician – everything is energy and it requires our being able to experience that energy in order for us to master it.

Which reminds me of when we were trying to find the right preschool for our son. I spent a few weeks tracking down what I thought was the right preschool near our place in Santa Monica. We drove by the school with his older sister Olivia in tow – she was about five at the time. The following morning Olivia said she had a dream and announced; "That's not the school that RJ goes to."

Chagrined, I looked at my wife Sherry. Most parents upon hearing their children describe some kind of dream would dismiss it – but as you can tell, not in Chez Martini. "Where is the school that he's supposed to go?" I asked.

Olivia said "I don't know. But it's not the one you showed me. He goes to a school not far from my school, and his teacher has long blonde hair." Well, that would be just about every preschool in Santa Monica. But since the school we signed him up for was beginning in a few days, we decided to take Olivia for a drive and see what we might find. We started at her present school and began driving in concentric circles away from her school. After about five minutes she said "There, that's it." She pointed to a small church in Santa Monica. I was not aware they had a preschool, but called them. The church told me they did not have a preschool, but there was one next door.

The Principal said they had normally had a long waiting list, but a student had dropped out unexpectedly that very morning. She had a question for me. "Is your child a boy or girl?" I told her a boy. She said, "We try to keep a mix of boys and girls, and we do have an opening for a boy. Is he ready to join the school this coming week?" I said he was, and then I said "Can I ask you an odd question? What color hair is your hair?" She paused a moment and said "It's blonde, why?"

As it turned out, it was one of RJ's teachers who had the long blond hair just as Olivia predicted and he developed a bit of a crush on her. Now, if we can just get Olivia to pick lottery numbers...

Frank Capra wrote "It's A Wonderful Life" after having a profound spiritual experience. A bald "faceless" man chewed him out for pretending to be ill when he had a purpose in this life - to make people laugh. He owed it to the planet to get out of bed and do what he was born to do. Perhaps we should all follow suit.

We've come to the end of the first volume of "It's A Wonderful Afterlife." If you've come this far, you know there's more adventures that lie ahead in Volume Two. All you need to do is turn the record over.

Welcome to the flipside.

"The water will always be ok."

APPENDIX –"What's It All Add Up To?"

(Photo: Author with friend outside Mt. Kailash in Tibet) This is reprinted from the Flipside: A Tourist's Guide on How to Navigate the Afterlife." It still applies. A summation of what this research shows:

1. *Souls don't die.*

We've been around for millennia, our souls continue on for mlllennia. In between lives we are fully conscious, with all of our memories intact. Yes, our bodies die, our loved ones depart from us in this life. But we reconnect with them in the Afterlife.

2. *After death we return to our soul group, where we recognize those we've been reincarnating with for eons.*

There's anywhere from 3-25 people in our individual group and we usually plan our next life with these same folks. We share laughs and memories of the life just lived and eventually plot with them our next adventure. We may even recognize them during this lifetime; usually identified with the thought "I felt like I always knew this person the moment I met them," or "I knew we would marry."

3. *In between lives, we all have a life planning session where we choose our next life; we are able to pick and choose what kind of life we want to lead for various reasons, as well as choose our parents.*

"Why would I choose those people who've made my life miserable?" is a familiar refrain. The answer is that you chose them so that you could be where you are today. Either far, far away from them - which is a gift in some cases, or their influence had directly put you in the place you're supposed to be on the planet. It puts a different spin on your parents behavior when you consider you chose them because of it. As well as why your own children chose you.

4. *We each have our own "council of elders" who oversee our lifetimes, and engage with us in Socratic debate about how we did.*

Everyone has a council of elders, and everyone goes to see them at least twice; once upon our return so they can help assimilate all the lessons from that lifetime, and once again just before we take another trip into human form. They don't sit in judgment; rather they help you discern your path. Usually there are 6-12 people on any given council; it seems the younger souls have fewer.

5. *No humans are born without a soul, and we don't arrive at our chosen body until the fourth month (or sometimes later).*

Consciousness is something we've retained from our life between lives. Some kind of veil, or filter, prevents us from remembering those previous lives. However, through the process of deep hypnosis, we're able to bypass these filters and access these previous memories. The idea that we don't join the body until the fourth month would be controversial to advocates who believe life begins at conception. The human animal life may begin at conception, but the spiritual life does not.

6. *We don't reincarnate as other animals.*

Each species comes back with in its own pantheon; i.e. birds of a feather, fish in the sea, and animals on land can swap places with those in their group, but not within other groups. To the concept of being reborn in a "lower life form" as a result of negative karma - that's not what is reported. All life forms are sacred; there are no pejoratives when it comes to life. However, its reported you can access your animal friends at any time in the life between lives – they're an energy pattern as well, and can spend hours playing fetch once again. In all the cases I've examined, I've only know of one where a person recalled in detail a previous life as an animal. I imagine it's possible, but statistically extremely rare.

7. *When we return to our home base, with our soul group, all actions and effects are left behind - we return to a pure state where we enjoy a world without pain, sin or suffering. There is no hell per se, nor a Satanic like region or persona.*

Those who've caused pain, sin or suffering experience the pain they inflicted fully – as if they were the person being hurt during their life review. Afterwards they may choose (or it's decided for them) to be isolated from others in order to learn from their mistakes. There is no Satan or hell per se. Once you depart this plane, you no longer have access to the negativity here, or those who might perpetrate it. (For those Satanists out there, sorry, don't mean to offend.) According to the thousands who've journeyed into the afterlife, there's no evil waiting for us. But we may experience our own form of hell based on how we've treated other human beings.

8. *The process of reincarnation is planned by us, not subject to karma, past mistakes, or past injustices. People choose to be gay, choose to be crippled, or choose to be blissful depending on their spiritual depth.*

We don't travel up or down in any fashion, going from peasant to rich person, or unhappy soul to happy soul. Free will is the law of the Universe, and it's up to us who we want to return as, or even if we want to reincarnate. But inevitably, the pull of helping your loved ones and friends, brings us back time after time. Our life choices are up to us. That includes sexuality, physical type, body shape, etc. We may choose to struggle with these issues in order to progress spiritually, or to help those around us to progress. Those who live on the fringes of society are frequently older souls who chose to be there.

9. *Bad experiences, including suicide, murder, mayhem and other events are frequently worked out in advance, with the agreement of all souls involved.*

They claim there's no such thing as random violence. This may sound controversial, but according to the research, pretty universal. When examining a life between-life session, we get an opportunity to see those details, however heinous or upsetting, to be true.

10. *Our friends in our soul group frequently show up as pals in this life, relatives, brothers, sisters, loved ones or even as adversaries.*

In the "Gospel of Judas" (National Geographic 2006) Judas claims Jesus came to him and asked him to turn him over to the Romans. "If you truly love me, you'll do this for me." There are many reasons to be on the planet, we benefit from all our own experiences, but the main role might be one of assisting a loved one.

11. *Our progression in the afterlife can be charted, in part, based on what color we see ourselves as - the earlier souls are closer to white, and through the spectrum, they wind up into the violet realm. But there is no hierarchy.*

As therapist Jimmy Quast put it; "No one gets to hoard the jelly beans." The idea of someone being smarter, better, richer, happier, more famous, more revered, more anything is just not the case. You are the perfect self you're meant to be. All paths are sacred, and none is judged lesser than another. Just older.

12. *We all have a spirit guide or "Guardian Angel," sometimes more than one.*

Every one of us has a spirit guide who has agreed to watch over all of our incarnations. It gives new meaning to the sacrifice one does at the service of others - can you imagine becoming a mentor to a soul for all of their lifetimes? But the journey many of us are on is to eventually be a guardian angel (spirit guide) for another soul; no time like the present to start treating others like they might be a future candidate.

13. *All of this movement and planning is based on energy.*

Every thought, action, word or deed contains it, every emotion as well. Treat it with sacred intent, whether praying for deliverance, or to help another soul. If you think it, believe it, pray for it, sing it, act it or create it, you've put that personal energy out into the Universe. It can help, heal, or in negative cases, harm others.

14. *There are other Universes and places we can reincarnate. Some religions have spoken of them, various planes in different dimensions Religion is a construct that mirrors the afterlife.*

Earth is the best school, the best playground, the best place to advance our souls. "You'll learn more in one day of tragedy on Earth, then perhaps 5,000 years on another, simpler planet," according to one interview. The argument has been raised, "There aren't enough souls to reincarnate. Where'd the new souls come from?" According to Newton's patients, there are other places to reincarnate and new souls are reportedly being born. When we graduate from our many lifetimes, the graduation ceremony includes being rewarded with (and offering to guide through many lifetimes) a new soul.

15. *Love and compassion turn out to be not just religious concepts, but words that explain how the Universe actually works; from energy transfer to why we choose a particular life.*

Love is the wheelwork of nature, and that attraction and energy is what keeps us going. Compassion is part of the fabric as it's included in many examples of what we give our loved ones by reincarnating by their side. The Golden Rule is actually golden for a reason, because it represents how the Universe works. Loving your neighbor as yourself, nature as yourself, your fellow beings on all levels as yourself, turns out to be not only a spiritual maxim, but a physical one as well.

16. *Religion is a man-made experience based on our god like nature.*

In light of this research, world religions seem to be echoing the same thing; in the afterlife we have eternal qualities, and experience a heaven-like state of bliss. And while we're on Earth, we try to recreate or relive that experience. One could say we're "trying to get back to the Godhead," or "return to God." Religion expresses the inexpressible, examines the unexamined, and finds truth in the nature of all things. Science aspires to take the same journey, by making logical sense of what we are doing on the planet, how we got here, and where we are going. For those who believe that life ends in death, that's not what's reported. For those who think the stress of this lifetime is based on karma from a previous one; that too doesn't bear up under this form of scrutiny. Forgiveness, compassion and love for all people and things appears to be the universal law of the Universe.

17. *We have both an animal ego and a spiritual ego.*

According to this research, we started incarnating on Earth millennia ago. Perhaps when humans became upright or adept; our spiritual energy melded with the human's, and thus began consciousness. Perhaps this event coincided with the formation of societies 60,000 years ago and is our "missing link."

Human life appears to be an agreement between the animal and spiritual ego. That fact helps to underline why people act a certain way, and could have a profound influence on the criminal justice system – if a person is struggling in this life with animalistic tendencies is there a way of examining a healing process that's not "Clockwork Orange[199]" but based on helping souls discover their purpose? As mentioned, in Holland, they've already [200]begun to bring in psychics and past life regressionists to help cure career criminals.

18. *Curing and healing people is part of the work done by others in the Afterlife.*

People choose their lifetimes before coming here to continue their work in a particular field. Musicians may return to further their music knowledge, perhaps explaining child prodigies like Mozart and others. Doctors and Nurses are involved with healing energy transfer, and may have had many lifetimes where they continued their practice. Just the way Tibetan lamas might spend a lifetime studying esoteric practices, and then remember them in their ensuing lifetime, we can all tap into the knowledge of our previous lifetimes to help with our current one.

19. *There are no coincidences.*

What appears to be a matter of amazing coincidence, upon examination, turns out to be an incredible planned sequence, like a complex 3D chess or "Second Life" game being played on multiple planes where each move affects the other players. As a butterfly's wings in a rain forest may cause a hurricane in Asia, everything can be linked in cause and effect if one looks long and hard enough. And by the way, is the reason you've picked up this book.

---

[199] The book by Anthony Burgess mocks criminal rehab in the future where prisoners are reprogrammed.
[200] The Telegraph 22 Nov. 2010 "Dutch prisons use psychics to help prisoners contact the dead."

20. *You are doing pretty much what you set out to do.*

Time and again, people report the spiritual journey they're on was laid out in advance. This is annoying for anyone with a remote control - we all have the inclination to change the channel, to want to change our circumstance, get richer quicker - but the answer is: "You're doing fine, you're on the right path, relax." As hard as your path may seem, you're on it for a spiritual reason.

21. *This research is the tip of the iceberg.*

For those who are interested in finding their soul's purpose – the reason they chose to be here on the planet – I can't think of a more effective way. Here's some collected insights from the therapists I interviewed:

People come in because there may be a relative who recently died, or emotional trauma from losing a child. This work is not to supplant therapy they should receive from a licensed trained professional; it's intended to provide them with answers about their inner being. One of the things clients don't understand until they experience it is that there is a dual nature to all of us. We have our brain ego if you will, and we have a soul ego, and when they are combined it creates one personality and one lifetime.   Michael Newton

Someone can have a strong religious belief that doesn't include reincarnation, but when you take someone through one of these sessions, they have this mind boggling experience - it's a visceral experience on a soul and body level – they emerge knowing this to be true. It's far beyond a concept or belief. That's profound. One other common occurrence is a feeling of reconnecting to the whole. To know you and I are of the same essence makes it much more difficult for me to cause you harm, because it's harming me and the whole as well. That's a message for the entire planet; how we cause harm to others. It's more difficult to do knowing we are all the same. I'd love to see everyone have the opportunity to go through one of these sessions. It's wonderful that it's not a dogma, it's not a religion, but it's open to everyone.   Paul Aurand

I believe we are spiritual beings that live on this Earth. We're not Earthly beings who happen to be spiritual, but the other way around. So for me, this past life work, soulful work, is about that fact that at our core, we're this beautiful diamond and the mud that covers it are experiences in other lifetimes we've encountered. And we create these negative beliefs we have about ourselves, whether it's shame or self-hatred or unworthiness, and sometimes we have to go all the way back to the beginning - our past lives - to wash away the mud so we can uncover the beautiful diamond we are. Until you get to the source of it, you're going to be in conflict with nature until you find the source of the diamond within you.   Debbie Haynie

Always wisdom is uppermost in mind. We choose to incarnate to harvest wisdom from the lifetime, to gain direct experience and knowledge so that we are improved as beings, so that we are expanded as beings, so that we have more wisdom, understanding and compassion. Colleen Page-Joy

There's this very bright light everywhere I look; I'm part of it. He's showing me I'm part of a universal plan, I'm part of that light and it's everywhere, there's nowhere in the universe there isn't this light. He says "That's what you're working with, keep it as part of you and bring it back." We need to know there's nothing else but light and love. The work we're doing (as hypnotherapists) is about light, because it opens us up to understanding. We're on a mission to clarify and create more light and love and it's available to everyone; all we have to do is open ourselves to it. The light is clear and cleansing, loving and peaceful. Eventually when we become light all the other things go; sadness and such. It's very healing. Morrin Bass

To date it's the single most important modality I can offer anyone. It gives them a sense of their immortality, of the importance of their life and journey, and it gives a sense of belonging to something greater than themselves. It's not a gifted psychic telling you who you are or what you've been, or going to a "Channeler" to tell you your past and background; it's experiential, the clients become their own channel. After every single client has an LBL, they aren't the same – some part of them has changed in a positive way and it's a resource that remains for them long after their Life between Lives journey is complete. Chanda Nancy Berlatsky

I think traditional belief systems are breaking down all over the world; people are looking for something more, for a greater understanding of themselves, rather than being told by other people what to believe. If you can look at what you have within, that's got to be the real stuff because it's your own. If you can tap into that, have access to that, it's very empowering. The world is picking up pace and if we can have something that's centering, like an awakening and understanding of your immortal identity, that seems to be the most centering you could ever have. The more people discover the beautiful compassion and wisdom we hold within, that's got to be good for the planet. Peter Smith

REFERENCES & LINKS:

Scott De Tamble – LightBetweenLives.com
Peter Smith – NewtonInstitute.org
Rajiv Parti - DrRajivParti.us
Eben Alexander – EbenAlexander.com
Robert Thurman – BobThurman.com
Mario Beauregard – DrMarioBeauregard.com
Jean Charles Chabot – JcChabot.com
Peggy Carey – PeggyCareyMeditation.com
Olivia Shelkey - MentorsForChange.com
Chuck Frank – HypnosisArts.com
Gary Schwartz – DrGarySchwartz.com
Dr. Medhus – ChannelingErik.com
Carol Bowman – carolbowman.com

RECOMMENDED READING

"Voyage of Purpose" by David Bennett. An amazing NDE from a science officer.

"Children's Past Lives" by Carol Bowman. Excellent case studies.

"Life Before Life" by Dr. Jim Tucker. Amazing studies from Dr. Tucker at UVA.

"Life After Life" by Dr. Raymond Moody. The book that inspired others to write.

"Tibetan Book of the Dead," translated by Robert Thurman *"The Jewel Tree of Tibet,"* by Robert Thurman. "Essential Tibetan Philosophy" is equally terrific.

"Many Lives, Many Masters" by Brian Weiss. A Yale psychiatrist explores many cases of patients who spontaneously regressed during hypnotherapy.

My Son and the Afterlife: Conversations from the Other Side" by Dr. Elisa Medhus. Dramatic stories and interviews from the afterlife with her son Erik.

"After the Light: What I Discovered on the Other Side of Life That Can Change Your World." By Kimberly Clark Sharp. Her dramatic NDE.

"MindScience: An East-West Dialogue" by the Dalai Lama, Robert Thurman, etc. The Dalai Lama joins scientists in a discussion of consciousness.

"Journey of Souls" and *"Destiny of Souls"* by Michael Newton Based on over 7000 interviews with patients, he lays out a powerful case for his vision of the afterlife, and how to get there.

"Life Between Lives" and *"Memories of the Afterlife"* Edited by Michael Newton. A must read for all hypnotherapists.

"The Afterlife Experiments" and *"The G.O.D Experiments"* by Gary Schwartz with William Simon *The* scientist explores scientific evidence of what ESP and psychic ability might be about.

"Just When I Thought I'd Heard Everything! Humorous Observations on Life in America" by Charles Grodin. Prolific actor, writer, pundit and humanitarian.

"Brain Wars," by Mario Beauregard. Neuroscientist Beauregard proves there's not a single "God spot" and other case studies.

"The Near Death and Life of Jeremy Kagan" by Jeremy Kagan. The film director has a profound near death experience.

"The Soul of Wellness" by Dr. Rajiv Parti. Dr. Parti describes how his life changed dramatically after his NDE from "Hummer to hybrid."

"Heaven is For Real" by Todd Burpo, Lynn Vincent. Colton Burpo's father recounts his son's NDE which has become a feature film.

"Proof of Heaven" by Dr. Eben Alexander. Dr. Alexander's fascinating NDE account which he has shared with many in the near death community.

"Once Upon a Car: The Fall and Resurrection of America's Big Three Automakers-- GM, Ford, and Chrysler" by Bill Vlasic. Excellent tale of present life intrigue.

"Journeys Out Of the Body" by Robert Monroe. Monroe is the Godfather of "astral projection" and has written many books on the subject.

"Linked: How Everything Is Connected... and What It Means" By A.L. Barabasi How clustering is one of the laws of the Universe, apparently for souls as well.

"My Life After Life - A Posthumous Memoir" by Galen Stoller. Written by a young boy who passed away, edited by his father who is a renowned doctor.

"Afterlife of Billy Fingers" by Annie Kagan. Author's brother died and contacted her to prove that there's life after death.

"Irreducible Mind: Toward a Psychology for the 21st Century" Edward F Kelly, Emily Williams Kelly and Bruce Greyson. A hefty scientific investigation of consciousness done by scientists at the Division of Perceptual Studios at the University of Virginia.

ACKNOWLEDGMENTS - *A THOUSAND THANKS*

First and foremost Scott De Tamble. Scott, I bow to your skills as a therapist, a teacher and student, as well as your and Diane's friendship. We've had many laughs during these sessions, and there's nothing quite like hearing something that's profound and astounding, and being able to laugh about it. He's in Claremont, CA at LightBetweenLives.com. Michael Newton, thank you for your work and your research, and your kind words about the documentary.

This book was crowd funded. There are many crowds to thank: you folks who wrote reviews on Amazon, who attended talks I've given and passed the word along. Thanks to George Noory and his Coast to Coast radio show "Flipside" went to #1 at Amazon after both shows. My appearance on his "Beyond Belief" (2nd highest rated show in its history), and now Gaiam TV is distributing the film. Thanks to you folks who donated money to help me continue the research via gofundme.com, or paypal including, but not limited to: Billy Hunter, Billy Vlasic, Nick Milo, Ian Meyer, Linda Castellani, Maureen Cook, Rosemary O'Leary, Wendy Williams, Diana Takata, Asami Ishimaru, Laurie Yehia, Savarna Wiley, Marcus Latham, Richard Grilli, Janet Elleard, Tom Fox, Vivienne Scheil, Dani Dennington, Marie Groh, Jeanette Vigne, Lyn (Tigg) Boyce, Mary Beth Bronk, Chuck Frank, Rajiv Parti, Nat Bernstein, Mitchel Katlin, Martin Richardson, Yaniv Rokah, Camille Alcasid, Maureen Johanson, Tess Moore, Will Zigler, Alexander Broskey, Jan DeAngelis, Carin M Levee, Sarah Jensen: Thank you!

Thanks to Bruce Greyson, Mario Beauregard, Gary Schwartz, Jean-Charles Chabot, Ed Kelley, Jim Tucker, Eben Alexander, Robert Thurman, David Bennett & Cindy Griffith-Bennett, Jeremy Kagan, Pete Smith, Jo Krasevich, Joel Gotler, Laurence Becsey, Debra Skelly, Ken and Galen Stoller, Dave & MaryAnn Patlak, Tim & Nancy Meinelschmidt, Chuck and Elissa Grodin, Doug Martin for his artwork and friendship. Habib Sadeghi, BeHiveOfHealing.com; an early and ardent supporter of my research.

And to those of you who helped, Dick, Cheryl, Elisa, Erik, Jaimie, Kearie, Linda, Laurie, Scherry, Valerie, Robert, Jeff, Jeffry, Jeremy, Cindra, Sue, Scott & Diane... Thanks. To Bob Shaye, Phillip and Vuyo Noyce, Matt Palmieri, Bruce Haring, *miei fratelli* Jeffry, Chas & Roberto and their families – my parents, Anthy and Charlie; thanks for all your support in this lifetime and others... And to my wife Sherry (who edited both volumes!), Olivia and RJ – I love you. Thanks for choosing me.

Richard Martini is a journalist, author and award winning filmmaker. With a BA in Humanities from Boston University (Magna Cum Laude 1978), he was at USC Film School 78-80, returned for his Masters of Professional Writing 2008. He's written and/or directed eight theatrical films including "You Can't Hurry Love," "Limit Up," and "Cannes Man." Documentaries include "Journey Into Tibet with Robert Thurman" and "Tibetan Refugee." He wrote for Variety, Premiere and Inc.com. His previous book "Flipside: A Tourist's Guide on How to Navigate the Afterlife" (FlipsideTheBook.com) is available at all online outlets.

The documentary film "Flipside: A Journey Into the Afterlife" is available through Gaiam TV and Amazon. For further information, or to contact Richard, please visit RichMartini.com. He's married and has two children and lives in Santa Monica, California.

For Chuck

(Photo: Me with Charles Grodin. While Charles remains a skeptic about the afterlife, he introduced me to the work done at The Monroe Institute and Division of Perceptual Studies at the University of Virginia. Many thanks for his contribution of the foreword and other fun episodes in this lifetime.)

For further info: RichMartini.com, FlipsideTheBook or FlipsideTheFilm.com

This is Volume One of "It's A Wonderful Afterlife." Volume Two is being released simultaneously.